Fonts

A Guide for Designers and Editors

Fonts

A Guide for Designers and Editors

Gerald E. Jones

———

toExcel

San Jose New York Lincoln Shanghai

Published by toExcel
an imprint of iUniverse.com, Inc.

For information address:
iUniverse.com, Inc.
620 North 48th Street
Suite 201
Lincoln, NE 68504-3467
www.iuniverse.com

ISBN: 1-58348-768-9

Printed in the United States of America

Acknowledgments

Many dedicated and talented people worked to bring you this book. At SYBEX, credit for making this project both credible and creditable goes to editors David Krassner and Michelle Nance. Len Gilbert, a desktop publishing specialist in the SYBEX production department, lent his early support and enthusiasm to the project and provided helpful technical advice.

Thanks also to David Clark and Kenyon Brown for first seeing potential in the subject. My heartfelt personal thanks to Georja Oumano Jones for perisisting in seeing potential in me.

An overall technical review was provided by my friend and colleague Gary Palmatier, whose book design firm Ideas to Images (Santa Rosa, CA) has filled many shelves with outstanding typography.

I owe my grateful appreciation to two other notable experts who were kind enough to review specific chapters and offer suggestions. Tom Reynolds, Chairman and CEO of The Reynolds Group (Burbank , CA), which specializes in retail signing systems, reviewed Chapter 7. Si Becker, Director of Engineering for the Society of Motion Picture and Television Engineers (White Plains, NY), reviewed Chapter 8.

The material in Chapter 9 benefited from work I had done previously on color slide imaging, assisted by Cliff Leach and Dallas Wright of Autographix (Burlington, MA).

Thanks to the following vendors for their fine cooperation in providing the fonts and software used in the examples: LaVon Peck and Celia Cobb, Adobe Systems Incorporated (Mountain View, CA); Rebecca Ellington and James F. O'Gara, Altsys Corporation (Richardson, TX); Kirk Matfuo, Ares Software Corporation (Foster City, CA); Sherri Wangler and Mike Kilroy, Atech Software (Carlsbad, CA); Stefan Wennik, Bitstream, Inc. (Cambridge, MA); Janie Sullivan, Corel Corporation (Ottawa, Ontario, Canada); Bryan T. Kinkel, Lose Your Mind Development (Norristown, PA);

Collins Hemingway and Shelly Womack, Microsoft Corporation (Redmond, WA); Bruce Newman, Precision Type, Inc. (Commack, NY); and Christy Thiele, Swfte International Ltd. (Rockland, DE).

The illustration that appears in the front endpapers is from the True-Type® Font Pack for Windows™ *User's Guide* and is reprinted with permission from Microsoft® Corporation.

The scanner font that appears in Chapter 4 is from the "Instruction Sheet for Microsoft TrueType Font Pack for Windows 720K Disk Offer," Part No. 30188, reprinted with permission from Microsoft® Corporation.

The quotations in Chapter 5 from H. M. Stanley's famous story in the *New York Herald* can be found in John Carey, Ed., *Eyewitness to History* (Cambridge: Harvard University Press, 1988), 389.

The quotations used in Chapter 6 are excerpts from the essay "My Début as a Literary Person," by Samuel L. Clemens. The selection can be found, among other sources, in *The Family Mark Twain* (New York: Harper & Brothers, 1935), 1443–1444.

The television test pattern in Figure 9.5 is Copyright © 1989 by the Society of Motion Picture Engineers and is reprinted by permission.

The sources of other proprietary material reproduced by permission are acknowledged in the figure captions.

Contents at a Glance

Table of Contents

CHAPTER 3 Writing a Report

OR *Time to 'Fess Up!* **79**

CHAPTER 4 **Preparing Practical Printed Documents**

CHAPTER 5 **A Copy Editor's Guide to Preproduction**

xiv

CHAPTER 6   ## Publishing Newsletters and Books

CHAPTER 7   Selling at the Point of Purchase

OR *Listen to the Talking Sign*   **219**

CHAPTER 12 Love Notes for the Technically Inclined

OR *How to Cope with Some Ugly Characters* **351**

Introduction
Fonts Can Be Fun (or Not)

> This book refers to version 3.1 of the Microsoft Windows operating system. However, the principles of TrueType and PostScript fonts described here also apply to later versions of Windows.

The Windows operating environment for PCs has built-in capabilities for generating attractive typography on the computer screen and in printed documents. And, if everything is working as advertised, the composition of fonts on the screen and in printed output will match beautifully. That's WYSIWYG technology (short for What You See Is What You Get). However, in some unfortunate circumstances, WYSIWYG goes haywire and the wrong font gets printed, the spacing is off, or perhaps nothing prints at all!

Diagnosing and fixing problems with fonts is a major focus of this book, but the tips and advice don't stop there. Beyond simply suggesting ways to fix what's wrong, I'll show you how to get the most attractive results—how to make your correspondence, reports, and presentations more effective, more creative, and more persuasive!

So, there's much more to this book than fonts. Its main purpose is to help you *enhance your business message,* no matter which software application or output medium you're working with.

Each chapter in the book centers around a specific business-oriented task, such as writing an effective letter or designing a persuasive report. For each task, I give examples using one of the more common Windows applications: for example, using Microsoft Word for creating correspondence or Harvard Graphics for generating charts. Along the way, I'll point out the most likely problems and pitfalls, but I'll also suggest ways to make your work easier and your results more pleasing to the eye.

How to Use This Book

Since chapters are organized around specific tasks, you may choose to proceed directly to your area of interest—or to the source of your trouble. Cross-references within the chapters direct you to relevant background material that is covered in greater depth in another chapter.

If you choose to read this book from cover to cover (bless you), you'll find an orderly progression of typographic topics. Most of the basics of fonts and page composition are covered in the first two chapters. Chapter 1, "Composing Business Letters and Memos," deals mainly with the choice and composition of text fonts in word-processing applications such as Microsoft Word. The chapter also covers some common printing problems and solutions, which apply to the Windows environment in general.

Chapter 2, "Designing Persuasive Print Ads," is mostly about getting creative with display typography in CorelDRAW, but also covers techniques for composing text fonts, such as columnar layouts and runarounds.

Chapter 3, "Writing a Report," deals with the combination of text and graphic elements that must be brought together in a typical report to management; for example, combining spreadsheet data (analyzed in Microsoft Excel), charts (created with Harvard Graphics), and the report narrative (written in Word).

Chapter 4, "Preparing Practical Printed Documents," is all about simplifying the familiar and generally bothersome task of laying out manual forms. An example of the layout procedure is done in CorelDRAW. Computer-based forms using Excel are also discussed.

The next two chapters are a crash course in newsletter and book production. Chapter 5, "A Copy Editor's Guide to Preproduction," focuses on preparing written copy and text files for typesetting. Chapter 6, "Publishing Newsletters and Books," deals with the mechanics of fitting copy within a specified number of pages, different approaches to page design, and production of finished pages.

The subject of Chapter 7, "Selling at the Point of Purchase" is the special design challenge of the retail sign. Techniques for composition, layout, and production of signs are discussed using examples in Word and in a special-purpose application called WinSign, which can be used for high-volume signmaking.

Chapters 8, 9, and 10 deal with composition of titles and word lists for business presentations in various media. Each medium has its own unique requirements. Chapter 8, "Designing a Screen Show," tells how to construct a screen show, a presentation that will be viewed on the computer monitor. The application examples are done in Harvard Graphics, highlighting the use of its Outliner module to compose the text. Chapter 9, "Generating Video Titles," covers aspect ratios, color selection, and contrast ranges of images that must be composed for videotape recording and television. The application used is CorelDRAW. Chapter 10, "Producing Color Slides and Transparencies," points out how the requirements change when images will be recorded on color film. The application example covers printing images from CorelDRAW to PostScript files for submission to an Autographix service center.

Getting wild and crazy with your own font designs is the subject of Chapter 11, "Dressing Up Fonts." Topics include creating custom characters such as fractions and logos. The application used is Fontographer, a Windows utility for manipulating TrueType and PostScript Type 1 fonts.

More complex issues that I purposely omit from prior chapters are relegated to Chapter 12, "Love Notes for the Technically Inclined." If the printing solutions covered in Chapter 1 don't do it for you, or if you just want to delve more deeply into the fascinating world of computer typography, look no further. Avoid this chapter, however, if you're the least bit squeamish about viewing the insides of your .INI files!

Installing Windows Fonts

There are two main categories of Windows fonts: TrueType and Adobe Post-Script Type 1. A selection of TrueType fonts comes along for the ride when you install Windows. To use PostScript Type 1 fonts, you must install a separate piece of support software, Adobe Type Manager (ATM), which also includes a selection of fonts. In general, you can intermix TrueType and Type 1 fonts in the same Windows document. (With ATM installed, your printer need not support PostScript to be able to print Type 1 fonts.)

You can expand your selection of fonts by purchasing sets of TrueType or PostScript Type 1 fonts from commercial vendors. Here are the basic procedures for adding them to your system.

In the steps below as well as in the rest of this book, I often use a kind of shorthand for describing a sequence of Windows commands. For example, instead of saying, "From the File pull-down menu, select Run," I'll just say something like "Do File ➤ Run." Sometimes, the less said, the better!

Installing TrueType Fonts

All installations of TrueType fonts must be done through the Control Panel. If you simply copy font files from the vendor's distribution disks, you will not be able to use them successfully in Windows.

To Install a TrueType Font

1. In Windows Program Manager, open the program group Main.

2. Open the Control Panel application.

3. From the Control Panel icons, choose Fonts. The Fonts dialog box will appear, with names of previously installed fonts shown in the Installed Fonts list box.

4. If the font you need is not listed, select the Add button. The Add Fonts dialog box will appear.

5. Insert the vendor's distribution disk in drive A (or B) and change the Drive setting to log on to that drive and display the font files in the List Of Files box.

6. From the List Of Files box, select the name of the font you want to install. (You can select multiple fonts by holding down the Ctrl key as you click each name. Or, hold down the Shift key as you click the top and bottom names in a range of fonts.)

7. Select OK. Windows will copy the selected fonts to the WIN-DOWS\SYSTEM directory, generating separate files for screen fonts in the process.

8. Close all open dialog boxes and windows.

In step 4, you can select a font name and the Remove button to uninstall a font. The check box Delete Font File From Disk will appear. Marking the box causes not only the font to become inactive but also its files to be deleted. Leaving the box unmarked makes the font inactive but leaves the file intact so that it can be reinstalled later. Select Yes to confirm the procedure. Removing a font name from the list conserves memory. Removing its files, as well, frees up both memory and disk space.

Installing ATM

To be able to use PostScript Type 1 fonts in Windows, the ATM program must be started when you start Windows. If you install ATM correctly, this will always be done automatically.

To Install ATM

1. Be sure that no other font-manager program is currently running.

2. Use the command Control Panel ➤ Printers to select and install your printers in Windows.

3. Insert the ATM Program Disk in drive A (or B).

4. In Program Manager, select File ➤ Run.

5. In the Command Line text box, type **a:\install** (or **b:\install**).

6. Select OK.

7. If you wish to change the default location of font files on your hard disk, enter new paths for fonts and font metrics files in the ATM Installer dialog box, then select Install.

8. Select OK. ATM and its fonts will be copied to your hard disk.

9. Before you can use Type 1 fonts, you must exit and restart Windows.

To Control ATM

1. In Program Manager, select the Main program group.

2. Select the ATM Control Panel application.

3. To make ATM inactive (making no other changes), select ATM Off. Otherwise, make sure the setting is On.

4. To unload a font from the current set, select the font name from the Installed ATM Fonts list box, then select Remove and Yes to confirm the removal.

5. To adjust the size of the font cache, click the ↑ or ↓ buttons. (See Chapter 12 for suggested settings.)

6. To use bitmap fonts that reside in your printer, mark the check box Use Pre-Built or Resident Bitmap Fonts. (See the section *Preventing Those Pesky Printer Problems* in Chapter 1.)

7. Select Exit.

8. If you changed the setting of the ATM Off check box in step 4, you must restart Windows for the change to take effect.

To Add Type 1 Fonts

1. Do steps 1–3 of *To Control ATM*.

2. Select Add.

3. If font files are located somewhere other than in the default directories, enter the correct paths in the Target Directory text boxes.

4. Insert the vendor's font distribution disk in drive A (or B).

5. Make selections from the Directories (including device letters) and Available Fonts list boxes.

6. Select Add.

7. Select Exit to close the ATM Control Panel.

8. Exit Program Manager and restart Windows.

All installed fonts, whether TrueType or Type 1, will be available to all Windows applications and will appear in their font selection lists. So, how do you select them, change their attributes, and lay them out on a page attractively?

For the answers to these and other intriguing questions, explore the rest of this book.

Writing a book on fonts is an ambitious endeavor, spanning many different Windows applications, not to mention a variety of professional disciplines. Although I've had my own work here double-checked by an impressive list of experts, there is always the possibility that I misunderstood their patient explanations or that I stated something incorrectly.

If you think I could make something clearer, if you don't find the solution to a particular font problem, or if you find that, despite my sincere efforts to avoid it, I just plain screwed up, please write to me at the following address:

Gerald Jones
c/o SYBEX Inc.
2021 Challenger Drive
Alameda, CA 94501

I'll try to incorporate your tips and suggestions in the next edition of this book.

CHAPTER 1

Composing Business Letters and Memos

OR

How to Address Them with Class

ERHAPS THE BIGGEST factor motivating people to buy laser printers these days is the simple and sincere desire to produce crisp, clean business correspondence. Laser-printed type is jet black and has no funny bumps or jagged edges. The lettering is very attractive, looking like the stuff you see in the glossy magazines. It's slick, it's professional, and it can enhance a business message.

After all, the purpose of writing a letter or memo is to get results—even if the result is just a good impression of your business.

And with the advent of Windows and its family of software applications, it is now possible for users of PCs to get much better looking type from dot-matrix and ink-jet printers, as well. (The Mac world had a head start—but the gap has closed!) In Windows, there is now a wide variety of lettering styles for creating professional-looking documents of all kinds.

What Type of Impression Will You Make?

Even in a document as straightforward as a business letter, the way you choose and compose the type can make a big difference on the impression you make.

There's an acting coach in Los Angeles who says that if you can change your voice, you can change your life. It's a prescription for being more persuasive on the telephone and in meetings. But where the written word is concerned, it can be a matter of changing your type! For example, consider the effect of that dreaded (and now completely unnecessary) "dot-matrix look":

```
To Whom It May Concern:

        This letter was printed by a computer
that generates thousands of these things every
day, so don't expect the personal touch from us.

Mechanically yours,
```

Compare that with the impression given by this example, composed in Windows and output on a laser printer:

Dear Ms. Penworthy,

> This elegant Jouillard type suggests that our organization has the good taste and judgment to serve the discriminating tastes of a person of your fine sensibilities.

So, assuming that you are using Windows and one of its word processing applications, how can you get such attractive and impressive type out of your computer and on paper?

That's the purpose of this chapter—to help you make your correspondence more presentable by dressing it up nicely with judiciously selected fonts.

There's that word: *font!* Before you read much further, you and I had better agree on what we mean by that.

What Type of Type Is a Font?

To a professional typesetter, a *font* is a particular design of lettering in a specific size. The design is called a *typeface* (or just *face*).

Type size is usually measured in *points*. In Windows, one point is $\frac{1}{72}$ inch.

The point size of a font is measured from the tip of the lowest *descender* (such as the tail of a *p* or a *q*) to the tip of the highest *ascender* (such as *b* or a *d*), with a small amount of extra space above and below, depending on the font design. (See the diagram on the inside front cover of this book.)

A standard typeface on typewriters is Courier, which is also available for use in Windows applications. Courier Elite on a typewriter is the 10-point size in Windows, and Courier Pica is the 12-point size:

```
Courier Elite

Courier Pica
```

 *The exact specification used in conventional typesetting is 72.254 points to the inch, so a point equals 0.128 inch, or 0.349 cm. That's just one reason— one of many—why conventional typesetting might not match your computer-generated output, even if the specifications for typeface and size are the same.*

All Upstanding Fonts Have Character

A font generally includes all of the letters of the alphabet in capitals (A–Z) and in lowercase (a–z), as well as the numeric digits 0–9, punctuation marks, special characters such as the dollar sign ($), and perhaps some characters used in other languages (usually referred to as *international characters*). All of the characters in a font constitute its *character set.*

All of the characters in the Arial font are shown in Figure 1.1. This Windows font is similar to Helvetica, which is probably the most widely used set of letters in the Western world.

Fonts differ in the number and variety of characters that they contain. For example, some special-purpose fonts have only capital letters. Most English-language fonts include the British pound sign (£) but often do not have the copyright symbol (©).

FIGURE 1.1

The character set of the Windows font Arial

	!	"	#	$	%	&	'	(	)	*	+	,	-	.	/	0	1	2	3	4	5	6	7	8	9	:	;	<	=	>	?
@	A	B	C	D	E	F	G	H	I	J	K	L	M	N	O	P	Q	R	S	T	U	V	W	X	Y	Z	[	\	]	^	_
`	a	b	c	d	e	f	g	h	i	j	k	l	m	n	o	p	q	r	s	t	u	v	w	x	y	z	{	|	}	~	□
□	□	‚	ƒ	„	…	†	‡	ˆ	‰	Š	‹	Œ	□	□	□	□	‘	’	“	”	•	–	—	˜	™	š	›	œ	□	□	Ÿ
	¡	¢	£	¤	¥	¦	§	¨	©	ª	«	¬	-	®	¯	°	±	²	³	´	µ	¶	·	¸	¹	º	»	¼	½	¾	¿
À	Á	Â	Ã	Ä	Å	Æ	Ç	È	É	Ê	Ë	Ì	Í	Î	Ï	Ð	Ñ	Ò	Ó	Ô	Õ	Ö	×	Ø	Ù	Ú	Û	Ü	Ý	Þ	ß
à	á	â	ã	ä	å	æ	ç	è	é	ê	ë	ì	í	î	ï	ð	ñ	ò	ó	ô	õ	ö	÷	ø	ù	ú	û	ü	ý	þ	ÿ

When Is a Font Just a Font?

In Windows and its applications, the term *font* usually means just *typeface,* without reference to size. That's because most Windows fonts are *scalable,* or can be adjusted continuously over a wide range of point sizes, typically from 1 (very small) to 999 (very big).

In software manuals and in books like this one, you will sometimes see the term *font* used rather loosely to refer to the whole set of appearance options, or *attributes,* that are available for a particular typeface.

Attributes Are the Spice of Type

Attributes are ways of varying the appearance of a typeface. In Windows, font attributes can be applied to individual letters, or characters, or to groups of letters, such as words or even entire paragraphs or documents. Examples of font attributes include bold, italic, underline, double underline, strikethrough, color, hidden, small caps, all caps, letterspacing, superscript, subscript, and drop shadow. There are examples of each in Figure 1.2.

The particular set of attributes that are available to you can vary from one font to another, from one Windows application to another, and also from one printer to another.

FIGURE 1.2

Font attributes provide many ways to alter the appearance—and the impression given by—a single typeface. The font used in this example is Times New Roman.

Roman

Bold

Italic

Single underline

Single underline, words only

Double underline

Hidden doesn't print!

~~Strikethrough~~

SMALL CAPS

ALL CAPS

Here's the (Microsoft) Word on Using Fonts

Changing fonts in Word for Windows is a snap (actually, a click). Other Windows word processing applications work much the same way, so the following examples using Microsoft Word will be fairly typical.

In Word, options that control the appearance of text are called *character formatting.* Many of the most often used options for character formatting are found in the *ribbon,* a set of graphical controls shown in a bar near the top of the screen (Figure 1.3).

FIGURE 1.3

The ribbon at the top of the Word screen has controls for changing fonts and their appearance.

Left tab stop

Center tab stop

Right tab stop

Bold

Italic

Underline

Style box   Font box   Points box

| Normal | | Times New Roman | | 12 | | **B** *I* U | | | | | |

Justify

Align right

Align center

Align left

Decimal tab stop

Show/Hide codes

If you don't see the ribbon at the top of the Word screen, someone turned it off. To make it reappear, select View from the menu bar, then select Ribbon (View ➤ Ribbon).

These Styles Are Ready-Made

The three rectangular openings, or text boxes, on the left side of the ribbon show settings that affect the current font. Each of these is a drop-down box, containing a set of options that opens up, or drops down, when you click the ↓ button on the right side of the box:

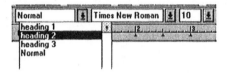

The Style box, located on the left end of the ribbon, usually shows the name of the current *template.* In Word, templates are empty documents with ready-made formatting, including font selections. Templates are a handy way to get professional-looking results without having to sweat the details of character and document formatting.

Not surprisingly, the normal, or default, template is called Normal. It's popular for doing memos and reports. Clicking the button of the Style box reveals five options for text styles within a Normal document: Headings 1–3 (for three sizes of titles), Normal (for the text body of the document), and Normal Indent (for bulleted items and the like).

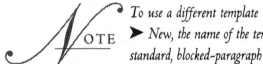 *To use a different template when you begin a document in Word, select File* ➤ *New, the name of the template, then OK. The name of the template for a standard, blocked-paragraph business letter is LETBLOCK.*

The two drop-down boxes to the right of the Style box show options that are preselected for the current style (the style showing in the Style box): The Font box shows the typeface and the Points box shows the type size in points.

For the Normal text style used for the body text of a memo or report, the preselected typeface is Times New Roman and the preselected size is 10 points (about the size of typewriter Elite). With these settings showing in the ribbon, if you start typing, the body text will look something like this:

Times New Roman in the 10-point size is the Normal text in Word.

Remember that you shouldn't press ↵ at the end of each line as you would on a typewriter: Word makes the text *wrap* from one line to the next. You need only press ↵ at the end of a paragraph or a block of text. (See the sidebar *Timely Typing Tips* in this chapter.)

For most business correspondence, reset the normal point size from 10 to 12, as described later in this section. Among your more influential readers may be older business executives —or people of any age who have misplaced their eyeglasses. They will appreciate your considerate choice of the larger, more legible type size.

Having typed a paragraph and pressed ↵, you can change the font quickly to type a heading on the next line. (Headings are appropriate for memos but are not good form in business letters unless you're doing a direct-mail piece.) To change to one of the other ready-made styles, just select it from the Styles box and start typing. For example, click the ↓ button on the Styles box and select Heading 1. Notice that the typeface in the Font box changes to Arial and the size in the Points box changes to 12. Type the next line, and it will look like this:

First-Level Heading

Notice also that the heading appears in **bold** and <u>underlined</u> because the Bold and Underline options have been preselected for this heading style. These options appear as buttons that are depressed in the ribbon:

Set Your Own Style

You can override the preselected styles in the template anywhere in a document. Your changes will apply only to the current document, unless you make an extra effort to change the template, as well. (See *Go Ahead, Play Favorites* in this chapter.)

You're never stuck with your font selections. You can change fonts either

> ¶ Before you start typing, or as you are creating text (on the fly)

> ¶ After you have typed the text, as a way of editing it (as an afterthought)

Changing Character Formatting on the Fly

To change fonts *on the fly,* or as you are typing, you can select a different typeface in the Fonts box, or perhaps a different size in the Points box, and click any of the other buttons on the ribbon to change the formatting. The next character you type will reflect these changes.

For example, it's often necessary to change the font to Italic formatting in the middle of a sentence. You might change to italics to emphasize a word or to show the title of a book. So, just before you type the italicized word or phrase, click the Italic button in the ribbon:

Type the italicized word or phrase, then click the Italic button again, turning the option off this time, and resume typing in the Normal style. For a quick exercise, look at Figure 1.4.

In this example, the typeface remains the same, and its appearance is changed from normal (a Roman typeface) to italic. It's also possible to change the typeface any time, even in mid-sentence.

FIGURE 1.4

To make font changes, as you are typing, click your changes in the ribbon, type the altered text, then reset the options you changed in the ribbon and resume typing in Normal style.

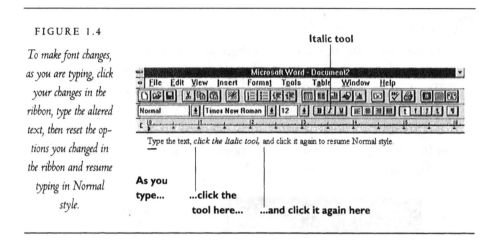

Stay Away from Those Comic Books!

Changing the Font selection in mid-sentence is not something that you should do in business correspondence. It's not that you *can't* do it, you just should avoid it. If you get over-eager with different fonts, your message can acquire what I call the Comic Book Look:

When you **intermix** fonts, you get that **Comic** Book LOOK!

This technique isn't always a wrong choice. For example, used with some discretion, it might be very effective in a magazine ad. It also works well in ransom notes, but I won't testify to this. (If you're looking for this effect, try the Ransom font in Microsoft's TrueType Font Pack 2. For you lazy kidnappers, Ransom generates the jumbled-font effect automatically—without your having to format characters separately.) Later chapters in this book explore some of the more creative uses of fonts.

11

Changing Fonts as an Afterthought

Rather than changing the Font setting as you are typing, it is more common to try a changed look as an afterthought, when you are editing the text. In Word, you can change a single character, a word, a block of text, or an entire document—with just a drag of the mouse and a couple of clicks.

To change a hunk of text—no matter how small or how large—select it first by dragging over it with the mouse. The letters will appear in reverse video (usually, white text on a black background):

Selecting text is a drag. Missed me!

With the text highlighted this way, click the ↓ button on the right end of the Font box. The box opens by dropping down, and a list of all of the available Windows fonts will appear.

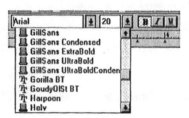

If the list of installed fonts is longer than the open box, scroll bars will appear on the right. Drag the slider or click the arrow buttons to move up and down the list.

Click on a font name, and the highlighted text will change accordingly. It's that simple.

When you have highlighted a block of text, you can change any of the character formatting options in the ribbon: Style (perhaps affecting all the other options), Font, Size, Bold, Italic, and Underline.

TrueType and PostScript: Those Funny Font Symbols

When you open the Fonts drop-down box, the list shows only the fonts installed *for the current printer*. Font names preceded by the *TT* symbol are True-Type fonts supplied with Windows:

ᴛᴛ Arial

TrueType fonts can be reproduced on just about any printer—except some old dot-matrix models that don't do graphics and even older daisy-wheel printers that work like typewriters.

Fonts preceded by a little printer symbol are—you guessed it—supported only on specific types and models of printers. PostScript fonts, the other most commonly used category of Windows fonts, are printer-specific:

🖶 Arial MT

The PostScript outline fonts used in Windows applications are referred to as Adobe PostScript Type 1. Another variety, called Adobe Type 3, is termed "user-defined" and is handled by PostScript as bitmaps, or arrays of dots. (For obscure reasons, Adobe Systems had intended for there to be a Type 2, as well, but it didn't happen.)

Fonts for which the little symbol is missing are probably Windows 3.0 fonts such as Modern, Roman, and Script. You can use these if you want, but there are usually better alternatives in TrueType or PostScript.

So—which fonts should you use? TrueType? PostScript? Bob's Fonts? The short answer is: As long as you're going to print the document on the same printer, you can select any of the fonts you see in the list. (And, yes, it's usually okay to mix TrueType and PostScript fonts in the same document.)

However, there is a longer answer—at least one book longer. Dealing with differences between TrueType and PostScript is a recurring topic throughout the chapters that follow. (Hey, if it were simple, you wouldn't need a book!)

Go Ahead, Play Favorites

You can change the preselected font for any style of any Word template so that it will be used for all new documents.

Select the style you want to change in the Style box. For example, if you wanted to change the font of the first-level headings in the Normal template, you would select the style Heading 1.

Then, from the menu bar select Format ➤ Character. The Character dialog box will appear, as shown in Figure 1.5. Select the Font, Points, and Style options you want. To make them more or less permanent, click the Use As Default button. When Word asks you to confirm the change to the template, click the Yes button. (If you don't click the Use As Default button, your changes will apply only to the current document.)

FIGURE 1.5

You can reset the font options for the current template and style in the Character dialog box.

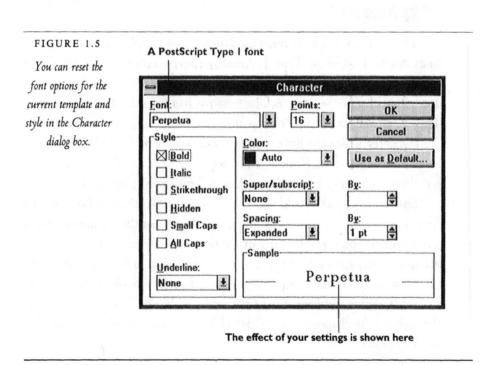

A PostScript Type I font

The effect of your settings is shown here

Learn How to Pick 'Em

As you can see from the foregoing examples, there's nothing particularly difficult about selecting or changing fonts in Word for Windows. It's just as easy in other Windows applications, although the commands and procedures might be different.

So, working with fonts can be like buying fine art: You don't have to know much about it; you just have to know what you like. Since there are literally hundreds of fonts available for use in Windows, the real challenge can be choosing a typeface that both makes a favorable business impression and also conveys something distinctive about you or your company.

Take a closer look at a business message set in 12-point Courier New (the TrueType version of Courier):

```
        Earnings for the year were up, due to increased
    sales volume. Cash flow improved due to the sale and
    lease-back of the company's plant in Lower Slobbovia.
```

Neat, clean, businesslike—it's a correct but also a very conventional choice. Courier has been so common on office typewriters that it is now the "expected" typeface in business letters.

Take an even closer look at Courier New. There's something about it that's, well, uninteresting. One reason for this is the fact that the lines of each letter have a single, uniform thickness:

Earnings

Courier (an Adobe PostScript Type 1 font) and Courier New are called *stroke* fonts because all the characters are composed of single lines and curves, or strokes.

 *Another distinguishing characteristic of Courier and Courier New is that each letter takes up the same amount of horizontal space. For example, there's extra white space if either side of the letter i so that it has the same width as the letter*

m. *(For more of the subject of letterspacing, see* Careful How You Space Those Letters! *in Chapter 2.)*

Compare the stroke letters of Courier New with the thick-and-thin design of the default font for Word body text—Times New Roman:

Earnings

This font is patterned after Times Roman, a very readable typeface that was developed by Stanley Morison in 1931 for *The Times* of London newspaper. Times New Roman is an *outline* font. It is built and stored in the computer as a "hollow" outline, so that the form of a character can have considerable variation in thickness. To make the character solid when it is displayed or printed, the computer software fills the outline with black—or any other color you select.

Most Windows fonts are outline fonts—for two reasons. First, fonts created as outlines can have more interesting and varied designs. Second, outline fonts can be *scaled,* or sized, readily so that the letters remain attractive and readable whether the size is large or small.

So, here's the same business message set in 12-point Times New Roman:

> Earnings for the year were up, due to increased sales volume. Cash flow improved due to the sale and lease-back of the company's plant in Lower Slobbovia.

Classy, dignified, professional—these are the words you might use to describe the impression of Times New Roman. If it looks like the type in the magazines, that's no coincidence—since its predecessor Times Roman is perhaps the most-used typeface in print journalism.

Maybe Times is your cup of tea, or maybe not. Quite a different impression is given by 12-point Arial:

Earnings for the year were up, due to increased sales volume. Cash flow improved due to the sale and lease-back of the company's plant in Lower Slobbovia.

Modern, straightforward, no nonsense—does it say those things to you? Look back at Times New Roman, which is a *serif* face. There are little frills at the ends of the letters. Serifs are an aspect of the design that make it more complex, which for some people means more interesting. But Arial is a *sans serif* face—no frills:

Earnings

Courier New, Times New Roman, and Arial are all included in the standard set of TrueType fonts that come with Windows. Before leaving this topic of taste and tastefulness in type, consider one more face— Garamand (a variation of Garamond), which is similar in many respects to Times Roman:

Earnings for the year were up, due to increased sales volume. Cash flow improved due to the sale and lease-back of the company's plant in Lower Slobbovia.

Garamand has all of the class of Times New Roman, but for many people it also conveys elegance. It's an excellent choice for a business letter. But you won't find it in the standard Windows fonts.

If you want something more, you usually have to pay a price. The Garamond face shown here is included in the Typecase assortment of additional TrueType fonts from Swfte International.

Timely Typing Tips

No offense to your beloved typing teacher, but you may have to un-learn some of your old habits when you are composing typeset-quality text on a computer. Here are some guidelines:

- As I hinted already in this chapter, don't press the carriage return (↵ or Enter) at the end of each line of text. When the words you are typing reach the right edge of the screen, bravely keep typing and let the word processor wrap the text to the next line. The only carriage returns should be at the ends of paragraphs and bulleted lines. If you omit the extra carriage returns, the software will be able to recompose your paragraphs prettily if you later decide to change the margins.

- Don't double-space after a period (or after other punctuation marks, for that matter). One space will do nicely. If you include the extra space, varicose-like white veins, or *rivers*, will appear to wend their way through your otherwise shapely paragraphs.

- In general, don't use the Spacebar in place of the Tab key. For example, press Tab to indent the beginning of a paragraph. Also use Tab to move from one column to another in a table. If you use blank spaces instead, the vertical alignment of your text might look somewhat ragged. (And don't build tables manually at all—unless you have no better alternative. To let Word set a nice table for you, the command is Table ➤ Insert Table. You might also have a look at *Building Tables* in Chapter 3.)

- Don't use an asterisk (*) or a lowercase 0 in place of a bullet to mark items in a list. Most computer fonts have special bullet characters—and some extra-special fonts have nothing *but* fancy bullets! (See *Where Are Those Special Characters?* below.) In Microsoft Word for Windows, you can get a "generic" bullet by holding down the Alt key while you press 0, 1, 4, and then 9 on the numeric keypad (Alt-0149, with Num Lock on).

¶ Other special characters should be used in place of stuff you learned to improvise only because there were no equivalents on the typewriter: en dashes (short dashes slightly longer than a hyphen), em dashes (long dashes you got used to typing as two hyphens), the ellipsis (… to show omitted material), fractions (use $\frac{1}{2}$ instead of 1/2), and quotation marks (use " and " instead of the accursed ditto mark "). Key codes for these special characters you will probably use a lot are given in Table 1.1.

¶ Use the *superscript* and *subscript* features of your word processor to type numbers that are used in footnotes, mathematical expressions, and chemical formulas. Superscript characters are shown slightly above and subscript characters slightly below a line of text, typically in a smaller point size. The Word command for inserting a superscript or subscript is Format ➤ Character ➤ Super/Subscript. This command creates the correct alignment and point size automatically in relation to the current font.

CHARACTER	CHARACTER NAME	ANSI KEY CODE
…	Ellipsis	Alt-0133
"	Open quote	Alt-0147
"	Close quote	Alt-0148
–	En dash	Alt-0150
—	Em dash	Alt-0151
$\frac{1}{2}$	Half	Alt-0189

T A B L E 1.1: *ANSI Key Codes for Commonly Used Special Characters*

Where Are My Fonts?
(Did You Install Them?)

As of Windows version 3.1, several TrueType fonts come with the installation, including Arial, Courier New, Symbol, Times New Roman, and Wingdings.

Get a List of Available Fonts

To see a list of these fonts, open the program group Main and select Control Panel ➤ Fonts.

The Fonts dialog box will open, as shown in Figure 1.6. The fonts that are available to your Windows applications are listed in the Installed Fonts

FIGURE 1.6

*Selecting Main ➤
Control Panel ➤
Fonts displays a list
of available fonts.*

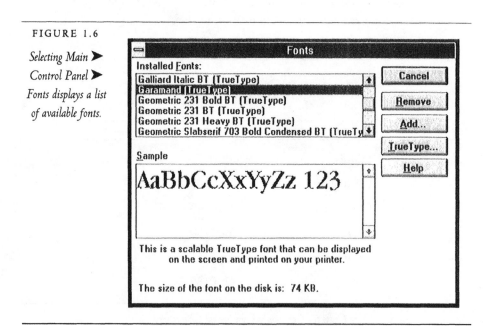

box. When you select a font name from this list, you get a preview of it in the Sample box, along with a brief explanation.

TrueType fonts in this list are identified with the notation (TrueType) after the font name.

Using PostScript Fonts

To use PostScript fonts in Windows with non-PostScript printers, you must install a separate program, Adobe Type Manager, (ATM). ATM includes an assortment of PostScript Type 1 fonts. Once installed, this program is normally loaded along with Windows and runs all the time during your work sessions. It permits PostScript fonts to be printed on non-Post-Script printers, improves printing speed, and improves the resolution, or fineness of detail, in fonts that are displayed on the screen.

ATM is provided with many Windows applications, including all applications from Lotus Development Corporation. These include Ami Pro, 1-2-3, Improv, and Freelance Graphics.

There's more about ATM, including technical notes, in Chapter 12.

Exchanging Text and Formats with other Applications

One of the nifty features of Windows is the ability to exchange data quickly and easily among applications. Depending on the capabilities of the applications, you can exchange text and graphics, as well as *multimedia objects* such as sound recordings and movies (animated sequences).

In Windows parlance, the application you get the data from is called the *source* and the application that receives it is called the *destination.* To copy data

Hiring a Good Font Manager

ATM is one of several available programs called *font managers*. If you never plan to venture outside the realm of TrueType, you might not need to hire a separate font manager because you can inspect, add, and remove TrueType fonts through the Windows Control Panel.

The main reason to install a font manager is to be able to use fonts that are in other formats, such as PostScript. Examples of formats that cannot be used in Windows without a font manager or conversion program are Post-Script Type 1 and Type 3, Nimbus Q, Intellifont, and Bitstream Speedo.

Particularly for people who acquire lots and lots of fonts, font management software also can provide another valuable service. When many fonts reside on your system, Windows can take a very long time to load and your applications can slow down generally. It can also be tedious to scroll through a long list of fonts just to pick one that you use all the time. To resolve these problems, some font managers permit you to create *application groups* of fonts, or sublists of the specific fonts that you use most often in each application.

Limiting the number of fonts available to an application has another important benefit: It can make your documents print faster, as noted below in *Preventing those Pesky Printer Problems*.

There's more on font management software in Chapter 12.

from one application to another, you normally select the data in the source application, then do the command Edit ➤ Copy to put it on the Clipboard (a scratch-pad area of memory). You then switch to the destination, select the point of insertion, and do Edit ➤ Paste.

If you have tried this type of data exchange with text, you probably have noticed that appearance attributes, including fonts, don't necessarily come along for the ride.

To get the fonts as well as the text in an application such as Word, you must do Edit ➤ Paste Special instead of Edit ➤ Paste. The Paste Special dialog box will appear:

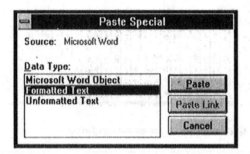

If your text selection in the source application contains appearance information, such as fonts, the option Formatted Text will be listed. Select it and then select the OK button to close the dialog box and insert the formatted text into the destination document.

If your selection is a table, it may include other appearance formatting such as spacing, grid lines, and shading. To insert such a table as well as its appearance formatting, select Edit ➤ Paste Special in the destination and select Formatted Table in the dialog box, then select OK.

Where Are Those Special Characters?

As I've said, each font can have its own assortment of special characters. And some fonts are nothing *but* special characters! It's not difficult to grab one when you need it.

Grabbing a Special Character in Word

If you're working in Word, select Insert ➤ Symbol. The Symbol dialog box will open, as shown in Figure 1.7.

FIGURE 1.7

This dialog box appears in Word when you select Insert ➤ Symbol.

Insert selected character in document

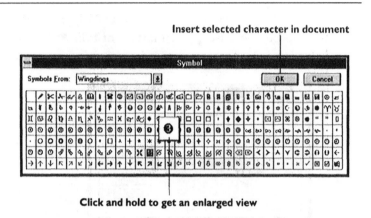

Click and hold to get an enlarged view

The default selection in the Symbols From drop-down box is Symbol, one of those font sets that has nothing but special characters. If you click a character and hold the mouse button down, the character will appear in an enlarged view. To pick one of these, just select the character in the table and then click OK, and it will appear at the insertion point in the current document.

To pick a character from the font that is currently selected in the Font box in the ribbon, select (Normal Text) in the Symbols From drop-down box. All of the characters in the current font (such as Times New Roman) will appear in the table. Click your selection, then click OK.

Snagging Special Characters in Windows

If you are working in a Windows application that doesn't have its own command for retrieving special characters, you can get them anyway by using the Character Map application.

In Program Manager, open (or switch to) the Accessories application group. Select the Character Map application. The Character Map dialog box will open (Figure 1.8). It looks much like the Symbol dialog box in

FIGURE 1.8

*You can copy
sequences of special
characters to the
Clipboard from this
dialog box, which
appears when you
select Accessories ➤
Character Map.*

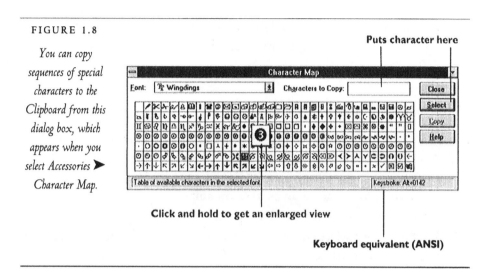

Puts character here

Click and hold to get an enlarged view

Keyboard equivalent (ANSI)

Word, but it has an extra feature that can be very handy: You can select an
entire sequence of special characters and copy them to the Clipboard, from
which you will then be able to retrieve them into any Windows application.

In the Character Map dialog box, first select the Font that contains the
characters you want. To view a character more closely, click and hold on it.
An enlarged picture of the character will pop up.

To select a character for copying, click it, then click the Select button.
The character will be inserted in the Characters To Copy text box.

Select the rest of the characters in a sequence the same way. Each will
be inserted in the Characters To Copy text box.

When all of the characters you want are showing in the Characters To
Copy text box, click the Copy button. The characters will be copied to the
Clipboard.

Select the Close button to exit the Character Map application, then start
or switch to the destination application and document. Then do Edit ➤
Paste to retrieve the characters from the Clipboard, which places them at the

insertion point. (In some applications, it will be necessary to use the Paste Special command instead to make sure that the font stays the same.)

What About Those Silly Fractions?

You can use the procedures just described to retrieve the ready-made fractions that are included in a font. Text fonts such as Times New Roman generally have $\frac{1}{4}$ (Alt-0188), $\frac{1}{2}$ (Alt-0189), and $\frac{3}{4}$ (Alt-0190).

If you need a fraction in another amount, you can construct it in Word. Select Format ➤ Character ➤ Superscript and type the numerator (top number). Then select Format ➤ Character ➤ None (for Superscript/Subscript) and type the slash character (/). Then select Format ➤ Character ➤ Subscript and type the denominator (bottom number). Do Format ➤ Character ➤ None (for Superscript/Subscript) to change back to normal text and resume typing.

If you use nonstandard fractions a lot, you might consider using a font manipulation program such as Fontographer to actually construct those fractions as custom characters in the font of your choice. See Chapter 11 for more on creating your own characters. (Some special-purpose fonts consist of digits for numerators and denominators.)

Preventing Those Pesky Printer Problems

None of this advice will be much good to you unless you can get your documents to print properly. Here are some of the most common reasons why fonts cause trouble in printers and vice versa.

Printing Takes Too Long

Printing in Windows is generally slower than in its counterpart DOS applications, just because the documents are so much fancier—even text is handled like graphics to accommodate all those lovely fonts. But there are a few things you can do to speed things up.

Turn off Print Manager. This *print spooling* feature of Windows is supposed to let you work on other applications while a document is being printed. In practice, it might be quicker all around to get the printing over with, then resume your work. From the Main program group, select Control Panel ➤ Printers. The Printers dialog box will open. Unmark the check box Use Print Manager, then click the Close button.

Try using printer-resident or bitmap fonts. If your printer stores fonts internally, or if you have a set of fonts for it as a plug-in cartridge, printing can go faster if you permit the Windows printer driver to use these instead. To use printer fonts instead of ATM's PostScript Type 1 software fonts, open the ATM Control Panel in the Main program group and mark the check box Use Pre-Built Or Resident Fonts. Select the Exit button and restart Windows. The procedure for using printer fonts instead of TrueType varies by type of printer, so follow the printer manufacturer's instructions. If you try this approach, however, beware that you are more likely to encounter a different problem: The fonts on the screen might not match the printed ones exactly.

Try printing fonts as graphics. If you are using version 2.5 or later of ATM, it can be more efficient to print all fonts as graphics. In the Main program group, open the ATM Control Panel and mark the check box Print ATM Fonts As Graphics. Click the Exit button and restart Windows. To print TrueType fonts also as graphics, select Windows Control Panel ➤ Printers. Select the name of the printer you will be using from the Installed Printers list. Procedures from this point onward vary among printer drivers. For example, if you are using a Hewlett-Packard LaserJet II, click the Setup button, then the Options button. Mark the check box Print TrueType As Graphics. Select the OK button in each of the two open dialog boxes, then the Close button in the remaining one. If you are using a PostScript printer, such as the Apple LaserWriter, click the Setup button, then the Options button, then the Advanced button. In the TrueType Fonts section of the dialog box, change the Send To Printer As drop-down box to Bitmap (Type 3), and unmark the check boxes User Printer Fonts and Use Substitution Table. Select OK in each of three dialog boxes, then Close to exit the remaining one. (This approach won't work if the options for your printer don't include the equivalent of "Print TrueType As Graphics.")

Use no more than six fonts in a document.   Six fonts may seem like a lot, but consider that, depending on the font, bold and italic attributes might count as separate fonts.

Change the size of the font cache.   If you are using ATM, you can vary the amount of memory set aside for handling fonts. Adobe Systems recommends 64K for each megabyte of system RAM in excess of 1 Mb. Another rule of thumb is to use 32K for each font that you use routinely. Use the setting that is the smaller of these two formulas.

The Screen Font Doesn't Look Like the Output

You are not likely to encounter this problem with TrueType fonts, provided that you are actually sending TrueType to the printer rather than using "equivalent" printer-resident fonts. With TrueType, the same set of computer font files is used to generate the display on the screen as well as the printed output.

This is not the case with PostScript fonts. ATM actually has one set of fonts for the screen and one matching set for printing. So, one problem might be that you moved font files or directories and didn't tell ATM about it by reinstalling the fonts.

Mismatches are most likely to occur when you are using printer-resident fonts instead of software fonts. Follow the procedure described above, *Try Printing Fonts As Graphics*. If that solves the problem, the printer-resident fonts are probably different from the screen fonts installed in Windows.

A related problem is that the printer driver might be switching fonts on you. If the setup options for your printer include the option Use Substitution Table or the like, turn it off. (However, substituting one font for another might be required when you are printing to a disk file that will be loaded onto another computer system. The purpose of the substitution table is to overcome incompatibilities between systems that might have different sets of installed fonts.)

Document Prints Okay on One Printer but Not on Another

In Windows, each printer can have a different list of installed fonts. You can inspect the list by looking under the printer name—such as [HP Laser-Jet Series II,LPT1] or [PostScript,LPT1]—in the WIN.INI file. You can use the Notepad text editor to open this file, which is found in the WINDOWS directory.

Please don't make changes in the WIN.INI file unless you are sure you know what you are doing. Most of the time, you need not make changes directly to this file. You can usually make the required change through the Windows Control Panel or in an application, which, in turn, will update WIN.INI. If you feel you need to mess around with this stuff, have a look in Chapter 12, which has some pointers. Even then, make a backup copy of the unchanged file as protection in case you screw things up.

When you have the WIN.INI file open in Notepad, select File ➤ Print to print it out. Then you can study the font lists for each of your installed printers. If the fonts that are not printing successfully are found in the lists of the printers involved, the cause of the problem lies elsewhere.

If you don't find the names of the required fonts listed for one of the printers, you shouldn't change the WIN.INI file directly. Instead, follow the printer manufacturer's instructions for reinstalling the fonts you need.

As another approach, follow the procedures under *Try Printing Fonts As Graphics*, above. This should work for any printer driver that can handle fonts as graphics. However, without a font manager such as ATM that can compose font graphics on the fly, you might not be happy with the printing speed.

PostScript Font Crashes the Printer

The straightforward answer to this one is that the printer may not support PostScript. You must generally do one of two things to be able to use PostScript fonts on a non-PostScript printer:

Install ATM.   This program translates PostScript Type 1 fonts for most printers for which there is an installed Windows printer driver. Optionally, ATM can send fonts to the printer as instructions for the closest-match resident font or as graphics, as described above.

Install a PostScript emulation card in the printer.   This conversion might be available as a plug-in cartridge. PostScript emulation software is also available *for the computer* and may be less expensive than converting the printer. But, ATM is a better solution if the main concern is simply being able to print fonts. Upgrading the printer might be necessary, however, if you want to be able to use it with PostScript graphics applications such as Aldus PageMaker or Adobe Illustrator.

Even after you've installed ATM or upgraded the printer to handle PostScript directly, you could still have problems. Again, the list of installed fonts for the printer in WIN.INI might not match those you have installed in Windows or in the application. If there is no font substitution table to take care of font names the printer driver doesn't recognize, the font won't print.

To resolve this for a printer that uses the PostScript printer driver, you might mark the check box Use Substitution Table in Advanced printer options—and perhaps also click the Edit Substitution Table button to change the names of fonts to be substituted. Beware, though, that font names assigned by type vendors, Microsoft Windows, and the PostScript language might all be different—for the same font! As you might expect, messing around with font substitution tables is not for everyone. Read more about it in Chapter 12.

CHAPTER 2

Designing Persuasive Print Ads

~ or ~

Getting Fancy with Fonts

HAPTER 1 DEALS mainly with *text fonts* such as Courier and Times New Roman. Text fonts are used for creating the body of letters, reports, newspapers, books—and print advertisements.

This chapter introduces another category of typefaces—*display fonts.* Display fonts are intended primarily for titles, headlines, logos, and other decorative uses.

Designing a Sales Message

You might say that working with display fonts is the creative side of typography, but the design of an effective magazine ad uses both display and text fonts in careful combination, as shown in Figure 2.1.

The reader's eye is drawn first to a headline in a display font. In a good design, the purpose of the ad is conveyed not only in the words of the headline, but also in the style of the display font used to create that headline.

The body of the ad is composed in a highly readable text font. Just as it does in a business letter, the design of the font should convey an impression of the product or company represented by the ad.

But unlike business correspondence, the body text of an advertisement uses white space—or gaps within the text—more creatively. This element

FIGURE 2.1

This magazine ad uses display typography in the headline along with carefully composed body text to make a well-coordinated impression on the reader.

of text *composition* is just as important to the overall creative effect as the design of the headline.

In longer ads, the body copy may be further broken up by the insertion of *subheads*. Subheads are decorative headlines that highlight the main topics of the ad, subdividing the page into blocks, or areas of interest.

Careful How You Space Those Letters!

An important difference between the composition of text and display fonts is in the *letterspacing*, or amount of white space between the characters of a word.

Letterspacing can vary even among text fonts. Consider Courier New and Times New Roman.

```
Courier is a monospace font.
```

Times New Roman is a proportionally spaced font.

Typewriter fonts like Courier and Courier New are called *monospace* fonts because each character and its surrounding white space always take up the same amount of overall space. So, an 80-character line of Courier 12-point is always the same length, whether it is composed of wide characters like *m* or narrow characters like *l.*

```
mmmmmmmmmm
llllllll
```

The amount of white space varies between letters because wide characters like *m* take up almost the full width of a monospace character, and narrow characters like *l* get the same amount of room and have lots of white space surrounding them:

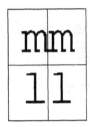

Monospace fonts are very convenient for some purposes. For example, aligning letters and numbers vertically in a table is greatly simplified with monospace fonts. Computer displays that have a fixed number of character positions (such as 80-column displays) can show only monospace fonts.

In contrast, typeset-quality fonts use *proportional* letterspacing. Times New Roman is an example. The amount of white space between letters is variable, depending upon whether the characters are wide or narrow. The effect is more pleasing, because words don't appear to have internal gaps; also, the characters of words appear to flow together better to form a group. Proportional fonts are thought to be more readable because these groups can be recognized more easily as entire words—and the ideas those words represent—than as collections of individual characters.

While proportional spacing is prettier, it greatly complicates the process of composing type. What's more, proportional spacing, by itself, doesn't always produce the most attractive results.

The Joys of Kerning

If you were always to insert the same amount of space between letters, some combinations of characters would show unsightly gaps. Consider a capital *T* and a lowercase *o*. If you use the same letterspacing for this pair as for a pair of m's, there will be too much white space between the *T* and the *o*:

Today

Seeing this makes you uneasy, even if you don't know why. Why is the poor little *o* running away from the big *T* ? They don't seem to make a single, cozy word.

If you try to solve this by decreasing the letterspacing between all the other characters in a line or paragraph, everything will look cramped:

Today

The solution is to make an exception for such problematic pairs of letters and draw just these special combinations closer to one another. In typography, closing up the space between letters is called *kerning*, and the letters in a font to which this special spacing must be applied are called *kerning pairs*. Here we see just the *T* and *o* have been kerned, leaving the other letters alone:

Today

The designer of a type font must identify the letter combinations that will be treated as kerning pairs and then determine the amount of space to be inserted between each of these pairs to make an attractive combination. Approaches to kerning vary widely among fonts. Some fonts have a large number of kerning pairs, while others—including all monospace fonts—don't bother with kerning at all.

Most of the time, and especially when you're composing business correspondence, you don't have to be concerned about the effects of proportional letterspacing, including kerning. The Windows software takes care of it. For example, if you type a paragraph in Times New Roman in Microsoft Word, the characters will be proportionally spaced automatically.

But you do need to worry about custom letterspacing when

- You don't like the result of a block of body text in a particular font. The easiest solution can be to select a different font that makes your words prettier, perhaps a font with more kerning pairs.

- You are trying to achieve an attractive design using a display font to create a headline or a logo, as described later in this chapter. In such cases, you will want to use an application that makes it possible to adjust kerning of display type, such as CorelDRAW.

Learning to Love Ligatures

Particularly for display fonts, there's a solution to the ugly letter-pair problem that goes kerning one better. A *ligature* is an otherwise difficult pair of stand-offish characters that are made to connect, or touch one another, and are included in the font design as a separate character. The *ae, fi, fl,* and *oe* letter pairs often were designed as ligatures in old-fashioned text fonts. Ligatures can be particularly stylish when they appear at either the beginning or end of a logo in letter pairs such as *ph* or *th*. The most common use of ligatures today is to create stylish and distinctive corporate and product logos.

These days, only a few of the fancy display fonts include ligatures. However, with some font manipulation programs, such as Fontographer, you can control the letterspacing and even modify the character outlines to create special characters such as ligatures in Windows fonts.

Designing Headlines with Special Effects

Some Windows applications permit you to manipulate conventional fonts—whether they are intended for text or for display—to create appealing special effects.

You can compose headlines in a display font and add attractive graphics, such as borders and shadows, in the Microsoft Draw graphics application, which is included with Word. However, the letterspacing capabilities of Word are rather limited.

The first set of examples here are a bit more ambitious. They are done in CorelDRAW Release 4 for Windows. You can create your headlines in one of these applications, then use Edit ➤ Copy in the application to place the graphic object on the Clipboard and Edit ➤ Paste Special in an application such as Word to retrieve the graphic into a text document.

Or, since CorelDRAW can also produce body text, you could do an entire ad page in that application. I'll show you some examples in Corel-DRAW, then give you some tips on doing much the same work in Word.

To begin, here are just a few examples of the wide variety of special effects for display type that can be produced with CorelDRAW.

Creating and Kerning Display Type

CorelDRAW provides two different text-creation modes: For creating display type, you use the Artistic Text tool. For creating body text, you use the

Paragraph Text tool. These tools appear when you click and keep holding the mouse button down on the Text tool:

When this tool menu pops up, you can click the tool you want, or you can keep holding the mouse button down as you drag the highlight to the tool. If you simply click once on the Text tool instead of holding the mouse button down, the Artistic Text tool will be selected.

To create display type in CorelDRAW, select the Artistic Text tool (Figure 2.2). The mouse pointer will change to small crosshairs in the drawing area. Click the place in the drawing at which the text will begin. Then, type the text.

To set the font and other text attributes, use the Pick tool to select the text and do Text ➤ Character. Or, set options in the Text roll-up menu (Text ➤ Text Roll-Up), then click its Apply button. Click the Zoom In tool and drag a small area around the text to get a closer view as you adjust the letterspacing. To return to a full view of the page, click the Show Page tool. (Both of these tools are found in the Zoom pop-up tool menu, as shown in Figure 2.3. Click on the Zoom tool to select from this menu.)

To adjust letterspacing, click the Shape tool (the second tool from the top in the toolbar):

FIGURE 2.2

*Use the Artistic Text
tool in CorelDRAW
to create text, espe-
cially for display type
such as headlines
and logos.*

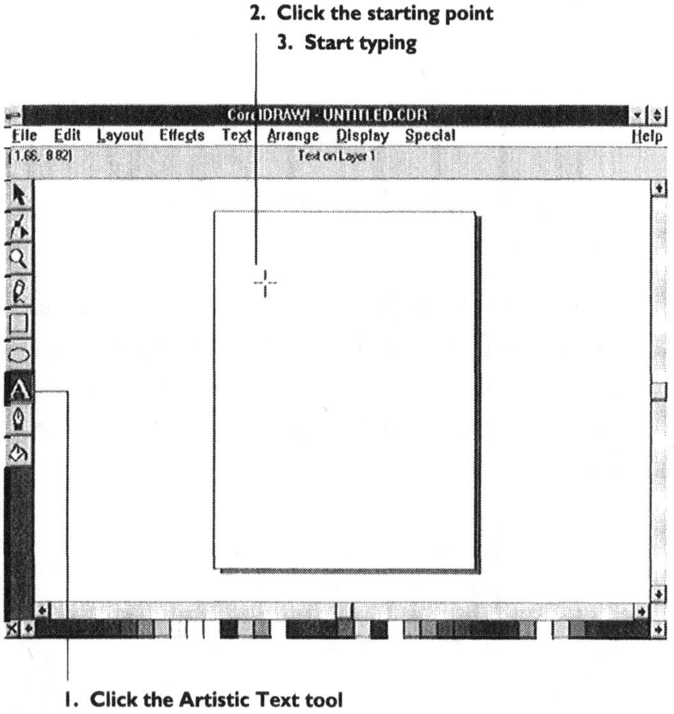

2. Click the starting point

3. Start typing

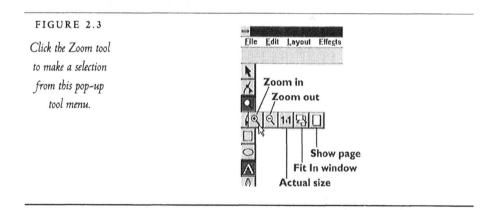

1. Click the Artistic Text tool

FIGURE 2.3

*Click the Zoom tool
to make a selection
from this pop-up
tool menu.*

Zoom in

Zoom out

Show page

Fit In window

Actual size

Then, click the text object you want to modify. A small, hollow handle (called a *node*) will appear at the lower-left corner of each letter:

Click the node of the letter you want to move. To move several letters together without changing the spacing between them, hold down the Shift key while you click each of their nodes. The selected nodes will change from hollow to solid. Drag the nodes to move the letters and adjust the letterspacing:

Don't be concerned if you move the letters above or below the *baseline*, the imaginary line on which the letters sit. Once you've got the spacing you want (with the nodes still visible), do Text ➤ Align To Baseline, and the letters will be realigned properly. If you decide that you want to return to the default letterspacing—canceling your adjustments—do Text ➤ Straighten Text.

For a creative effect, you might want to move individual letters above or below the baseline. This effect is called *bounce*, and it's usually done to add some silliness to the message:

Today!

Sizing, Stretching, and Mirroring Text

In CorelDRAW, these three types of transformations are done in much the same way:

> **Sizing** makes a text object larger or smaller, retaining its original proportions.

> **Stretching** distorts the text in one dimension only—horizontally or vertically.

> **Mirroring** creates a reverse image of the selected text.

Scaling, stretching, and mirroring—like many other types of transformations in CorelDRAW—can be done on most kinds of objects, including text. In CorelDRAW, the text will remain fully editable after the transformation. For example, you can stretch a word, then while it is still selected do Text ➤ Edit Text to change its spelling or even replace it with a different word, and the edited word will be displayed with the same stretched effect as the original. (Some other drawing programs don't permit text editing after it has been transformed.)

Picking a Text Object

To transform text object in CorelDRAW, select it by clicking the Pick tool, then clicking the object once. (If you click it twice, it will be selected instead for skewing and rotation, as explained below.) Besides the already familiar little letter nodes, you will also see eight larger, solid handles surrounding the object:

Monster Movie

Move the mouse pointer to one of the object's solid handles until the pointer shape changes to small crosshairs. Then, drag the handle in the direction of the transformation. The type of transformation depends on which handle you drag and where you drag it.

If you drag one of the four corner handles, you will resize the text proportionally (without distorting it). This action has the same effect as doing Text ➤ Character and changing the point size of the font. The benefit of dragging a handle is that you can adjust the size by eye to fit a headline exactly within your page layout.

Monster Movie

If you drag one of the four middle handles, you will stretch (distort) the text in that direction.

Monster Movie

If you drag any of the handles past the handle on its opposite side, you'll get a mirror-image of the text. (Think of this operation as folding the text back over on itself.)

Monster Movie

Holding down the Ctrl key as you drag a handle will constrain the transformation to increments of 100 percent of the object's size. Holding down the Shift key causes the object to grow or stretch from its center—in two opposite directions at the same time. You can hold down both the Ctrl *and* Shift keys as you drag to get both effects.

To specify sizing by numeric point size, select the text with the Pick tool and do Text ➤ Character instead. Or, specify font options in the Text roll-up menu and click its Apply button. To specify stretching by horizontal and vertical percentages, select the text and do Effects ➤ Stretch & Mirror (or press Alt-F9).

Skewing and Rotating Text

Skewing is a kind of slanting distortion. As in some other drawing programs, skewing an object in CorelDRAW is closely related to rotation, turning an object clockwise or counterclockwise around its center point. For example, you might rotate a headline to place it at an angle in relation to the body text below it or to create a *banner* that cuts across the corner of a magazine cover.

After clicking the Pick tool, clicking a text object *twice* selects it for skewing and rotation. (Or, if handles around the object indicate that it is already selected for sizing, clicking it once more selects it for skewing and rotation.) Either way, a different set of handles will appear:

Each of the handles appears as a small, double-tipped arrow. When you move the mouse pointer to one of these handles, the pointer shape changes to small crosshairs. Dragging one of the four corner arrows will rotate the object:

Dragging one of the four middle arrows will skew the object:

You can adjust the *center of rotation* simply by moving the mouse pointer to it (the circle symbol) and dragging it. To constrain the rotation movement, hold down the Ctrl key and the rotation will be constrained to increments of 15 degrees.

NOTE *To specify rotation or skewing by typing the number of degrees by which the object will be turned, select the text and do Effects ➤ Rotate & Skew (or press Alt-F8).*

Adding Perspective to Text

Another special effect in CorelDRAW that is similar to skewing is *perspective*, which can change the shape of a text object so that it appears to recede toward an imaginary *vanishing point:*

To add perspective to an existing text object, select the text by clicking the Pick tool and then the text. Do Effects ➤ Add Perspective. Move the mouse pointer to the selection handle that is closest to the vanishing point you want to create. When the pointer is over the handle, it will change to small crosshairs. Drag this pointer to the vanishing point, as shown in Figure 2.4. When you release the mouse button, the text will be redrawn according to this perspective.

FIGURE 2.4

To make dimensional text, select the text, do Effects ➤ Add Perspective, and drag a handle to the vanishing point. (When positioned directly over a handle, the pointer will change from the arrowhead shown here to small crosshairs.)

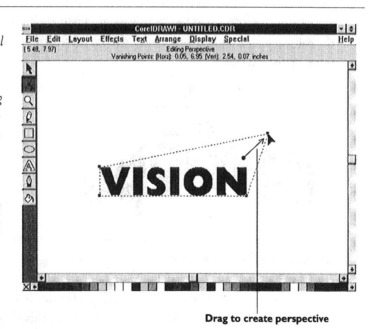

Drag to create perspective

When you're applying perspective, you need not be limited to a single vanishing point. You can drag any of the four handles at the corners of the selected text to distort the object in that direction.

Creating Envelope Distortion

In CorelDRAW Release 4, an *envelope* is an imaginary bounding box that can be used to define the shape of an object, including text. You can distort the object to almost any shape by dragging the contours of the envelope.

To add an envelope to a text object, click the Pick tool and then the text. Then, do Effects ➤ Envelope Roll-Up. The Envelope roll-up menu will appear, as shown in Figure 2.5.

Click the Add New button in the roll-up menu. An envelope with a set of handles will surround the text object. Click one of the Editing Mode buttons in the roll-up to determine how the envelope will be reshaped. Drag any of the envelope's handles to reshape it. Then click the Apply button in the roll-up menu, and the text object will be transformed to fit the new contours of the envelope:

You can do many types of transformations with envelopes—too many for me to try them all here. Have fun experimenting—that's what this feature is for!

Another important use of the Envelope feature is to make body text flow around illustrations. More about that later in this chapter.

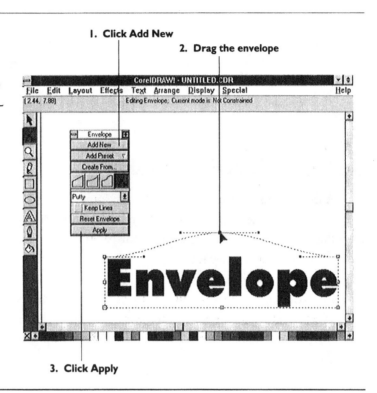

FIGURE 2.5

You can change the shape of an object by manipulating the contours of an imaginary bounding box, or envelope.

Adding Drop Shadows for Emphasis

A *drop shadow* is a duplicate copy of a text object that is placed behind its original, offset slightly. The offset is usually down and to the right:

A drop shadow creates a dimensional effect by making the text object appear as if it were raised off the paper and casting a shadow. Also, when a drop shadow is in a sharply contrasting color, the readability of the text on top can be improved because the edges of the letters are highlighted. For these reasons, drop shadows can be very effective on headlines.

Drop shadows work best on larger type. In general, don't use a shadow on text that is smaller than 24 points. An exception might be adding a shadow to a small label that must be placed over another object that is similar in color. In that case, a contrasting shadow could make the label more legible.

Adding a Mysterious Shadow

Although this is an automated feature in some other graphics programs, you won't find a menu command in CorelDRAW for creating a drop shadow. But don't despair. There's a quick way to do it.

Create the shadow text first as an Artistic Text object, say, in black. Select it with the Pick tool.

Now, here comes the magic. Press the + key on the numeric keypad, which creates another copy of the object on top of the first. Then, press the ↑ arrow and then the ← arrow to move the copy up and to the left. (Using the arrow keys when moving an object is called *nudging*.)

Finally, click a different color in the palette at the bottom of the screen for the face, or top, text.

The distance by which the shadow is removed from the face, or top, text is called the offset. You can control the amount of offset by doing Special ➤ Preferences and entering a distance for the Nudge option. This is the distance by which a copied object will be moved each time you press an arrow key. (For positioning type, you might want to change the units from Inches to Points). For an even quicker solution, also in the Preferences dialog box, adjust the Horizontal and Vertical distances for the option Place Duplicates And Clones, which can determine the exact offset of copied objects. Remember, though, that resetting either of these options will affect the positioning of all copied objects, not just text; so use with care!

Creating the Amazing Floating Drop Shadow

A floating drop shadow uses three rather than two images of a text object:

Using the procedures just described, create the third, or back-shadow, text object first, then the drop shadow, and finally the face text. Make the color of the shadow the same hue as the top color, but darker. The back-shadow should be darkest. For example, if the top color were yellow, its drop shadow might be gold or yellow-orange, and the back shadow might be black. For monochrome output, the top color might be light gray, the drop shadow medium gray, and the back shadow black.

When you are creating drop shadows and floating drop shadows, you should create the back shadow first, because the copying operation will put the copy in front of it (that is, on top). If you had created the face text first, you would have to select it and change its order, or overlay priority. To bring an object at the back to the front, select it with the Pick tool and do Arrange ➤ Order ➤ To Front (or press Shift-PageUp).

Try These Other Tasty Text Treats

CorelDRAW permits some other transformations on text that can be used to create stunning headlines and logos.

Fitting Text to a Path

In some Windows graphics applications, including CorelDRAW, you can make a text object "bend" to follow the shape of a nearby object. In CorelDRAW this is called *fitting to a path:*

To fit text to a path, first use the Artistic Text tool to create a text object. Then, use a tool such as the Ellipse tool to create the object or shape to which the text will be fitted.

Now, select both the text and the shape. Click the Pick tool, then hold down the Shift key as you click both the text and the shape. When the two objects are included in the same selection, a single set of handles should surround them.

With both objects selected (the text and the shape), do Text ➤ Fit Text To Path. The Fit Text To Path roll-up menu will appear:

In the roll-up menu, select options that will affect the shape of the text in the two drop-down boxes: The top drop-down controls how the letters will be transformed, and the bottom one controls the placement of the text on the surface or edge of the selected shape.

There's also a four-sided square button in the roll-up menu. Click the segment of the button to indicate the side of the selected shape to which the text will be attached. To place the text on an inside rather than on an outside edge of the selected object, mark the check box Place On Other Side.

Normally, the text will be placed directly on the selected object. Optionally, to control the amount by which the text is separated from it, click the Edit button. The Fit Text To Path Offsets dialog box will open. Enter distances for the offset in the Horizontal Offset and Distance From Path boxes. Then, click OK to close this Offsets dialog box.

When you have set all the options in the roll-up menu, click its Apply button, and the text will be redrawn fitted to the shape.

Extruding 3D Text

Letters can be made to look like three-dimensional blocks in CorelDRAW. Create the text with the Artistic Text tool. Then, click the selection tool and click the text so that handles surround it. From the menu, do Effects ➤ Extrude Roll-Up. The Extrude roll-up menu will appear:

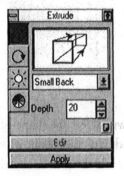

There are quite a few Extrude options—too many to cover here. The four buttons on the left side of the roll-up control the options categories of (from top to bottom): Depth and Type of extrusion, Rotation, Light Source, and Colors. When you click one of the buttons, its options will appear within the roll-up.

The only option you must be sure to reset when extruding text is the coloring so that the text on the face of the extrusion is different from the extrusion itself. Otherwise, you won't be able to read it. Click the Colors button, then the Shade check box. Click the From color and select a different, usually lighter, color from the menu that appears, as shown in Figure 2.6.

FIGURE 2.6

*Recolor the face of
extruded text so that
it is legible.*

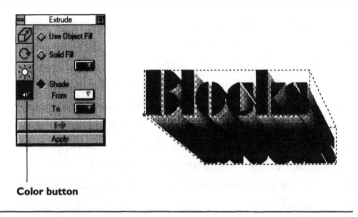

Color button

> *As with the Envelope feature, there are far too many ways to use Extrude than
> can be shown here. To get detailed help on any command or menu of
> CorelDRAW, press Shift-F1. The mouse pointer will change to a question
> mark. Move the question mark to the thing you're doing (such as into the open
> Extrude roll-up menu) and click. An explanation of the options will appear
> in a Help window. When you want to resume drawing, select File ➤ Exit
> from the menu bar of the Help window.*

Feel free to experiment with the other Extrusion options. When you
have made your selections, click the Apply button in the roll-up menu, and
the text will be transformed in the drawing.

Body Building

Now that you have a snazzy headline, it's time to concentrate on composing
the text message that it advertises.

At this point, you might want to review the *Timely Typing Tips* section of Chapter 1, which applies to all typography that you compose on the computer. These tips involve typewriter habits that must be broken. For example, you don't press ↵ at the end of each line with the same paragraph; and you use one, not two, spaces after periods and other punctuation marks.

In general, there are fairly strict rules for composing business correspondence. For example, there are a few variations in the formal block letter, but all letters pretty much look the same. (And if yours don't follow the rules, it might reflect badly on you or your company.)

For sales messages of any kind except those in formal letters, there is just one rule of composition: *There are no rules!* As long as you don't break any laws or hurt anyone, you are free to be just as creative with the body of an ad as you are when designing its headline.

Your main objective in composing a print ad is to deliver an overall message to the reader at a glance. Anyone seeing your ad should immediately understand what it's about. This subject should be interesting or even intriguing to that person because it relates to some fundamental business need they have. The purpose of the ad is to tell how your product, service, or company can fulfill the reader's specific need.

To deliver on this promise, the body of an ad must be composed so that it is easy to read and easy to understand.

Readability has to do with the look of words and sentences. Does the text seem to flow? Can the eye scan the words and recognize them quickly and without effort? Does the design of the font used for the text body promote this readability, making an appropriate impression, without drawing attention to itself? (A font design like music in the movies: You should remember only the effect it had on you, not the details of its construction.)

A quality we might call *understandability* describes the overall composition, such as the way blocks of text can be arranged by topic, each topic identified by a subhead. For example, if the product being advertised has five benefits, you might expect to see one block of text with a subhead for each of those benefits, as the example in Figure 2.1 shows.

If all this seems subjective and terribly arty, you're right. Remember, there are no rules. Of course, there are fashions and fads in advertising design. For periods of time, there might seem to be rules. But when all the ads start looking the same, it's time to break the rules again.

Readability: Using White Space

Perhaps the most important element of readability is the use of the white space that surrounds printed text. Already discussed in this chapter is letter-spacing, or the amount of white space between characters. (You can also vary *wordspacing*, or the amount of white space between words.)

Another element of white space is called *leading* (rhymes with *bedding*). Leading is vertical spacing, or the amount of white space between text lines. The term is derived from the practice, in days of yore, of inserting thin strips of lead between lines of metal type that were set by hand.

Single- or double-spacing on a typewriter is an example of leading. In business correspondence, the rule is pretty simple: You single-space letters and memos, double-space reports. Single-spacing is more difficult to read than double-spacing. The main reason for the single-spacing rule in correspondence is to keep the typical letter or memo to a single page. Because reports usually have many pages, it is a courtesy to the reader to double-space the text.

Again, in print ads, flyers, and brochures, there are no strict rules. But, depending on the font you select, readability usually can be improved by opening up the spacing between lines. So, letterspacing should be tight and lines should be loose. But do either to the extreme and readability actually gets worse. If the letterspacing is too tight, the words look cramped. If the lines are too loose, the paragraphs fall apart visually, and your topic-oriented composition is no longer perceived as a unified and readily understandable block of text.

A pleasing design might use 1.5 times normal single-spacing between lines, with wider gaps, perhaps double-spacing, between paragraphs, which further highlights them as blocks of text.

 *Although it's not a hard and fast rule, there should be a relationship between leading and line length. (The length of the line, of course, depends upon the type size and the letterspacing.) Longer lines and smaller type require more leading. Less leading can be used for narrow columns, as is done in daily newspapers.*

Planning Pretty Paragraphs in CorelDRAW

In CorelDRAW, you create body text with the Paragraph Text tool.

To get to this tool, recall that you click the Text tool, then select it from the little mini-menu of three tools that pops up. The mouse pointer will change to small crosshairs in the drawing area. Drag a box that will contain the paragraph text. Then, start typing. The text will flow into the box you've drawn, starting at its top-left corner.

 *As with Artistic text, you can change the font options for Paragraph text by doing Text ➤ Character or by resetting options in the Text roll-up menu (Text ➤ Text Roll-Up). To work up close with text in smaller point sizes, click the Zoom In tool and drag the area that contains the text. Click the Show Page tool to restore the full view. (Have another look at Figure 2.3.)*

You can have different sets of default options for artistic and for paragraph text so that changing fonts for the display type won't affect your preferences for the body. Everything you always wanted to know about setting options for paragraph text in CorelDRAW can be found in the Paragraph dialog box, which appears when you select the text with the Pick tool and do Text ➤ Paragraph (Figure 2.7).

FIGURE 2.7

The Paragraph dialog box in CorelDRAW appears when you do Text ➤ Paragraph; it contains all of the font and layout options for paragraph text.

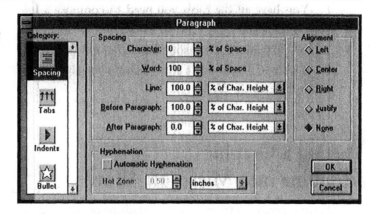

When the Spacing icon is selected in the Category list on the left side of this dialog box, letterspacing for characters or words can be set as a percentage of the *blank space* character in the current font. Leading between lines, as well as before and after paragraphs, can either be set as a percentage of character height or set in points.

The height of a line is the same as the point size of its largest type. The point size is measured from the tip of the lowest descender (such as a *p* or *q*) to the tip of the highest ascender (such as a *b* or *d*) with a small amount of extra space above and below.

The check boxes on the right side of the Paragraph dialog box control alignment of the paragraph margins. (See *Justifying Your Righteous Words* later in this chapter.) Notice that the Justify option produces full justification, or alignment both left and right.

Other sets of options appear in the Paragraph dialog box, depending on the Category icon selected: Tabs for setting tab stops, Indents for indentation distances and page margins, and Bullet for picking a symbol that will be used for marking bulleted lists.

You have all the tools you need to compose a full-page ad, including both display and body type, in CorelDRAW. However, since more people rely on their word processors than on graphics software for composing all kinds of text, here follows a more complete explanation of laying out body text in Microsoft Word.

Pasting a Graphic Headline into Microsoft Word

Having created a truly dynamic headline or logo, you might very well want to move it into a text document in a word processing application. For example, having created a headline with one of the techniques just described in CorelDRAW, you might want to paste it into Word so that you can build the body of an advertisement beneath it. (As alternatives, you might simply create a headline in Word or a headline with graphics in Microsoft Draw.)

In the application you used to create the headline, you must select it and place it on the Windows Clipboard. Select the text object and then do Edit ▶ Copy.

Start or switch to the application, such as Word, that will receive the headline. Then, do Edit ➤ Paste Special. The Paste Special dialog box will open:

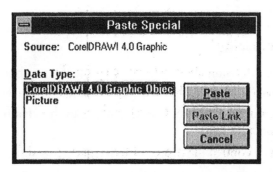

Depending on the source application and the type of graphic, you have your choice of pasting the object in a variety of formats. In this example, the drop-shadowed text can be pasted from CorelDRAW as a CorelDRAW Graphic Object or as a Picture. Other selections that might appear include Unformatted Text and Bitmap. In general, you'll get the best results—the best graphic resolution and the closest matching colors—if you choose the named application format. Otherwise, choose the Picture option. Then click the Paste button to insert the graphic object into the document.

In Word, you might not necessarily see the pasted object unless you reset the program's display options. By default, a thin rectangle will surround the area of the document that holds the pasted headline. When you click the rectangle and handles surround it, you can drag the object to reposition it on the page, but that's about all the changing you can do. Although you might not be able to see it in the Word document on the screen, the headline should appear on printouts.

To be able to see pasted graphics in Word, do Tools ➤ Options ➤ View, unmark the Picture Placeholders check box, and click OK.

Getting Spaced in Microsoft Word

Here's how to set the letterspacing and leading in Microsoft Word.

Adjusting the Letterspacing

Your most important decision about letterspacing for the text body is the choice of the font itself. Either you like the way a font handles letterspacing or you don't. There's more about font selection later in this chapter under *Shopping for Just the Right Text Font.*

You can, however, control the degree of letterspacing used for any text selection, whether the selection is a word, the entire document, or just a few adjacent characters within a word.

To adjust the letterspacing, drag the text to be affected so that it becomes highlighted in reverse video:

Spacing Selection

(If you want to select all of the text in the current document, do Edit ➤ Select All instead. This command will not affect a headline you pasted into the document, because the program regards that as a graphic, not as text.) Having selected the text for which the letterspacing will be adjusted, do Format ➤ Character. The Character dialog box will open, as shown in Figure 2.8.

The options that affect letterspacing are in the Spacing drop-down box. The default setting is Normal. You can reset it to Expanded or Condensed, which will spread out the selected characters or draw them tighter together. The amount of uniform spacing is controlled with the By option, from 0–1.75 points. The arrow buttons beside this box adjust the setting up or down by increments of 0.25 points, or you can type a number. (Recall that in Windows there are 72 points to an inch.)

FIGURE 2.8

This dialog box will open in Word when you do Format ➤ Character. Letterspacing for the current text selection is controlled by options in the Spacing drop-down box.

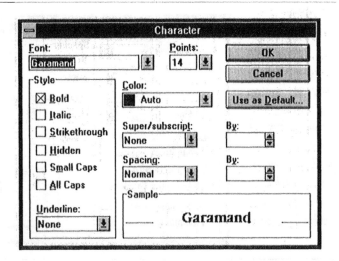

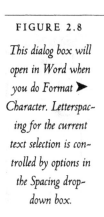

Expanded   Condensed

Adjusting Spacing between Lines and between Paragraphs

The command for controlling the space between lines and between paragraphs is Format ➤ Paragraph, which opens the Paragraph dialog box (Figure 2.9).

The portions of the document to be affected by this command depend on the cursor location when you do it. If the cursor is at the top of the document, the command affects the entire document. If the cursor is within the document, the command affects all paragraphs from that point onward. If you have selected (dragged) a paragraph, the command affects that selection only.

63

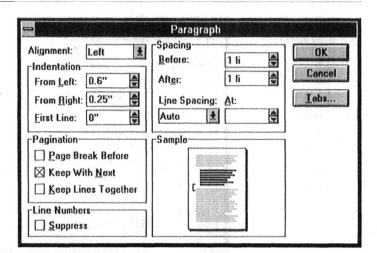

Here's a description of the spacing options in this dialog box.

Spacing Settings in the Before and After boxes control the amount of vertical space before and after a paragraph. The numbers in each box must range from 0–132 lines (li). The number you enter multiplies whatever you set for the Line Spacing option below. So, if Line Spacing were set at Single (6 text lines per inch, or $\frac{1}{6}$ inch per line), a Before setting of 1.5 lines would put $1.5 \times \frac{1}{6}$, or 0.25 inch, before the paragraph. You can set either the Before or the After spacing, or both. If you set both, the spacing between paragraphs is the sum of the Before and After values.

Line Spacing Options in this drop-down box control the amount of vertical space between lines of text. The setting also affects the space between paragraphs, as just described for the Spacing options.

The default line spacing is Auto, which places lines as closely together as possible without touching. Word adjusts the height of each line to be just a bit taller than the tallest character in that line.

The Single option puts one line-height of space between lines (single spacing), the 1.5 option adds one and one half, and the Double option adds 2 (double spacing). With these settings, Word can increase the space if necessary but will not decrease it.

Two other options permit you to specify the line spacing as a decimal number in the At box. The setting is in terms of the height of lines of type, from 0–132 lines (li). If the Line Spacing setting is At Least, this number is a minimum spacing that Word can increase. If the setting is Exactly, the spacing is fixed and Word will not adjust it.

The Short Story of the Points and Picas

Standard single-spacing on a typewriter is 6 lines to the inch. This is also the definition of the unit of measure called the pica. In conventional typesetting, the point unit is used with type, and the pica is used for measurements on a page, such as leading and the widths of lines and columns.

However, in Microsoft Word, all numeric settings—including type size, letterspacing, and leading—are calculated as if they were in points. In Word, vertical spacing is controlled as a multiple of the height of a line, which depends on the point size of the type: The bigger the type, the more space between the lines. So, single-spacing in Word will produce 6 lines per inch only if the type size is 12 points ($6 \text{ li/in} \times 12 \text{ pt} = 72 \text{ pt/in}$).

It should come as no surprise, then, that 12-point typewriter type is called Pica: This font is one pica tall.

Shopping for Just the Right Text Font

Most of the pointers in Chapter 1 about choosing a font apply to composing the body of an ad. Simply put, you want to pick a font that gives the right impression. Refer to *Here's the (Microsoft) Word on Using Fonts* in that chapter for procedures on making your selection.

Although, as I've insisted, there are no rules, here are some very broad guidelines for picking text fonts:

Use a proportionally spaced font. For attractive letterspacing and good readability, pick a proportional font. There's just no good reason to use monospace fonts for presentation-quality text.

Use a serif font. The serifs, or curlicues and doodads, at the ends of letters can further enhance the legibility of the font, as well as add a distinctive impression. Much of the uniqueness of a typeface can come from its serif design. Sans serif fonts are no-frills designs, and that's the impression they give—stark and minimal. (Sans serif faces can be good choices for headlines, though.)

Don't intermix fonts in the body. You might very well use one display font for the headline, a different one for the subheads, and yet a different text font for the body. But intermixing fonts within the body itself is usually unattractive, resulting in the Comic Book Style described in Chapter 1. Also, changing to a larger font size for some words within the same line of text can cause vertical spacing problems. In Word, spacing is determined by line height. Line height, in turn, is determined by the distance between the lowest and the tallest characters in the line. (You can overcome this, if necessary, by specifying Exactly for the Line Spacing option, but you run the risk of tall characters overlapping those in the line above or else having all the spacing look too loose.)

Use upper- and lowercase letters. While readability refers to the ease of recognizing words and sentences, *legibility* refers the ease of recognizing individual characters, or *letterforms*. Legibility is increased if you use upper- and lowercase letters. In particular, the ascenders and descenders of lowercase letters are an aid to quick recognition.

b d f h k l t   g j p q y

Monospace Fonts: An Endangered Species

Are monospace fonts threatened with extinction? The only reason for the persistence of Courier and its clones in business correspondence is that people have entrenched expectations that go back at least as far as the 1960s and the first IBM Selectric typewriters. As far as I know, there are only a few reasons to use monospace fonts—ever:

- When you are building a table, monospacing makes it easy to align the entries vertically. (See *Setting a Nice Table* in Chapter 3.) Even proportional fonts may have monospaced numeric digits, for this reason.

- If you are writing a manuscript and must be concerned with the word count, monospacing can simplify that. The number of characters per page will be more consistent than with proportional type. However, now that you have a computer to count characters for you, what's the point? (Word reports the character count in the document in the lower left corner of the screen after each File ➤ Save operation. To get the word count, divide the character count by 8, unless you're using every long word in your vocabulary to write a scholarly dissertation.)

- You are writing computer program code and need to be concerned with limitations such as fixed 80-character line lengths.

Justifying Your Righteous Words

In typesetting, *justification* refers to the vertical alignment of text lines. The usual options are to align the lines on their left ends, on their center points, or on their right ends.

Left aligned

Centered

Right aligned

Justified Both Right and
Left

As a rule in a game that I already said has none, body text is usually justified left. If an indented list or text block includes a column of numbers, the numbers are usually justified right. (However, for decimal values with a varying number of places, the decimal points themselves, rather than the rightmost digit, should be aligned vertically.)

Text Left	Numbers Right
Monday	$1,634.00
Tuesday	564.00
Wednesday	3298.00

If body text is justified left, there may be no fixed right margin. Rather, the text will wrap to the next line at approximately the same point, without dividing (hyphenating) the last word in the line. This type of left justification is called *ragged right*—because that's just how the right margin looks. The raggedness can be reduced somewhat by permitting hyphenation of words—dividing the last word after a syllable, inserting a hyphen, then continuing the word on the next line.

NOTE *Microsoft Word can suggest word hyphenation. Select the word you want to break and do Tools ➤ Hyphenation. This command will not appear in the*

Tools pull-down menu, though, unless you chose the Hyphenation Help option when you installed the program.

Body text of formal business letters, newspaper and magazine columns, and books often is justified on both ends of the line—left and right. Such text is said to be *fully justified,* and composing it this way presents some special challenges.

*T*IP *Don't be compelled to use full justification just because you think it's the proper thing to do. True, it has been the accepted practice in formal documents. However, ragged-right composition is much easier to do attractively, and it's becoming more acceptable—in books and even in the stuffiest business letters.*

Difficult as it can be, full justification is somewhat easier to achieve—and certainly looks better—with a proportionally spaced font. To make each line begin and end in exactly the same place, lines usually must be condensed or expanded. To do this, a word-processing program will vary the word spacing, adding or subtracting small amounts of white space between the words on a line. This approach can work fine, especially if the line length is relatively long—almost the width of a page, say. And hyphenation usually improves the overall appearance, because it permits the line to be broken in smaller increments. (Just don't overdo it so that the right margin is littered with hyphens.)

For shorter lines, such as newspaper columns that might measure about an inch and a half, varying the spacing between words isn't enough. Big, unsightly gaps can appear to be running vertically through the text. The effect is made even less pleasing by the tendency of the eye to connect these extra white spaces throughout a block of text so that they appear to form rivers—and that's the technical term for this mess.

Software applications that are intended primarily for preparing pages for publication such as Aldus PageMaker or Ventura Publisher can take this variable spacing one step farther: Some programs can also vary the letterspacing *within* words automatically to achieve a more attractive fit for the line. Normally, the program will try to fit the line to the proper length by adjusting only the spaces between the words. But if this produces too much or too little white space between the words, the letterspacing will be varied also.

Even this more sophisticated approach doesn't always produce attractive results, and designers sometimes have to redo the justification, perhaps rebreaking the lines or adjusting the letterspacing of individual words.

In Word, justification is set through the Alignment option when you do Format ➤ Paragraph. The settings are Left, Centered, Right, and Justified. Notice that justified, in Word terminology, means aligned both left and right. In other Windows applications, this same option might be called Full, Spread, or Both (Left and Right).

If you select the Justified option in Word, the program will adjust the spacing between words only. Again, using hyphenation will improve the appearance of the justified lines. If you still are not satisfied with the result, recall that you can adjust letterspacing of selected words or portions of lines with the Format ➤ Character command, choosing Expanded or Condensed for the Spacing option.

When dividing words at the end of a line, be aware of the difference between *hard* (mandatory hyphens) and *soft* (discretionary hyphens). A hard hyphen is one that you type manually, followed by a hard carriage return (↵), forcing a line break where it might not be otherwise. A soft hyphen is inserted by the word processing program. If you recompose a paragraph, the program will remove soft hyphens that don't fall at the end of lines.

If you don't use the hyphenation help in Word, look up the word in a dictionary if you are unsure how to divide it. The correct division of the word isn't always what you'd expect. Remember also that, like a spelling checker, the hyphenation help feature doesn't necessarily know all the words you do—including slang, jargon, professional and technical terms, and proper names. You will find some proper names, shown properly divided, in the Biographical Names and Geographical Names sections in the back of some dictionaries. In others, you will find this stuff in a latter section called the Pronouncing Gazeteer.

Setting Page Margins

The largest and most striking amount of white space on a page is usually in the margins. Some designers believe that big margins, permitting a lot of space around the body, add a lightness to the page because the reader is not intimidated by a big mass of black type. Furthermore, a large amount of white space surrounding the body can make a few words seem very important.

If you are uncertain about line length, set the measurement 1.5–2.5 alphabets long. (In this sense, an alphabet *is the length, in points, of the entire set of lowercase characters from a–z in a font.) For typical type sizes used for text, the result should be 40–65 characters per line.*

Beware, though, that the bigger the left and right margins, the shorter the text lines in the body. Shorter lines are good for readability, but remember that getting attractive proportional spacing becomes much more difficult as the text lines grow shorter—particularly if the paragraphs are justified both left and right.

When you are working in Microsoft Word, the program keeps track of the page size that you intend to use. This is set up through the Windows printer driver. In Word, select File ➤ Print Setup ➤ Setup, make a selection from the Paper Size drop-down box, and click OK.

As of Windows 3.1, you have an alternative for setting the paper size. You can leave the printer set up for other applications and change only the Page Setup options in Word. At the time of printing, Word will reset the printer driver temporarily. To make these changes, do Format ➤ Page Setup ➤ Size And Orientation, change the Paper Size settings, and click OK.

Before changing the margin settings, you should make sure that the units of measurement match the paper size. For example, if you intend to print on standard letter-sized $8\frac{1}{2}\times 11"$ paper, the units should be inches. But if you were using a European size (such as A4, which is 210×297 mm), the

units should be centimeters (cm). In Word, the default unit is inches, but
you can change it by doing Tools ➤ Options ➤ General, choosing a different unit from the Measurement Units drop-down box, and clicking OK.
You can specify Inches, Centimeters, Points, or Picas. (However, text sizes
will still be expressed in points.)

To set the margins in Word, select Format ➤ Page Setup. The Page
Setup dialog box will open, as shown in Figure 2.10.

FIGURE 2.10

*In Word, you set
page margins in this
dialog box. The unit
of measure can be set
when you do Tools
➤ Options ➤
General.*

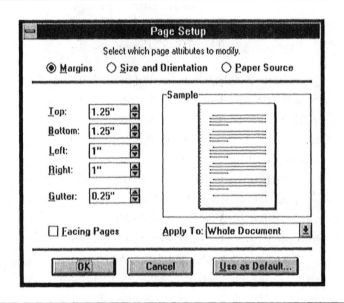

In the dialog box, enter measurements for the margins in the Top, Bottom, Left, and Right boxes. Optionally, you can allow some extra room for
binding at the left edge of the page by setting the Gutter. In a document that
is printed on one side of the paper only and also in right-sided (odd-
numbered) pages in two-sided printing, the Gutter measurement is added

to the Left margin setting. (The Gutter option can also be used for facing pages, or two-page spreads, as explained below. See this section also if you know that your one-page ad will be positioned on a left-sided, or even-numbered, page.) Make a selection in the Apply To drop-down box to indicate whether the new margins will apply to the Whole Document or from This Point Forward (from the insertion point location).

Setting Up Columns

Dividing the body into two or more columns can make the composition more attractive and can help you further divide its different topics into blocks of text.

Another benefit of composition in columns is that it can help the reader scan the text quickly. It's simply easier to grasp a whole line at a time if the lines are short.

Traditionally, multicolumn compositions are justified both left and right—newspaper style. But even in the more conservatively designed journals, the ragged right is gaining ground—especially in ads. And there's good reason to try it: Fully justified text and short line lengths are a difficult combination, composition-wise. It's hard to make those skinny columns look pretty without dividing words at the end of each line and permitting all kinds of variable spacing.

More important for readability and pleasing composition, the letter-spacing can be more consistent in a ragged-right paragraph because you don't have to fudge it to fit all the lines to a specific length.

For an ad or flyer on a letter-sized page, two columns can work nicely. And Word makes it easy to set them up. Do Format ➤ Columns, and the Columns dialog box will open, as shown in Figure 2.11.

FIGURE 2.11

Among the options in the Columns dialog box are the number of columns and their spacing.

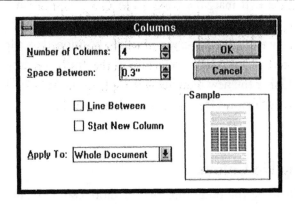

You can enter a number from 1–100 for the number of columns. Of course, the number of columns you can fit on a page attractively will depend on the point size of the body text, the width of the margins, and the size of the page. Set the white Space Between columns from 0–22 inches. (The default is 0.5 inch, which is about right for a letter-sized page.)

To place a vertical rule between the columns, mark the Line Between check box. If the insertion point is somewhere inside the document and there are other columns above it, mark the Start New Column check box if you want to change the column settings from that point onward.

Finally, set the Apply To option for your column settings here to affect the Whole Document, the current Selected Text portion, from This Point Forward, or to Selected Sections.

Runarounds

A particularly pleasing composition involves body text flowing around a picture, as shown in Figure 2.12. Graphic designers call this technique a *runaround.*

FIGURE 2.12

*A runaround makes
text flow around an
illustration or
framed text.*

In <u>portrait</u> orientation, the long dimension of the paper is vertical--the way you'd print a letter. In <u>landscape</u> orientation, the long dimension is horizontal--the way Van Gogh would paint a cow and a barn (and the way most big-sheet wizards want their stuff printed):

To produce a runaround in Word, you must create a *frame*, or bounding box, around a picture or graphic. Begin by selecting the page layout view (View ➤ Page Layout). Move the insertion point in the document to the point at the top-left corner of the frame. Then, do Insert ➤ Frame. Drag a box to create and size the frame. (You can draw the box around an existing picture, or create a frame and then paste a picture into it.)

To make text flow around the frame, also working in the Page Layout view, move the insertion point inside the frame and do Format ➤ Frame. The Frame dialog box will open. For the Text Wrapping option, select Around. Optionally, you also can set the distances to the text from the sides (Horizontal) and from the top and bottom edges (Vertical) of the frame. Select OK to close the dialog box.

In a Word document, there must be at least 1 inch between the frame and the page margin or column boundary. There must also be at least 1 inch between one frame and another.

Using a frame with a runaround is particularly effective in a two-column composition in which the columns are fully justified. You will pay a price for this attractiveness, though. The problem of letterspacing in short, columnar lines can get much worse in the shorter lines that flow around the frame. You may have to play with the letterspacing—and even insert hard returns (↵) to force some of the line breaks in different places—to avoid big gaps between words or too many hyphens at the ends of lines.

Getting the Runaround in CorelDRAW

Making paragraph text in CorelDRAW do the runaround thing requires a different procedure. You select the graphic and put an envelope around it as described previously in this chapter. (Select the graphic and do Effects ➤ Envelope Roll-Up ➤ Apply New.) Remember, paragraph text will follow the shape of the envelope, so you can have a lot of control over the shape of a runaround, because there are so many ways to manipulate envelopes in CorelDRAW.

Doing the Old Two-Page Spread

A type of magazine layout called a *two-page spread* covers two facing pages with the same ad or article. Many of the same composition issues are involved in designing books and reports that are printed on both sides of the page and bound.

The main challenge in designing a two-page spread is to permit just enough extra space in the middle, or in the gutter where the pages meet, to allow for the binding. Look back at the Page Setup dialog box in Figure 2.10. To do a two-page spread, mark the Facing Pages check box. The Sample display will change to preview the facing pages:

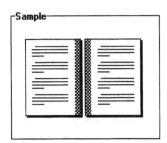

When you adjust the Gutter setting, shaded strips appear on the right and left margins of the previewed facing pages to show you how much the usable page width will be reduced by the gutter. Remember that, depending on the type of binding, some of the gutter might not be visible as white space but will be folded into the binding.

In two-sided printing—whether in a magazine or book—the first page of the document or publication is *always on the right*. So, odd-numbered pages will be on the right, and even-numbered pages will be on the left. If you are designing a two-page spread in Word and use the Facing Pages option with a gutter, leave page 1 of your document blank and start it on page 2. This page will be in the correct position for a spread—on the left. Then, put the facing page, which goes on the right, on page 3 of the document.

TIP   If your printer driver supports a page size that is large enough, you could compose a two-page spread on a single sheet in landscape orientation, allowing for a fold in the center of the sheet. To put one column on each page, you could use a two-column composition and set the gutter as the distance between columns. To change page orientation (and possibly paper size), do Format ➤ Page Setup ➤ Size and Orientation.

Putting It All Together

The two main elements of an effective print ad are a stylish headline and an attractively composed body. Enough said about both in this chapter; it's time for you to experiment!

You can also add subheads and highlighted text in a display typeface (use the Artistic Text tool in CorelDRAW). Look how the subheads improve the composition in the ad in Figure 2.1.

To insert graphics or illustrations, follow the procedure described previously for bringing a headline into Word: Select the graphic in the source application and do Edit ➤ Copy, then switch to the destination document and do Edit ➤ Paste Special. (In general, selecting Picture format for the pasted object will give you more control than bringing it in with the Bitmap option.)

If you paste a graphic into your ad, you might want to give it the runaround, but remember that your letterspacing problems might be multiplied thereby!

CHAPTER 3

Writing a Report

· OR ·

Time to 'Fess Up!

N THIS CHAPTER, we'll look at that time-honored burden of overworked staff and anxious middle managers—the written report. From the standpoint of page composition, there are two main elements of a report—the text and the illustrations. Typically, the illustrations include tables, spreadsheets, charts, and diagrams. I'll share some tips on using fonts for each of these presentation formats.

Let Microsoft Design Your Report

Microsoft Word comes with four designs for business reports. Each ready-made design, or template, includes layouts for the main title page, title pages of sections, and report pages. Some of the templates also provide an optional table of contents and an index.

To create a document using one of the business report templates, do File ➤ New. The New dialog box will open. In the Use Template box, select the name of the template that your document will follow. (To edit the template itself as a guide for making customized reports, click the Template option button.) Click OK to begin creating your report.

The ready-made templates for reports are

PROPOSAL This layout is more concise than the other formats, having no title page, table of contents, or index. You might use it for a brief report that has several relatively short, subtitled sections.

REPSTAND This is the standard report layout in portrait page orientation (long dimension of the paper is vertical). I used it for the examples in this chapter. This and the other templates beginning with *REP-* include a formal title page as well as an optional table of contents and index. (See Figure 3.1.)

FIGURE 3.1

The Word template REPSTAND produces a standard report in portrait page orientation.

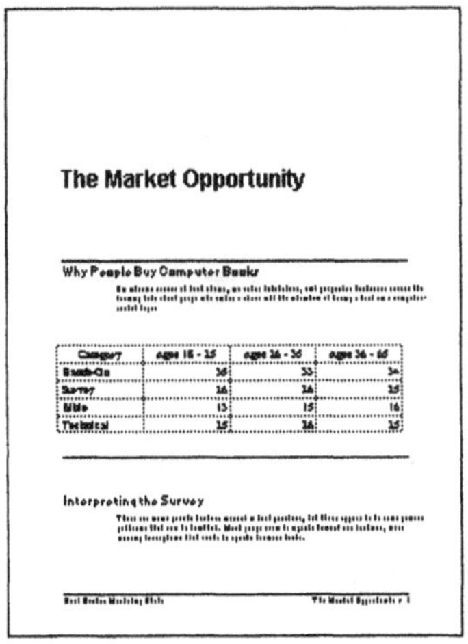

REPSIDE This report layout is also in portrait orientation, but it has wide right margins so that the headings can be placed to the side of the text rather than above it.

REPLAND This layout is similar to the standard report, but the paper orientation is landscape (long dimension of the paper is horizontal). This layout can be particularly useful if the bulk of the report is spreadsheets or charts, which can usually be made larger in landscape orientation. Putting the text in landscape as well would make things simpler for the reader, who would not have to keep turning the document to move between text and illustrations.

Macros Start the Report for You

If you use one of Word's templates to start a document, you can avoid seeing my worst nightmare—a totally blank page. After you click OK in the New dialog box, a set of startup *macros* in the template is activated. Macros are stored sequences of program entries. In the case of REPSTAND, the startup macros open the New Report dialog box, which prompts you for the report title, subtitle, your name (or, if you are a ghost writer, the name of the person who will have the byline beneath the title), and the name of your organization:

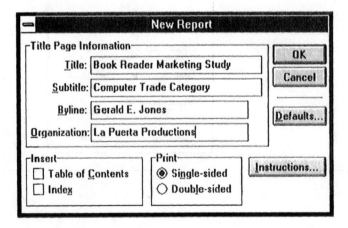

Click OK after typing this information, and the macros will enter it into all of the pages in the report that use it, including the main title page.

After the startup macros have entered this information, the title page of the report will appear in the Page Layout view. Press PageDown to start the text of the first section of the report. Then do View ➤ Normal, as well as View ➤ Zoom ➤ Page Width, to change to the enlarged screen display for typing.

What If I Don't Like the Fonts?

Each of the predefined report templates in Word uses two sets of fonts—a Normal font for body text and a Headings font for titles, subtitles, and section headings. By default, the Normal font is Times New Roman (a serif font) and the Headings font is Arial (sans serif).

By a single command, you can change these two typefaces whenever you want—either before you begin typing the report or any time thereafter. All of the custom commands for the current template are at the bottom of the Format pull-down menu. To change the font selections globally, or for the whole report, do Format ➤ Change Fonts. (You will not see these commands unless a template is open.) The Font Settings dialog box will appear, as shown in Figure 3.2.

Notice that you can change the Normal Font and Headings Font selections independently. Remember that you are setting only the typeface here; the size settings are part of the template design. Click OK to apply the new typefaces to the whole report. To change the typefaces in the template— affecting this and all future reports that use the template—click the Use As Default button, confirm the action by clicking OK, then click OK again to close the Font Settings dialog box.

FIGURE 3.2

*The Font Settings
dialog box appears in
Word when you
open a template and
do Format* ➤
Change Fonts.

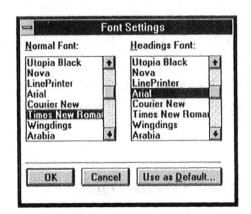

OTE *Remember that, regardless of the global font settings for the template, you can
change fonts for selected text by dragging it to highlight your selection and then
changing the settings in the Font and Points (typesize) boxes in the ribbon. (See*
Here's the (Microsoft) Word on Using Fonts *in Chapter 1.)*

The Style options that are already defined in the template can be viewed
and selected by opening the Style drop-down box in the ribbon:

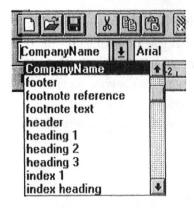

Recall that, when you make a selection from the Style drop-down box, the Font and Points settings for that style will be shown in the ribbon:

| heading 1 | | Arial | | 30 | | B | I | U | | | | | | | | | |

To change the default text attributes in the template, including type size, as well as font, for any style in the report, select a typical item in the report, such as a section title that is formatted in the Heading 1 style. Do Format ➤ Character. Reset the options in the Character dialog box, then click the Use As Default button. Confirm the change by clicking Yes, then click OK to close the dialog box.

Composing Pages They'll Want to Read

Here are some guidelines for laying out the text pages of a report:

Use subheads liberally to identify major topics Headings help break up the page and provide "signposts" to guide the reader through your material. In the REPSTAND template, there are styles for three levels of headings: Heading 1 (flush left, 30-point, bold), Heading 2 (flush left, 18-point, bold), and Heading 3 (indented, left aligned, 14-point, bold).

Don't use too many fonts If you stick with the two fonts in the template (the fonts you pick for Normal and Heading), you won't be in danger of over-designing the report. Also, use boldface, underlining, and italics sparingly within the body of the text. In general, the only mandatory requirement is to use italics for titles of books and other sources, as well as for referring to terms, such as "the word *eclipse*" or "the letter *f*." Remember, too, that putting too many fonts in a document might make it print much slower. Six fonts is about the maximum for good printing performance, counting boldface and italics as separate fonts.

Use tables to make explanations more concise Lengthy explanations of key relationships often can be condensed into a table. You can then use fewer words to simply highlight specific entries in the table or to draw overall conclusions about it. Be guided by the fact that business readers are always in a hurry—they don't read this stuff for pleasure. (For tips on composing tables, see the next section, *Setting the Table for Your Invited Number Crunchers.*)

Don't present data in a table or spreadsheet if a graph can show the same idea Raw data is seldom as interesting as a chart, which can make a trend or relationship understandable at a glance. If the source data must be shown, consider presenting it in a table beneath the graph. (There's more about creating readable graphs later in this chapter.)

Recap key points in brief lists Use bullets when presenting topics, especially if you are listing topics that will follow as subtitled sections in the report. Use a numbered list instead if you are presenting a sequence of steps. In the REPSTAND template, the List style is available for creating lists of text items. Use the Numbered List or Bulleted List tools in the toolbar to format the list.

Setting the Table for Your Invited Number Crunchers

Building a table within your report is straightforward in Word. Move the insertion point to where you want to place the table in the document. Then, do Table ➤ Insert Table. The Insert Table dialog box will appear, as shown in Figure 3.3.

The entries in the Insert Table dialog box permit you to specify the dimensions of the table: Number Of Columns wide (1–31) by Number Of Rows tall (1–32,767). You can also set the Column Width (0.25–5.49 inches) or leave this setting at Auto, which will divide the space between the

FIGURE 3.3

Specify the dimensions of a table in this dialog box, which appears in Word when you do Table ➤ Insert Table.

Insert Table

Number of **C**olumns: 4

Number of **R**ows: 5

Column **W**idth: Auto

OK

Cancel

margins evenly into the specified number of columns.

The program will present you with an empty grid for the table:

Why People Buy Computer Books

An informal survey of book chains, mail order distributors, and proprietor booksellers reveals the following data about people who enter a store with the intention of buying a book on a computer-related topic:

Leave the Column Width setting at Auto. You can always adjust the column width (or the row height) visually by dragging the grid lines on the screen. Simply move the mouse pointer to a grid line until the pointer shape changes to a two-way arrow. Then, drag the line in either direction to resize the table.

Each space within the grid is called a *cell*. Click inside a cell to move the insertion point there, and begin typing. If the text reaches the right boundary of a cell, it will wrap to the next line. If it reaches the bottom-right corner, it will continue to wrap, as the row height increases to hold the entry.

To move the insertion point to the next cell, click it or press the Tab key (Shift-Tab moves backward to the previous cell).

Controlling Text Size in a Table

Your goal in composing a table should be to make the text at least as large as the text in the body of the report. The default style TableText in the REPSTAND template is 10-point Times New Roman.

The limitation on text size in a table is the size of the individual cells. The bigger the cell, the bigger its text can be. Here are some tips on composing and recomposing a table so that you can fit legible text inside it:

Limit the number of columns The controlling factors on the number of columns are page width, margins, and text size. So, you can usually increase the size of the text if you use fewer columns. Often it is possible to eliminate a column that you might use for explanations by placing the information instead in a footnote to the table.

Stack text within cells Again, the more severe constraint is width, not height. So, instead of putting two words on the same line in a column heading, press ↵ to insert a hard return after the first word, dropping down to the next line in the cell.

Adjust column widths to just fit the entries As described in the foregoing Tip, you can drag the column width or the row height. In particular, make each column no wider than necessary for its longest entry, and stack (perhaps even divide and hyphenate) entries wherever possible.

Try to keep a table on a single page As discussed in the next section, you can run into trouble if a table spills over onto two pages. What's more, a page break in the middle of a table makes it that much more difficult for the reader to follow. Instead of breaking the table, consider placing it on a separate page, even if this means placing it away from its explanatory text. Give the table an exhibit or figure number and include that reference in the text.

Fixing Troublesome Tables

Typical troubles with tables can happen when:

❡ A table runs longer than a page.

❡ The dimensions of the table don't match the text indentations in the document.

Here are some suggestions for tackling these problems.

Multiple-page tables Should be avoided, but can be tolerated if you are careful. If the text in a cell at the bottom of a page runs longer than the row height, the text will seem to disappear from printouts. If this happens, move the insertion point into the problem cell, then do Table ➤ Insert Cells ➤ Insert Entire Row, and click OK. When you insert a new row, the program will put a page break between the rows. Then, move the offending text to the continuation of the table on the next page. If the table uses column headings, repeat them across the top of the next page before continuing the table entries. For more tips on multiple-page tables, see *Publishing Spreadsheets, If You Must* in this chapter.

Problem indentations Might be the cause if the text you entered in a cell isn't displayed or is stacked in a skinny column inside the cell, as shown in Figure 3.4. To fix this, move the insertion point inside the table. Then, do Table ➤ Select Table. Follow that command with Format ➤ Paragraph. The Paragraph dialog box will open. Reset all of the Indentation options to 0" and click OK to close the dialog box.

Rules for Justifying Alphabetic and Numeric Data

By default, Word will align text entries in a table along the left edge of each cell. This alignment might or might not be satisfactory. Here are the rules for aligning table entries with respect to cell boundaries:

❡ Align alphabetic text, such as labels, left.

89

FIGURE 3.4

Skinny stacks of text inside a table might result from a mismatch between the table dimensions and the text indentation options for the document.

Does your table look like this?	Skinny stacked text can indicate incorrect paragraph indentation.		

❡ Align numeric values right, usually on the rightmost digit.

❡ If numeric values are decimals, align them vertically on the decimal points.

❡ Optionally, align column headings center.

To change the alignment of text within cells, drag the text (your selection can include multiple adjacent cells), then click the appropriate alignment tool in the ribbon:

Putting Decimal Tab Stops Inside Tables

Using just the alignment tools, you can align decimal values on the right only if they all have the same number of decimal places, which isn't always possible.

To align table entries on their decimal points, you must insert a *decimal tab stop* in the document. To set the decimal tab, click the Decimal Tab tool in the ribbon, then, click the tab stop location in the *table scale* of the ruler at the top of the document window, as shown in Figure 3.5.

FIGURE 3.5

Tab stops, margins, and indentations that affect tables are shown in the table scale *portion of the ruler.*

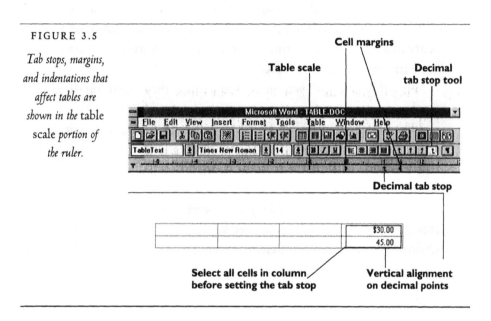

When you set a decimal tab stop within a table, any decimal values will be aligned on their decimal points automatically as you type them. Otherwise, to insert a tab character within a cell, press Ctrl-Tab. (Remember that pressing Tab just advances the insertion point to the next cell.)

To adjust a tab stop in the ruler, drag it with the mouse. To clear a tab stop, including a decimal tab, from the ruler, drag it off the edge of the ruler, and it will disappear.

91

Publishing Spreadsheets, If You Must

All the tips about tables also apply to spreadsheets—which, for the most part, are just big tables. You should try to avoid including spreadsheets in your reports because they are, well, just plain boring. Furthermore, the purpose of a report is usually to summarize information, and spreadsheets typically have too much detail. Again, you might communicate your message better in a graph of a few critical ranges in your spreadsheet, as discussed at some length later in this chapter.

But, if you must, you must. Sometimes they insist on seeing the numbers.

The basic rule of thumb for tables will work for making your spreadsheets legible: Limit the dimensions of the sheet. The larger the cells, the bigger you can make the type inside them. If you must show a large sheet, break it into several pages.

Here are some tips on making fonts work with worksheets in Excel, although other Windows spreadsheet applications such as Lotus 1-2-3 or Quattro Pro aren't much different in these respects. (Examples shown here use Excel 4 for Windows.)

Portrait or Landscape?

Before you print that sheet, you might give some consideration to the most important setup option—the orientation of the page. Unless the sheet has six or fewer columns, you'll be better off printing it in landscape mode (long dimension horizontal).

Use the File ➤ Page Setup command to switch between portrait and landscape printing in Excel. The Page Setup dialog box will appear, as shown in Figure 3.6.

FIGURE 3.6

Options in the Page Setup dialog box in Excel should be set before you print. The most important of these are Orientation, Centering, and Scaling.

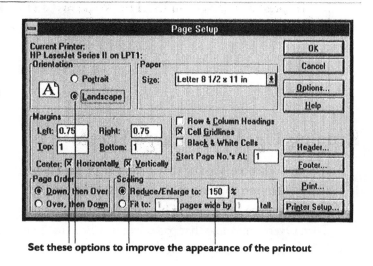

Set these options to improve the appearance of the printout

There are quite a few settings in the Page Setup dialog box, but you usually will have to be concerned with only three of them: Orientation, Centering, and Scaling. Reset these properly, and you can improve the appearance of most sheets.

Orientation Should be reset to Landscape for most purposes—even if the rest of your report is printed in Portrait.

Centering I don't know why Excel doesn't automatically center sheets on the page, but it doesn't. To compose the page nicely, mark both of the Center check boxes: Horizontally and Vertically. (This works best on smaller sheets, though.)

Scaling Your everyday worksheet—if it is about a screenful of information or a little more—won't fill a letter-sized page. The Reduce/Enlarge setting here is usually 100 percent. If your sheet is modest in size, try typing 150 in this box instead to enlarge your sheet $1\frac{1}{2}$ times. (You can reduce a bigger sheet to fit a page by entering a number less than 100, but it may be impossible to read.)

To print a worksheet in Excel for Windows, do File ➤ Print or click the Print tool:

Ripping Up Those Large Sheets

If your worksheet is so big that it can't be printed on a single page, you need to pay attention to some other Page Setup options.

In the Page Setup dialog box, the Page Order setting is normally Down Then Over—meaning that pages will be filled first going down all the rows in the sheet, then moving over one page width to the top of the sheet, and moving down again.

Resetting this option to Over Then Down proceeds from left to right across the sheet until the tops of all the columns are printed, then moving the height of one page downward and, starting again at the left border of the sheet, moving left to right.

The choice of Down Then Over or Over Then Down depends mostly on the way your sheet is constructed. When the sheets are bound in a report, which sequence of presentation will be easier for the reader to follow?

If the sheet runs to several pages, you might also reset the Scaling option to Fit To x Pages Wide By y Pages Tall. By entering whole numbers for x and y, you can control how many sheets are used in the down-then-over or over-then-down page-order sequence. Excel will adjust the reduction or enlargement so that the sheet fits the number of pages you specify.

Printing a large sheet on multiple pages attractively will require some trial and error. Experiment with these settings and print (or preview) until you're satisfied.

 *When you are working in the Page Setup dialog box, once you have changed the settings, you can print immediately. Select the Print button. The Print dialog box will appear, and you can select multiple copies or specific pages to print. To start printing, click OK.*

Breaking Pages Needn't Be Painful

To select a place in the sheet at which a page break will appear (forcing it at a spot where it wouldn't be otherwise), select a cell at the break and do Options ➤ Set Page Break. A dashed line will appear on the screen at the break. The line will be darker than the dashed lines that appear to indicate the page breaks that the program has set. (To get rid of a break you put there, put the pointer back in that row and select Options ➤ Remove Page Break.)

Pick Up Those Titles!

Some large sheets have one set of column and row headings and then tables of numbers that go on for pages. You can create such repetitive pages without having to reenter the column or row titles on each page of the worksheet. Select Options ➤ Set Print Titles. The Set Print Titles dialog box will appear. There are two text boxes here. Type a range reference for a row (A1:Z1) that contains titles to be used for column headings. Type another range reference (A1:A46) for a column that contains row titles. Click OK, and the titles that you've specified will appear on each printed page.

Fixing Fonts in Excel

Specifying fonts and their attributes is very similar procedure in Excel to the ways you control text in the other Windows applications covered in this book.

Selecting Fonts

The default font in Excel is MS Sans Serif, which is a screen font. On output, the closest printer font will be used instead. (See the discussion of font substitution tables in Chapter 12.) A better solution would be to select Arial, a scalable TrueType font, which should look the same on the screen as it does on printouts.

To change the font, drag a range (a group of adjacent columns and rows) that contains the text and numbers to be changed, then do Format ➤ Font. The Font dialog box will appear, as shown in Figure 3.7. Reset the Font, Font Style, and Size options, then click OK.

FIGURE 3.7

Control fonts in Excel through this dialog box, which appears when you select Format ➤ Font.

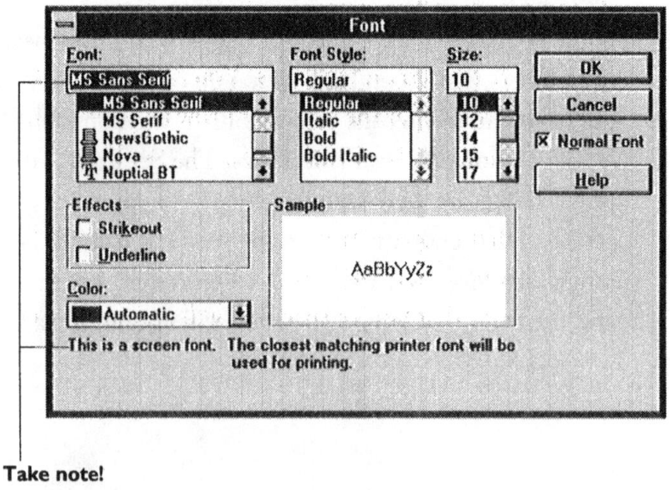

Take note!

A shortcut to this dialog box is to select the range, press the *right* mouse button, and select Font from the menu that pops up. Other shortcuts for setting the attributes of the current selection are these tools in the toolbar (Bold, Italic, Increase Size, Decrease Size):

Here's a Quicker Fix

The variety of fonts available for spreadsheets is usually less important than your ability to print them quickly. If you use other fonts that you might have installed with other Windows applications, they might or might not be printed as they appear on the screen. The quickest fix can be simply to use TrueType exclusively with Excel. In Windows Program Manager, open the Main program group, then select Control Panel ➤ Fonts. The Fonts dialog box will open. Select the TrueType button. Mark both check boxes in the window that appears.

Click OK to close this dialog box, then Cancel to close the Fonts window. Then click Close in the each of the control boxes of the windows Control Panel and Main. (If you are using a font management program such as ATM, you may also have to turn it off and restart Windows.) When you restart Excel, only the TrueType fonts will appear on the screen and in menu selections.

*If you reset Windows as just described to use only TrueType fonts, beware that this setting will affect **all** Windows applications, not just Excel. For example, you would not see any of your PostScript Type 1 fonts in Word.*

Preview That Sheet!

The normal document window in Excel is supposed to be WYSIWYG (What You See Is What You Get), but you might notice some slight differences in font sizes and spacing on output. To check the font situation—as well as any page breaks—in your sheet before you print, hold down the Shift key as you click the Print tool. (When you do this, the button changes into the Preview tool.) Clicking the Preview tool is the same as selecting File ➤ Print Preview from the menu bar. Excel will show you the first page of the printout, as shown in Figure 3.8.

If the printout will include multiple pages, you can click the Next or Previous buttons to advance or back up through the previewed page sequence.

FIGURE 3.8

Excel can present a screen preview of the printed sheet.

Opens the Page Setup dialog box (Figure 3.6)

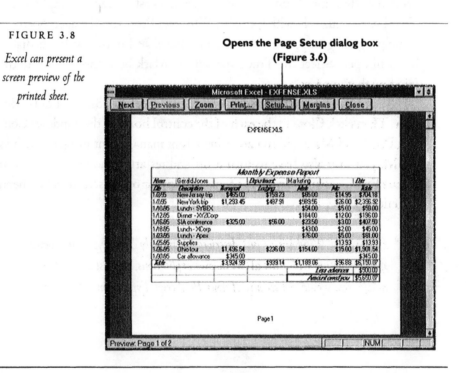

If you don't like what you see in the preview, click the Setup button, and your old friend the Page Setup dialog box will reopen. Then click OK to see the result of your changes on the preview screen.

Part of a Sheet Can Be Better than One

A good way to both make fonts bigger on output and make a sheet more concise is to select just a portion of it for printing. To do this, select the block of cells you want to print. Then, select Options ➤ Set Print Area from the menu bar. Or, click the Set Print Area tool:

The edges of the print area will be shown in the sheet as dotted lines. Whenever you click Print, just the portion inside those lines will be printed. This setting is also saved in the sheet file, so it will be there whenever you reopen the sheet.

To choose a different printing area, just repeat the command. To print the entire sheet, select it all as a block of cells, then choose Options ➤ Remove Print Area. (You will only see this command in the menu if the entire sheet is selected.)

Consolidating Your Holdings

If you are reproducing your report manually, you might simply want to let Excel print out your sheet and then collate it manually into the printed report. However, this approach won't work if you will be transmitting your report file electronically to another site—via e-mail or FAX, for example.

One solution is to paste the Excel sheet into the Word report document, routing it through the Windows Clipboard. Drag the range containing the sheet in Excel and do Edit ➤ Copy. Switch to Word, move the insertion point to the location in the document that will receive the sheet, and do Edit ➤ Paste Special. The Paste Special dialog box will open. Select Microsoft Excel Worksheet Object as the data type, then click the Paste button.

If page orientations of the sheet and the report differ, you will have to reset the orientation of the *destination report page only* before pasting. For example, if the sheet is in landscape and the report in portrait, move the insertion point in the report to the page that will receive the sheet and do Format ➤ Page Setup ➤ Size And Orientation. Select the Landscape option button, and from This Point Forward in the Apply To drop-down box. Then, click OK. When you need to switch back to portrait to type the rest of the report, advance to the next page and repeat the command, but select Portrait and This Point Forward.

Charting Your Way to a Brighter Future

The old proverb that a picture is worth a thousand words goes for numbers, too. Don't publish data in a table or in a spreadsheet that can be shown more clearly—and dramatically—in a chart.

Charting is a big topic—and the steps involved in choosing a graph type and composing it properly to convey a business message go way beyond the subject of this book. But, some aspects of charting depend on fonts, and these can be all the more difficult to deal with because you don't always have direct control over them in some charting programs. For example, almost all charting applications size labels for data and scales automatically, and it isn't always obvious how to make them bigger if the initial results aren't satisfactory.

There are quite a few Windows charting applications, including Microsoft Graph (provided with Word), Excel ChartWizard (a feature included within the spreadsheet application), CorelCHART (included with CorelDRAW), and Lotus Freelance Graphics. These applications vary not only in the types of charts they can generate, but also in the degree of control

It's Pretty, but So What?

The most important consideration in making a chart has nothing to do with fonts: You must exercise some careful judgment in selecting which data will be charted. No graphics software yet invented can make sure that the input data actually represent a meaningful trend or a key relationship. That's why programs that purport to generate graphs with a click of a button aren't necessarily a help. You might be able to make a chart quickly (and there's no reason why you shouldn't), but your understanding of the data, not the ease of making pretty pictures with it, will determine whether the result will make sense to anyone.

Being downright picky about the data becomes particularly important when you want to graph a spreadsheet. In any sheet, there is almost always too much information to make a single, understandable chart. Out of the whole sheet, you usually need to find just *one or two rows* of data that tell a story.

you have over the results. The examples here were created with Harvard Graphics Version 1 for Windows, which is not only a widely used application for this purpose but also gives you considerable flexibility in customizing the output.

Composing Charts in Harvard Graphics

Like most other business charting programs, Harvard Graphics reduces most of the chart creation process to your simply filling in the blanks on a data input form. You make some preliminary selections about the type of chart and its appearance, and the program does the rest, based on predefined chart layouts. When the program shows you the result, you can use the drawing and editing features of the program to customize the chart.

In Harvard Graphics, the basic working document is called a *presentation*. A presentation can contain multiple pages, called *slides*. Each slide is typically one chart, although you can show multiple charts on a slide, if you wish.

To create a chart in Harvard Graphics for Windows, start the program and do File ➤ New Presentation. The Add Slide dialog box will appear, as shown in Figure 3.9. Click one of the option buttons in the list on the left to indicate the type of chart you want to make. (The most commonly used types are Pie, Vertical Bar, and Line.) Then, click OK.

FIGURE 3.9

This dialog box appears when you do File ➤ New Presentation in Harvard Graphics.

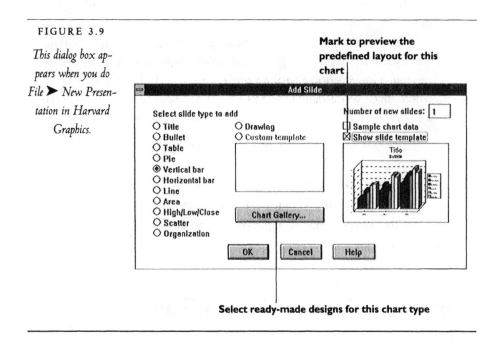

The Data Form, a data-entry worksheet, for the selected chart type will open, as shown at the top of Figure 3.10. Type a Title, and optionally a Subtitle and a Footnote, in the labeled text boxes at the top of the form, pressing Tab at the end of each entry to advance to the next box.

FIGURE 3.10

The Data Form is a worksheet-style document window in Harvard Graphics for input of chart data (top). The program shows a preview of the chart in the Slide Editor, where you can customize it, if you like (bottom).

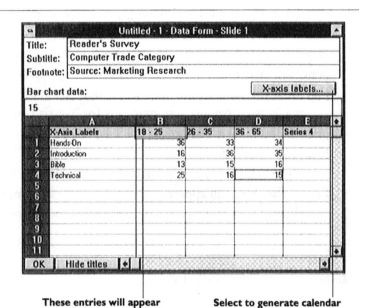

These entries will appear in the legend or data table

Select to generate calendar and time values automatically

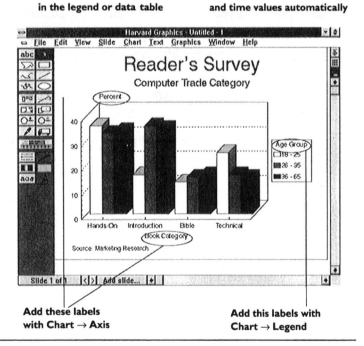

Add these labels with Chart → Axis

Add this labels with Chart → Legend

Notice that the Data Form is laid out like an electronic worksheet—with lettered columns and numbered rows. Just as in a worksheet, you can drag a range and then type the data. Each time you press ↵, the insertion point will drop down to the next lower cell. (Or, press Tab and the insertion point will move to the right, to the next cell in the same row.)

In a Vertical Bar chart, column A is for X-Axis Labels. The other columns are for numeric data series. Each data series is one set of same-colored bars or one trend line.

When you've entered the chart data, click the OK button in the Data Form. The chart will appear in the *slide area*, the document window of the Slide Editor view of the program, as shown at the bottom of Figure 3.10.

Changing Attributes of Titles

Changing fonts and text attributes in Harvard Graphics involves much the same procedure you use in other Windows applications.

To select a title, subtitle, or footnote for editing its attributes, click it once in the slide area. Handles will surround it:

Reader's Survey

When the handles are showing, do Text ➤ All Attributes. Or, click the Text Attributes tool:

The Text Attributes dialog box will open, as shown in Figure 3.11. Here are the familiar options of Font (typeface), Point Size, Color, and Style. Set the options and click OK.

FIGURE 3.11

All attributes for text in Harvard Graphics can be set in this dialog box, which appears when you do Text ➤ All Attributes.

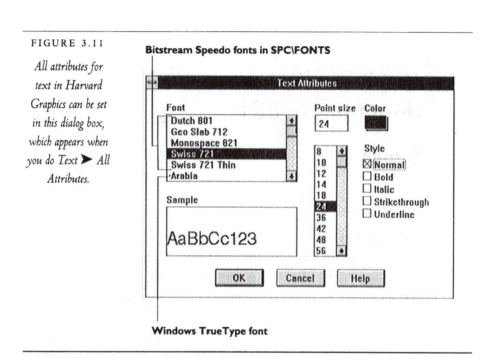

Bitstream Speedo fonts in SPC\FONTS

Windows TrueType font

Some other commands in the Text pull-down menu permit you to select specific categories of attributes, but these are the same options you'll find in the Text Attributes dialog box. These commands are: Text ➤ Font, Text ➤ Size, Text ➤ Style, and Text ➤ Color.

Some of These Fonts Are Special

The first five names in the Harvard Graphics font list are its own Bitstream Speedo fonts:

Dutch 801

Geo Slab 712

Monospace 821

Swiss 721

Swiss 721 Thin

Other fonts available in Windows, including TrueType and PostScript Type 1, follow in the font listing in alphabetical order. The "foreign" font names are preceded by a bullet character (●), so there is no way to tell True-Type from PostScript in the listing except by the font names. For example, Arial is TrueType; Arial MT is PostScript.

The Bitstream Speedo fonts are directly compatible with Harvard Graphics Version 3 for DOS. These fonts are in a special directory SPC\FONTS, which is shared by all Windows applications from Software Publishing Corporation.

In Harvard Graphics, only the Bitstream fonts can be rotated (Graphics ➤ Rotate command or the Rotate tool). If you attempt to rotate another Windows font, the program will permit the rotation but will change the text to one of the Bitstream fonts.

If you use Bitstream fonts in other applications, you may want to install a font management package such as Bitstream Facelift, which can make PostScript Type 1, as well as Bitstream Speedo, formats available to all your Windows applications.

106

It might be more convenient to consolidate all of your fonts in the same directory. If you copy the Bitstream Speedo fonts there, you must change the font directory setting in the HGW.INI file. In the [Utilities] section, edit the statement **Fontdir=C:\SPC\FONT** *to show the new path. However, if you are running other Windows applications from Software Publishing Corporation, you should not delete the SPC\FONT directory or its font files.*

Adding Data Labels

In Harvard Graphics, *data labels* can be generated above bars or points to indicate their numeric values. To turn on this option, select the chart in the slide area by clicking it once. Handles will surround the entire chart. Then, do Chart ➤ Labels. The Label Options dialog box will appear, as shown in Figure 3.12.

FIGURE 3.12

Options for data labels can be set in this dialog box, which appears when you click a chart and do Chart ➤ Labels.

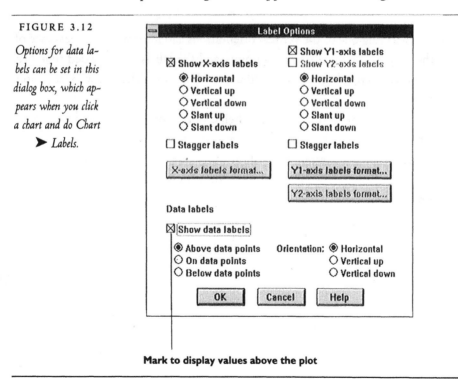

Mark to display values above the plot

To generate numeric labels above the plotted points, mark the Show Data Labels check box. The option buttons below the check box will become available. One set of buttons controls the positioning of the label in relation to the plot point—Above, On, or Below it. The other set of buttons controls the orientation of the label:

```
                    P           V
                    U           E
                                R
                    L           T
                    A           I
                    C           C
                    I           A
HORIZONTAL          T           L
                    R
                    E           D
                    V           O
                                W
                                N
```

Selecting one of the vertical orientations can improve the appearance of the chart if the plot has many points and the labels are crowded together. However, vertical orientation will usually be more difficult for most people to read.

In the top portion of the Label Options dialog box, you can select whether to show or hide labels on any axis (X, Y1, or Y2) by marking or unmarking the corresponding Show check box. Orientation of the scale labels can also be controlled. In addition to horizontal and vertical, the options are:

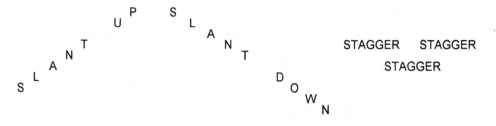

One reason to change the orientation of data or scale labels is to open up the space for making the label text bigger, as explained in the following section.

Changing Attributes of Labels

Harvard Graphics sizes labels automatically in relation to the overall size of the chart. However, any set of labels can be selected in the slide area for the purpose of changing attributes, such as font or text size. This involves a two-step procedure of *subselection.* Click the chart once to select it. Handles will surround the entire chart. Then, click once on the set of labels you want to change. A different set of handles should now surround just that set:

You can then do Text ➤ All Attributes to change the selected set of labels. When you do this, you have complete control over the font and text attributes. For example, the program will permit you to select any size, even if it is so big that the labels will overlap. Legibility of labels can usually be improved if you increase the size and also reset the Style attribute to Bold. (In general, stick with sans serif fonts for labels.)

Sizing and Scaling Charts to Improve Their Appearance

Since label size is related to the overall size of the chart, you might also be able to improve its appearance by making the whole chart bigger. In the slide area, click the chart once to select it. Then, drag one of the corner handles to resize the chart. To prevent distorting the shape of the chart, hold down the Shift key as you drag the handle. This forces the object to grow or shrink proportionally in both the horizontal and vertical dimensions.

Another important aspect of chart composition is the *scaling* of the axes, or the range from the lowest to the highest value on the axis scale. You can often improve the appearance of a chart, including making the scale labels fewer and bigger, by adjusting the axis scaling.

For example, as shown in Figure 3.13, a chart might have a Y-axis chart scale that starts at 0 and ends at 100. But perhaps all the data values fall within the range of 75–90. The scaling of the chart will be improved—and its graph fluctuations will be shown more dramatically—if the Y-axis scale is reset to start at 70 and end at 95 in increments of 10, as shown in Figure 3.14. Since this chart has fewer scale labels, it is possible to increase their text size and still have a well-composed chart.

To adjust the scaling of an axis, select the chart in the slide area by clicking it once. Handles will surround it. Then, do Chart ➤ Axis. The Axis Options dialog box will open. In this dialog box, click the Scaling button for the axis you want to change. The Scaling Options dialog box will appear, as shown in Figure 3.15.

FIGURE 3.13

This chart has a Y-axis scale that starts at 0 and ends at 100.

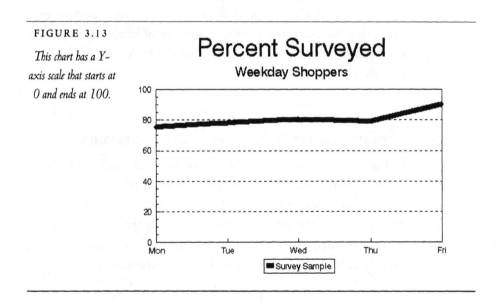

FIGURE 3.14

The axis scaling of the chart in Figure 3.13 has been adjusted to 70–95 in increments of 10.

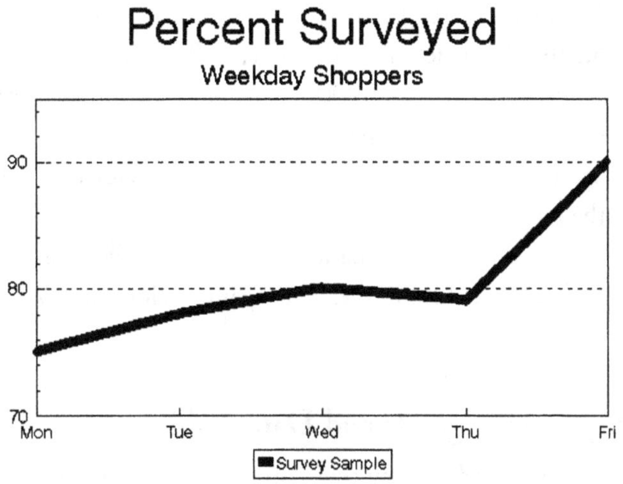

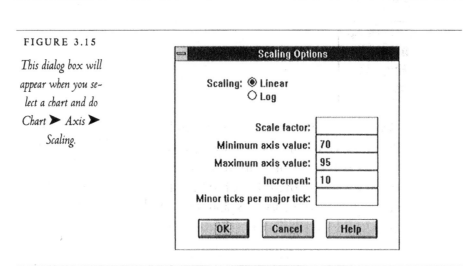

FIGURE 3.15

This dialog box will appear when you select a chart and do Chart ➤ Axis ➤ Scaling.

To adjust the scale, enter Minimum Axis Value (starting point), Maximum Axis Value (ending point), and Increment (number of scale divisions between labels). For example, you can reduce the number of labels on the

111

scale by changing the increment from 5 (a label every 5 divisions: 0, 5, 10, 15, 20...) to 10 (0, 10, 20...). Optionally, you can enter a Scale Factor, a number by which all scale values will be divided. For example, if the scale ran from 10,000 to 30,000, you could enter 1000 for the Scale Factor, and the axis would span 10 to 30. (Be sure to enter a descriptive axis title, such as "Thousands ($)" in the Axis Options dialog box to help readers interpret the factored scale.)

When you have made your entries in the Scaling Options dialog box, click OK to close it, then OK again to close the Axis Options dialog box.

Composing Legends and Data Tables

A chart *legend* is a key that correlates the colors or patterns of a plot to the name of its data series:

Age Group
■ 18 - 25
■ 26 - 35
■ 36 - 65

A *data table* shows the numeric values for each data series, usually beneath the chart area. It is customary to show a legend or a data table, but not both (although it's permissible in Harvard Graphics). In Harvard Graphics, if you turn off the display of the legend, a data table can show the color code. The coding of colors or patterns to plots, which ordinarily would be shown in a legend, will be incorporated in the data table instead.

	Hands-On	Introduction	Bible	Technical
18 - 25 ■	34	29	21	16
26 - 35 ■	42	34	13	11
36 - 65 ■	33	26	16	13

To turn on the data table, select the chart, do Chart ➤ Chart Options, mark the Show Data Table check box, and click OK. (Optionally, you can also mark Show Data Table Frame, which puts grid lines in and around the table.)

To display a legend, select the chart in the slide area, do Chart ➤ Legend, mark the Show Legend check box, and click OK.

The attributes of text in legends and data tables also can be reset through subselection. Click the chart once to select it, then click the legend or the table and do Text ➤ All Attributes, as described above.

Creating Free-Form Text Labels

Sometimes it might be necessary to annotate a chart or to add extra labels. To create such free-form text in Harvard Graphics, click the Text tool:

In the slide area, drag the size of a rectangle that would hold the text, and a text-entry box will open:

Type the text of the annotation or label, then click outside the box. When the box closes, handles will surround the text so that you can move it or change its attributes with the Text ➤ All Attributes command.

*When you drag a text selection handle in Harvard Graphics, you are resizing the **text block**, or paragraph boundaries, **not** the size or the shape of the text characters. To change the size, do Text ▶ Size. Distorted text is not permitted in Harvard Graphics Version 1 for Windows.*

Special Note for Organization Charts

Harvard Graphics provides the Organization chart type for showing managerial reporting relationships in a department or company. Unlike the other chart types, the organization chart type does not give you direct control over the sizing of text labels. Instead, the program calculates a best-fit text size based on these factors:

- Number of boxes

- Page width

- Length of longest label

The program sets only one text size for all of the labels in the chart. You can subselect the labels by clicking the chart and then clicking the labels, and you can reset all text attributes *except size*. To increase the size of the labels, you can do any or all of the following:

Eliminate some boxes from the chart Consider putting a large chart on two or more pages (slides).

Change the page and bottom-level orientations Most organization charts will lay out better in landscape orientation, which provides a wider page for longer rows of boxes. Controlling the bottom-level orientation of the chart along with the page can also help. As shown in Figure 3.16, changing the bottom-level (last row of names) orientation to Vertical can make more page width available for the next-to-last level, increasing the size of boxes and text overall. To set this option, click the chart in the slide area to select it, then do Chart ➤ Chart Options. Select the Vertical option button, then OK.

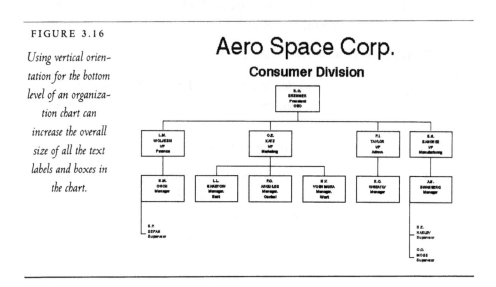

Reduce the width of text labels Shorten the entries by using initials only for first and middle names and by using abbreviations for job titles. Also, you can break entries into two lines—showing, for example, the given name on top and the surname name beneath it. To break a name or job title, press Ctrl-↵ at the point of the break when you are typing in the data entry form.

Putting It All Together

As in the spreadsheet example, you may wish to paste a chart you have created in Harvard Graphics into your report in Word. Use the same procedure described previously for passing a data object through the Clipboard:

1. Select the chart in the slide area by clicking it. (To include titles and other chart elements, hold down the Shift key while clicking each of them, or drag a box around all of them. Or, to select an entire slide, do Edit ➤ Select All.)

2. With the chart selected, do Edit ➤ Copy.

3. Switch to the Word document and do Edit ➤ Paste Special. The Paste Special dialog box will open. For best results when pasting Harvard Graphics charts, select Picture instead of Bitmap for the data type, then click the Paste button.

4. Make sure that the page orientations of the source and the destination documents are the same. If not, follow the procedure described in the preceding *Consolidating Your Holdings* section to change the orientation of selected document pages in Word.

CHAPTER 4

Preparing Practical Printed Documents

or...

Designing Forms for Fun and Profit

F YOU WORK IN AN OFFICE and you can't delegate the onerous task of designing forms, you must often create them yourself—for everything from employment applications to requisitions for supplies (including, no doubt, other forms). Nobody—neither you nor the form-fillers—thinks there's anything fun about it. And there's the guilt you must bear for feeding the paperwork monster that is eating what's left of our serious playtime.

But it's not like you have a choice. Here are some tips to make the task of laying out a form as painless as possible.

It's Not What You See, It's What You Don't See

From the standpoint of design, forms layout is largely a matter of arranging white space, or the empty areas to be filled in by the person completing the form. In fact, in every design problem covered in this book, the composition of the white space is just as important as the typography it surrounds. In the case of a form, not only must you be concerned with the legibility and readability of the preprinted type, but you must also plan the composition of lettering that isn't there!

Using white space effectively is the Zen of good typography: To make a perfect doughnut, you must construct a perfect hole!

Do It Backwards!

Most people quite naturally will be concerned with the content of the form before worrying about its design. That is, they will write the words of the preprinted questions first, then draw the lines or boxes that will hold the user's responses.

But if you actually build the form this way in a Windows application such as Word, Harvard Graphics, or CorelDRAW, you will be doing it the hard way.

Yes, you should start by making a list of the data entries you want the user to provide. But whether you type the list into a word processor or scrawl it on a napkin should make little difference in the steps that follow. You won't gain much by pasting the list into a graphics application, because—to achieve the best layout—each text item will have to be a separate graphic object.

Once you have your list, my admittedly low-tech suggestion would be to resort to pencil and paper: Make a sketch of the form, concentrating on the blank areas for the responses. Draw lines or boxes for each response. (Boxes are neater.) You might have to make several versions of the sketch to get everything to fit nicely on a page.

The next step is to draw *just the lines and boxes* in an application such as Harvard Graphics or CorelDRAW, as described in some detail later in this chapter. These programs include special tools that will help you compose the layout with the proper spacing.

To achieve a really spiffy layout with a minimum of pain, you need to work in a graphics application that has "grid" and "snap to grid" features. A grid in this case is an array of evenly spaced dots that serves as a drawing guide on the screen but doesn't show on printouts. The snap *feature forces the points or corners of anything that you draw to coincide with (snap to) points on the grid. So, if you set up the grid properly—with correct typewriter spacing of 6 lines per vertical inch, for example—all of your lines and boxes will be spaced properly because they will snap to the grid automatically as you draw them. You can also control vertical spacing in terms of line height: Line heights of 12, 18, and 24 points correspond to single, $1\frac{1}{2}$, and double typewriter spacing.*

In laying out a form, the most important question becomes: How much space do you give to each response?

Here's a straightforward solution: To make sure that you provide enough room, compose sample responses in type of appropriate size—even if the actual responses will be handwritten—and then draw the lines or boxes to fit the responses. This might seem an obvious approach, but many forms designers try to go at it the other way around, with less than satisfactory results.

The computer font and size that you pick for the sample responses (call it "ghost writing") will depend on the method by which the data will be filled in. However, no matter which data-entry method will be used, here are the secrets to composing the ghost writing:

> **Don't leave those spaces blank!** Include typical responses as well as the questions in your page layout. Save the form in two versions—one with the sample responses deleted that will serve as your printing master, and the other with the sample responses included. This version with the answers is more than a cheat sheet: It will come in handy if you ever need to revise the form, as happens all too often in the fast-changing business world.

Anticipate lengthy items If the question asks for a city name, use something like "Upper Horse Shoe Falls" to make sure you've provided enough room. If you need a more precise guideline, a 24-character field is typical for entries such as Name, Company Name, and City. A Street Address field should have two lines of at least 24 characters each.

Provide for differences in international conventions If it is possible that the form will be used by people from (or in) other countries, provide for variations in the number of digits in telephone numbers and postal codes, for example.

Use a monospace font for the responses Remember that a monospace font allocates the same amount of space for each character and will therefore more closely approximate the spacing of handwritten or typewritten responses. A possible exception is computer-generated forms, as described below.

Encourage users of the form to print in block letters Include a notice at the top of the form requesting responses in block letters (all capitals). You might also specify whether the responses should be in black ink. Red ink can be a problem for machine scanning, and blue ink might not be picked up well by photocopiers. Responses in pencil can get smudged, and there's the added risk of unauthorized alteration of responses. For example, you wouldn't want someone changing a purchase requisition after it had been approved and signed!

The typeface and size of the monospace font you use for the responses will depend on the data-entry method. Spacing requirements differ for

- ❡ Handwriting
- ❡ Typewriting
- ❡ Computer printing

Planning for Handwritten Entries

If data will be filled in by hand, use a monospace font such as Courier, Letter Gothic, or Orator in at least the 14-point size. To get the most realistic picture of a form filled out in block-printed letters, use all capitals.

TYPE THE USER'S RESPONSES IN ALL CAPS
IN A MONOSPACE FONT SUCH AS ORATOR

A feature that will help the user of the form is to subdivide the response area with a grid, one square of the grid for each letter.

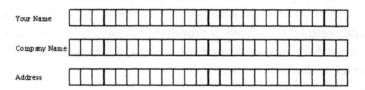

In some cases, such a preprinted grid will be absolutely necessary to assure relatively uniform spacing between the hand-printed letters:

- If the form is scanned optically for input to a computer information system, the ability of the equipment to recognize individual characters will be increased if there is uniform spacing between them.

- For optical scanning, use 20-point type for the responses. Provide a preprinted grid on the form that has 20-point boxes for the characters, with extra letterspacing between the boxes.

- If the form will be stored electronically in a pen-based computer, the preprinted grid will not only improve character recognition, but also will encourage users to keep responses within the mandatory character lengths of data-input fields.

Making Friends with Typists

Laying out a form for typists might seem easy, because you can compose the sample responses in 12-point Courier, by far the most common typewriter font. However, beware of differences among similar fonts. The computer font Courier is a PostScript Type 1 font, although it may also be available as a printer-resident font, especially on printers that do Hewlett-Packard (HPPCL) emulation. Courier New is a TrueType font. Pica is a generic printer-resident font on some dot-matrix machines. You might notice some differences in spacing among these and other typewriter-style monospace fonts—either on the screen or on printouts, or both.

Variations in similar fonts of the same point size typically show up in the letterspacing, or horizontal spacing. However, you also need to be careful about vertical spacing. The correct vertical spacing for single-spaced typewriting is 6 lines of text to the vertical inch. However, in a Windows application such as Word, spacing of 6 lines per inch will match typewriter spacing only if the text size is 12 points ($6 \times 12 = 72 \, pt/in$). For other text sizes, the vertical spacing is usually proportional to the type size. If you are using a type size other than 12-point, you must therefore specify the vertical spacing as exactly 6 lines per inch. In other applications, you can match typewriter spacing if you can specify 12-point leading exactly—regardless of type size.

If you want to make sure that your computer-produced form is spaced correctly for typewriting, print the same sample paragraph on both the computer printer and one of the office typewriters (with the same margins). Compare them by placing one page directly over the other and holding it up to the light.

If the spacing on the two sample pages doesn't match, one solution might be to use a printer-resident font, such as Courier or Pica and make sure that the vertical spacing is set at exactly 6 lines per inch (rather than letting the software set spacing based on line height).

When you are working with printer fonts, be aware that their designations differ from Windows fonts. For example, on an HPPCL printer such as the Hewlett-Packard LaserJet series, you will typically find:

```
Courier CPI 10
Courier CPI 12
```

The numeric designations of these printer fonts are in *characters per inch (cpi)*—not in points! The higher the CPI, the *smaller* the type size. To make things really confusing, Courier CPI 10 is 12-point Pica size, and Courier CPI 12 is 10-point, Elite size.

Epson LQ and FX dot-matrix printers provide these Courier sizes as well as two sizes of Prestige, which is also found on some typewriters. However, to use Prestige, the printer cannot be in HP emulation mode. Again, don't confuse points for CPI. The two sizes are Prestige CPI 12 (10-point, Elite) and Prestige CPI 20 (tiny! less than 4 points per character). Note also that some dot-matrix printer fonts are available only in portrait orientation, not in landscape.

Here are some tips concerning printer fonts:

Using Printer Fonts with TrueType If you are using mainly True-Type fonts without ATM, you can force the use of any printer-resident fonts by making sure that Windows is not sending those fonts to the printer as bitmapped characters. In Windows, select Main ➤ Control Panel ➤ Printers ➤ <printer name> ➤ Options. In the Options dialog box, make sure that the Print TrueType As Graphics check box is unmarked.

☐ Print TrueType as Graphics

Select OK to close the Options dialog box, and again to close the printer setup dialog box. Select Close to close the Printers dialog box.

(Click on the control box and select Close to close first the Control Panel application and then the Main program group.)

Using Printer Fonts with ATM If you are using Adobe Type Manager, you can force the use of printer fonts by marking the Use Pre-built Or Resident Fonts check box in the ATM Control Panel.

☒ Use Pre-built or Resident Fonts
☐ Print ATM fonts as graphics

Select the Exit button to close the ATM Control Panel. (You need not restart Windows for this change to take effect.)

Letting the Computer Do the Work

Designing electronic forms is relatively easy if you can use the same application to build the form that will be used to fill it in. (See *Paperless Forms! Now That's Progress!* later in this chapter.)

However, some complications can arise if the user requires a paper hard copy of the form. There may be some differences in typography if the user sends the output to a different printer from the one you had installed when you created the form. This problem situation is particularly likely if you are sharing files over a network and the user does not have access to the same printers you do.

For example, the form might not print properly if you use PostScript Type 1 fonts and the user's computer or printer cannot support them. To reproduce these fonts, the user must have ATM installed in Windows or must be using a PostScript printer (or one that can operate in PostScript emulation mode). Problems will most certainly arise if you use printer fonts, such as cartridge fonts, that are not installed on the user's printer.

It's therefore a more conservative approach to compose Windows-resident forms exclusively in TrueType. However, you need not restrict yourself to the default font set that comes with Windows. Most Windows applications can *embed* all required TrueType fonts in a document file, so the fonts will be available even on another Windows system that doesn't have those fonts installed, *but only for use with the document in which the fonts are embedded.*

Laying Out a Form in CorelDRAW

CorelDRAW is a good choice for laying out manual forms because it has extensive font-manipulation capabilities as well as the previously mentioned grid and snap features for constraining lines, boxes, and text to the spacing you require.

Setting the Paper Size

Start by setting up the program for the paper size and orientation on which the finished form will be printed. Do Layout ➤ Page Setup. The Page Setup dialog box will appear. Select the form size in the Paper Size drop down box, and Portrait or Landscape for the orientation. (If you are using a nonstandard paper size, you can select Custom and then enter the Width and Height in your selected unit of measure.) Select OK to close the dialog box.

Getting Your Grid Ready for a Good Snap

Before you type or draw anything, you should set up the grid—the framework within which your form will be created. Do Layout ➤ Grid Setup. The Grid Setup dialog box will appear, as shown in Figure 4.1.

For purposes of designing a form, leave the Set For Global Units check box unmarked. (This option is used to do proportional drawings, such as maps and floor plans. For example, you could set the global measurement so that 1 inch on the drawing represented 10 feet.)

FIGURE 4.1

The Grid Setup dialog box

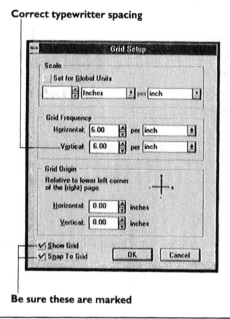

Correct typewriter spacing

Be sure these are marked

Your main concern in this dialog box is the spacing of grid dots, or Grid Frequency. The default setting is 6 dots per inch in both the Horizontal and Vertical dimensions. This is the correct Vertical setting for typewriter spacing, so in many cases you can simply accept the default.

The relationship of various measurements on a 6×6 dots-per-inch grid is shown in Figure 4.2. Typewriter single spacing is 12 points high—the vertical distance between two dots. The sample text in the figure is 10-point Courier New, for which each monospace letter is 6 points in width, or 12 characters per inch (cpi).

You might change the grid frequency if you wanted to use the grid as a guide for drawing a preprinted grid for handwritten responses to be scanned optically. (See *Preprinted Grids for Handwriting* below.)

127

FIGURE 4.2

*The required meas-
urements for
typewriter spacing all
converge happily on a
6 × 6 dots-per-inch
grid.*

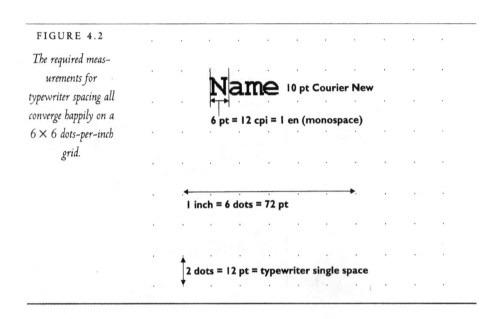

Normally, you need not change the Grid Origin settings, which control the starting point of the grid in relation to the edges of the *printable area* of the page. The printable area is controlled by the Paper Size setting in combination with the Windows printer driver for the current, installed printer. The drawing area that you see in CorelDRAW is the printable area of the page, not the physical edges of the page.

As an aid to drawing, mark the check boxes Show Grid and Snap To Grid. Then select OK to close the dialog box. (You can also turn Snap on or off at any time by pressing Ctrl-Y.)

The page will appear in the drawing area, as shown in Figure 4.3. If you accepted the default grid frequency, dots will be spaced in this full-page view at 1 per inch—not 6 per inch as you specified. However, the grids are there and operating, even if not visible. If you zoom in on a portion of the form, you will see more dots—now spaced at the expected 6 per inch.

FIGURE 4.3

A page in the drawing area

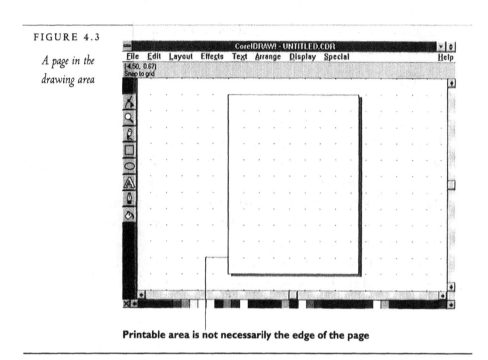

Printable area is not necessarily the edge of the page

Doing the Writing that Nobody Sees

Having set up the form and the grid, now is the time to do that ghost writing I talked about before. That is, start laying out the form by typing the sample responses first. Use a monospace font, and look back at the guidelines for types of input for the appropriate point sizes:

- 14-point for handwritten block letters

- 20-point if the handwritten input will be scanned optically

- 12-point Courier or a printer font such as Pica for typewritten responses (unless your office machines are standardized on something more exotic like 10-point Prestige)

Zoom in on the general area of the form that will hold the response. Do this by clicking the Zoom In tool.

Then drag a rectangle on the form to indicate the area you want to enlarge. You don't have to be too precise about this—you can move things around later. You just want to be working in an enlarged view to save your eyes when you're composing type, and it will be convenient if you're working in the general vicinity of the final location on the form.

Voila! There are the other grid points in the enlarged view—spaced, if you chose the default, 6 dots per inch.

Reset the default font and size for the type you will use for the responses. Do Text ➤ Character. The Character Attributes dialog box will open. Select OK so that your settings apply to both Artistic Text and Paragraph Text.

Let's assume that you are laying out a form for typewritten responses and that you don't have to worry about the special requirements of optical scanning. In the Character Attributes dialog box (Figure 4.4), select the font Courier New (or another monospace typewriter font) in the 12-point size, and select OK.

FIGURE 4.4

The Character Attributes dialog box

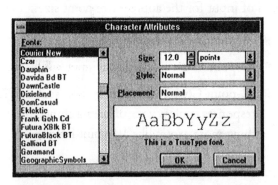

You need to be able to work with text blocks as separate objects so that you can recompose the form by moving them separately around on the screen. In CorelDRAW, use Artistic Text for both responses and preprinted questions. Paragraph Text would be suitable only for an essay-type response that is a single block (say, in response to "Please Summarize the Story of Your Life in 100 Words or Less") or for lengthy preprinted blocks such as instructions and legal disclaimers (if you must).

Type each response item (each text field on the form) as a separate Artistic Text object. To create an item, click the Artistic Text tool.

Then, click the starting point (by default, the left end) of the text string, and start typing.

```
.   .   .   .   .   .   .   .   .   .   .   .   .   .
Englebart Q. Von Rassmussen   .   .   .   .   .   .
.   .   .   .   .   .   .   .   .   .   .   .   .   .
.   .   .   .   .   .   .   .   .   .   .   .   .   .
.   .   .   .   .   .   .   .   .   .   .   .   .   .
.   .   .   .   .   .   .   .   .   .   .   .   .   .
```

Notice that, with Snap To Grid on, a line of Artistic Text—your ghost-written response— "sits" on the grid line, and its starting point (left end) coincides with a grid dot. Each line of text you type as a separate text object will be on a different grid line. So, like magic, the text objects will be spaced 6 lines to the inch.

```
    .   .   .   .   .   .   .   .   .   .   .   .   .   .   .   .
    .  Englebart .Q. .Von Rassmussen.   .   .   .   .   .   .   .
    .  .10001. Civic Center Drive  .   .   .   .   .   .   .   .
    .  Suite. 4050.   .   .   .   .   .   .   .   .   .   .   .
    .  Upper. Horse Shoe Falls.   .   . .CO.   .  55555-5555.  .
    .   .   .   .   .   .   .   .   .   .   .   .   .   .   .   .
```

However, if you now draw lines or boxes, these, too, will snap to the grid, leaving no space around the text. So, before doing any drawing, turn Snap off temporarily by pressing Ctrl-Y.

Move the text objects so that they lie vertically *between* the sets of dots. Do this by clicking the Pick tool.

Then drag a box around *all* the text objects. Solid, square handles should surround the text.

```
    .   .   .   .   .   .   .   .   .   .   .   .   .   .   .
    ■                             ■                      ■
    .Englebart .Q. .Von Rassmussen.   .   .   .   .   .   .
    ..10001. Civic Center Drive  .   .   .   .   .   .   .
    ■                                                    ■
    .Suite. 4050.   .   .   .   .   .   .   .   .   .   .
    .Upper. Horse Shoe Falls.   .   . .CO.   . .55555-5555.   .
    ■                             ■                      ■
    .   .   .   .   .   .   .   .   .   .   .   .   .   .   .
```

Click and hold on the mouse button, and the pointer will change to a four-tipped arrow. Drag this pointer to move the entire collection of text objects at the same time. Having turned Snap off, you can move the text any-where on the screen—but placing it vertically between the grid dots is a good idea, as you will soon see.

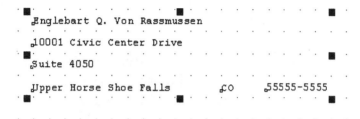

With the text repositioned, turn Snap To Grid back on by pressing Ctrl-Y again.

Now, you can draw boxes and lines that will snap to the grid, assuring the correct spacing. Click the rectangle tool.

And drag a rectangle around the set of responses.

```
    Englebart Q. Von Rassmussen
    10001 Civic Center Drive
    Suite 4050
    Upper Horse Shoe Falls       CO      55555-5555
```

Draw lines within the rectangle by clicking the Freehand tool.

And click each of the endpoints of the line. The Grid and Snap features will constrain the lines to the correct spacing.

```
    Englebart Q. Von Rassmussen
    10001 Civic Center Drive
    Suite 4050
    Upper Horse Shoe Falls       CO      55555-5555
```

You might say that designing a form is like playing Jeopardy. Having given the answers, you need to come up with the questions! So, having ghost-written the responses and drawn correctly spaced boxes around them, you need to add the question labels that will be preprinted on the form.

Do this also as Artistic Text, and reset the default first. Do Text ➤ Character. For the questions, you are not limited to monospace fonts. You can use any legible font, preferably a design that is open enough so that the letters won't become filled in if the form is photocopied. An excellent choice is Lucida Fax (a Microsoft TrueType font from the TrueType Font Pack for Windows). This serif font is elegant, but its characters have enough open space to permit good reproduction even when reproduced by fax or by photocopying.

The questions need not be nearly as big as the responses, as long as they will reproduce well. So, a choice of Lucida Fax 10-point might be appropriate. Select OK to close the Character Attributes dialog box after making your selection.

Now, turn Snap off again by pressing Ctrl-Y. Since you have your layout for the responses and the boxes, your positioning of the questions should be unconstrained.

Click the Artistic Text tool, click the starting point (left edge) of the first question, and type it. Make each question label a separate text object so that you can reposition it freely. Here's the result of adding the question labels to the sample. For purposes of discussion, let's call this completed unit a *response block*.

Name	Englebart Q. Von Rassmussen			
Address10001 Civic Center Drive				
Suite 4050				
City Upper Horse Shoe Falls	State	CO	ZIP 55555-5555	

Notice that the alignment of box labels here is poor. You can use the object-manipulation capabilities of CorelDRAW to align the labels. To align the question labels to the left edge of the box, select all of them by clicking the Pick tool, then holding down the Shift key while you click each label. Having selected the labels this way as a group, do Arrange ➤ Align ➤ Horizontal.

Name	Englebart Q. Von Rassmussen				
Address	10001 Civic Center Drive				
	Suite 4050				
City	Upper Horse Shoe Falls	State	CO	ZIP	55555-5555

Sizing and Moving a Response Block

Just before moving the response block, it's a good idea to make sure that it is sized correctly—mostly so that it will match the others you will be adding to the form.

To resize a rectangle or a line, use the Pick tool to select it. Move the pointer to one of the handles. The pointer will change to small crosshairs. Drag the handle to resize the object, as shown in Figure 4.5.

FIGURE 4.5

Resizing the text block

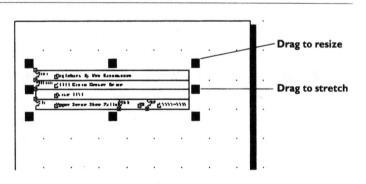

Drag to resize

Drag to stretch

Dragging one of the endpoints of a line or one of the side handles of a rectangle is called a *stretch* because it can distort the object's shape.

 *Decide the margins within the printable area of the form, then stretch and size response boxes to exactly fit the distance between the margins. If Snap To Grid is on, the boxes will be aligned exactly just by sizing or stretching them by eye.*

When you have created such a response block, you want to be able to move it around the form as a single unit—keeping this nice composition you've labored so mightily to achieve.

Before moving a finished response block, combine its objects as a group. Click the Pick tool, drag a box around all the objects, then do Arrange ➤ Group.

To compose the form, switch to the full-page view by clicking the Full Page tool (found in a menu of five tools when you click the Zoom tool).

The full-page view will be restored. Before moving a response block, turn Snap back on by pressing Ctrl-Y. This will assure that the response blocks will maintain the 6 lines per inch spacing in relation to one another.

With the response block selected (handles surrounding it) and Snap To Grid turned on, you can drag it anywhere on the grid to recompose the page.

If you're tempted to stretch those lines and boxes, don't try it while the text is grouped with the selection, or the text will become distorted. Select the grouped object and do Arrange ➤ Ungroup (or press Ctrl-U) before you do any stretching. (Be sure Snap To Grid is turned on to preserve the correct spacing!) If you nevertheless screw up your composition in the midst of a stretch, select Edit ➤ Undo Stretch (or press Ctrl-Z) before you do anything else. This will restore the previous version of the object so that you can try again.

Achieving a Harmonious Composition

You can build the rest of the form as a set of response blocks. In effect, you want to create each block as a mini-document, as just described. Then, group each block and drag the blocks around the screen to compose the finished form. Remember to ungroup before stretching if you need to adjust box widths or line lengths.

A completed form I did by this method (honest!) is shown in Figure 4.6.

Remember to do File ➤ Save to save the completed form with the ghost-written entries included. Then delete the entries and do File ➤ Save As, saving the file to a different name to be used as the master for printing the form.

FIGURE 4.6

A form produced with the methods described

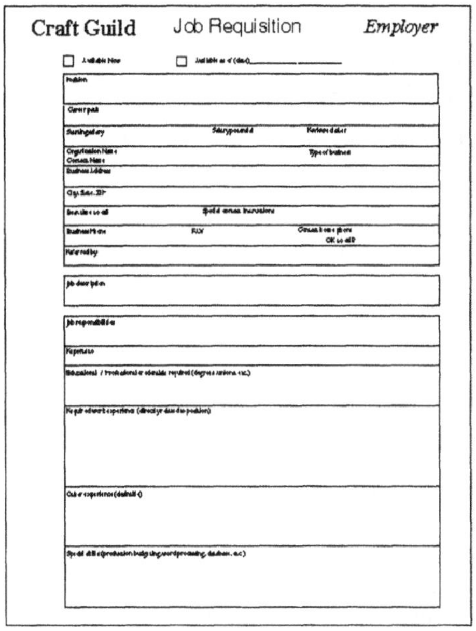

Getting Ready to Get Scanned

Optical scanners are typically much more fussy about what they read than people are. So, if your form will be fed to one of these machines, you must make allowances.

Special Fonts for Scanning

According to Microsoft, this is a font that represents the ideal handwritten input for optical scanning.

ABCDEFGHIJKLMNOPQRSTUVWXYZ
0123456789

Note especially the *O*, which looks like an inverted *Q*, and the stroke through the middle of the *Z* to prevent its being interpreted instead as a 2. Note also the serifs on *B* (to distinguish it from 8), *D* (to distinguish it from zero), *I* (to distinguish it from 1), and *J* (which might also be interpreted as a 1).

Microsoft prints this font at the top of its customer-response forms that will be scanned. A notice advises users to print in black ink and to use white correction fluid for making changes.

Machine-Readable Computer Fonts

Normally, you need not worry about the scanner's recognizing the question labels because the computer you're inputting the data to presumably has been programmed to interpret and process each response field correctly.

However, in some cases it might be necessary to include preprinted codes on the form that the scanner can pick up. Two fonts that have been designed specifically for optical recognition are Microscan A and Microscan

B, as shown in Figure 4.7. (These Swfte TrueType fonts are available in the font set Typecase II.)

FIGURE 4.7

Microscan A (top) and Microscan B (bottom)

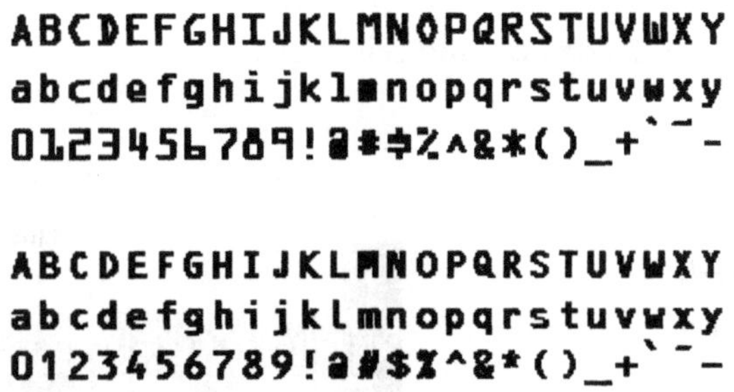

ABCDEFGHIJKLMNOPQRSTUVWXY
abcdefghijklmnopqrstuvwxy
0123456789!a#$%^&*()_+` ~ -

ABCDEFGHIJKLMNOPQRSTUVWXY
abcdefghijklmnopqrstuvwxy
0123456789!a#$%^&*()_+` ~ -

Microscan A is designed for older equipment that uses the same magnetic ink character recognition (MICR) fonts you'll see at the bottom of your bank checks. (Magnetic ink is no longer required. All the scanning is optical these days, but the fonts persist.)

Microscan B is a clean, sans serif typeface that should present no difficulties to later-model scanners. The font lacks the unusual character distortions and serifs that were designed into Microscan A to make each character unique.

Preprinted Grids for Handwriting

It's a simple matter to construct preprinted grids for handwriting in CorelDRAW. I suggest drawing a 24-character grid and storing it in a separate file so that you can retrieve and duplicate it later to your heart's content.

Start by doing Layout ➤ Grid Setup and change the Grid Frequency settings to 4 dots per inch Horizontal and 3 dots per inch Vertical. Then select OK.

To control the thickness and color of the lines you will draw, click the Outline Pen tool. Click the Line Weight tool shown in Figure 4.8. The Outline Pen dialog box will appear. Mark only the Graphic check box, and select OK. Click the Outline Pen tool again, and select the Shading tool (also shown in Figure 4.8). Confirm this selection for Graphic in the Outline Pen dialog box, and select OK.

FIGURE 4.8

The Line Weight and
Texture tools

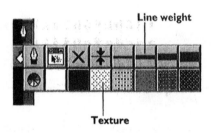

Having specified the thickness and color of lines, draw them by clicking the Freehand tool, then simply connect the 3 × 4 dots until you have a pattern that is 24 small rectangles wide, one for each character position.

Select your entire creation with the Pick tool and group the objects by doing Arrange ➤ Group (or press Ctrl-G). To duplicate the 24-character grid in a drawing, select it with the Pick tool and do Edit ➤ Duplicate (or press Ctrl-D).

Do File ➤ Save and name this graphic something imaginative like GRIDS.CDR. Use and reuse it as much as you want—there's no charge. To retrieve it, do File ➤ Open to reopen the file, select the object with the Pick tool, and do Edit ➤ Copy (or press Ctrl-C) to move it to the Clipboard, then Edit ➤ Paste (or press Ctrl-V) to insert your ready-made grid in the current drawing window.

Paperless Forms! Now *That's* Progress!

A more elegant approach than worrying about spacing on printed outputs can be to compose the form as an electronic document that will be stored and used in a Windows application such as Word or Excel. This is a particularly handy way of doing things if you and the form-fillers share the Windows environment, perhaps over a network.

Using Excel to design a data-input form has an added advantage: The user will be typing data items into a program that can also process them. Therefore, not only are the technical requirements of printing no concern of yours, but also you can forget your worries about catering to fussy input methods such as optical scanning.

Presumably, you're gathering all this data for a reason. You want to process the responses—to count them, summarize them, graph them—whatever. Excel is ready-made for such purposes. You can, for example, link the input form (a worksheet, or .XLS file) to an Excel database table (another worksheet) that would compile the results from many worksheets.

Figure 4.9 shows a form that has been set up in Excel as a template (.XLT file). A template is a preformatted reusable worksheet that has blanks for some of the data items. The template can include not only preprinted text labels, but also formulas that will perform calculations on the data that the filler-in of the blanks will provide.

FIGURE 4.9

An Excel template

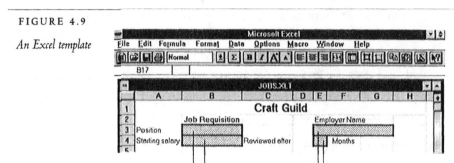

Add borders and shading to response fields

To create a template, start by building it as a worksheet in Excel. Then select File ➤ Save As. The Save As dialog box will appear, as shown in Figure 4.10. Change the setting in the Save File As Type drop-down box from Normal to Template. Type in a file name, and change the path to EX-CEL\XLSTART. You can type the path in front of the file name in the File Name text box, or you can navigate the Directories list box to change the current directory before you select OK to close this dialog box and save the file.

FIGURE 4.10

The Save As dialog box

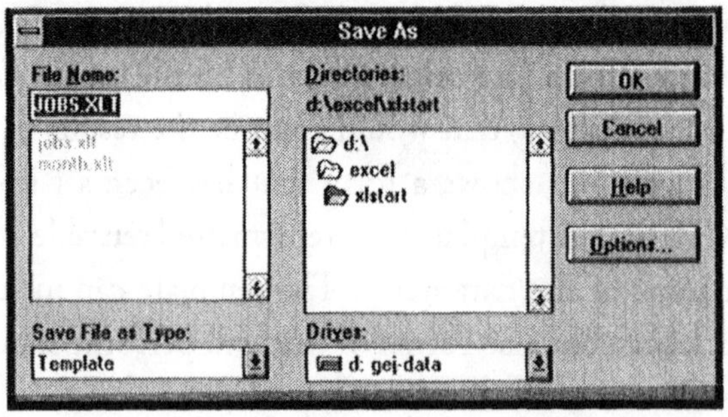

Controlling Text Size in Excel

Recall from Chapter 3 that the command in Excel for controlling font and point size is Format ➤ Font. Select the text by highlighting it in the worksheet, do the command, and the Font dialog box will open. You have all of the font options you have in other Windows applications, including True-Type and ATM font selections, if installed.

When you are creating your worksheet template, you may find that your text entries overflow the cell (little worksheet rectangle), especially if a text string is long or if its point size is greater than the height of the cell, as shown in Figure 4.11.

FIGURE 4.11

When the text is too large, its contents can flow into the next cell.

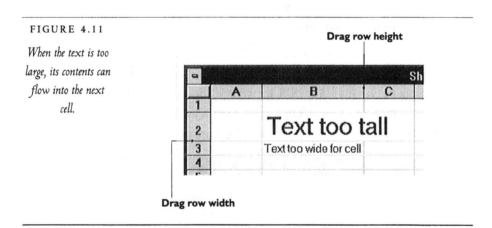

If you see such undesirable stuff, you can resize cells by dragging the column or row headings. To resize the width of an entire column, drag the right border of the column heading. To resize the height of an entire row, drag the bottom border of the row heading. To size a column or row automatically to fit the longest or tallest entry in it, double-click the border instead.

The Joy of Templates

If the template is stored in the program's startup directory EX-CEL\XLSTART (and if the user has access to this directory), the file name you gave to the form will appear when the user selects File ➤ New.

When creating a template as a form that will be filled out by others, select all of the cells that represent the blanks to be filled in by the user, and do Format ➤ Cell Protection. The Cell Protection dialog box will appear.

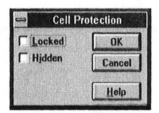

Clear both of the check boxes (Locked is usually on by default), and select OK. This command formats the selected cells so that they will remain unlocked even after you lock the rest of the sheet. To lock the rest of the sheet so that the user can put entries only in the blank spaces, select Options ➤ Protect Document. The Protect Document dialog box will appear.

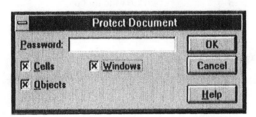

The Password here is optional. Type one in the text box if you want to prevent users from unlocking the form and making changes to the pre-printed entries. Normally, mark all three check boxes: Cells (for preprinted text, as well as formulas, if any), Objects (for charts and drawings you include in the form), and Windows (to prevent the user from resizing, moving, or minimizing the document window that holds the form). If you enter

144

a password, when you select OK to close this dialog box, Excel will ask you to reenter your password in confirmation before the lock is placed.

If you lock the preprinted portions of the form as just described, the user of the form can press Tab to move the insertion point from one blank field to the next (or Shift-Tab to move backwards). So, locking the pre-printed text makes the form both easier to use and less susceptible to un-authorized alteration.

Remember that if you design paperless forms in Excel, you will not only be saving yourself work by providing for automatic data input to forms processing, but you will also be doing us all a favor by putting the paperwork monster on a bulk-reduction diet!

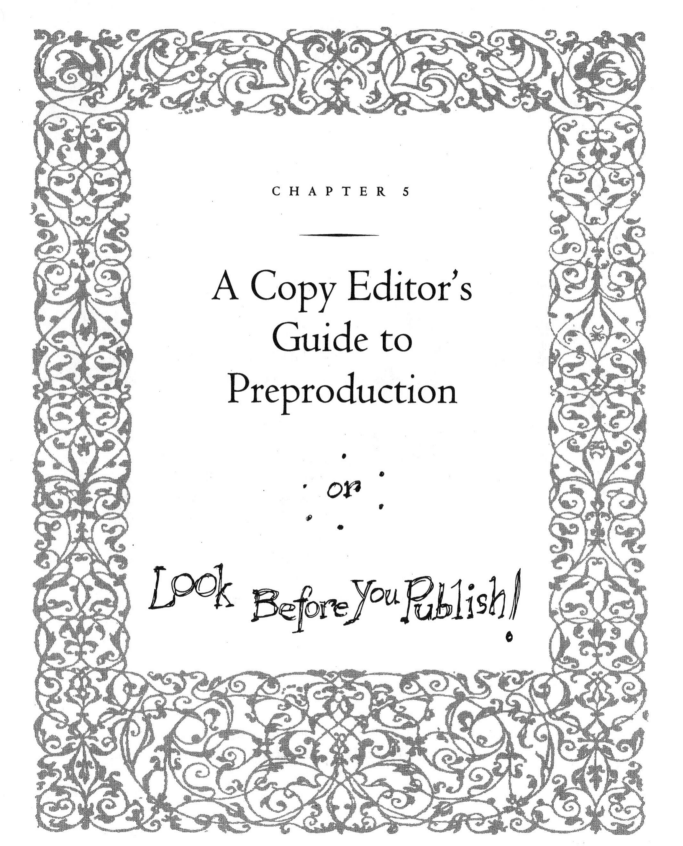

CHAPTER 5

A Copy Editor's Guide to Preproduction

or

Look Before You Publish!

HIS CHAPTER and the one that follows will help to make you productive in the field of desktop publishing. This chapter focuses on preparing written copy for typesetting. The next continues the process through page design and production.

The guidelines for preparing written copy apply equally well both to periodical journalism—such as newsletters—and to more lengthy published works such as books and manuals. Most of the differences show up at the production stage.

You will find that the material in this chapter extends beyond the subject of typography. Lots of issues besides the technical handling of fonts arise when you think about turning your words—or someone else's—into type for the rest of the world to read.

Copyediting Is Quality Control

The person who prepares manuscripts for submission to the production process is the copy editor. Even if you are publishing your own words, this quality-control step is essential to producing professional-looking results.

> ## Whose Script Is It?
>
> The term *manuscript* literally means *handwriting*. In the editorial offices of yesteryear when handwritten drafts were common, the term *typescript* was coined to refer instead to typewritten drafts. Today, drafts are typed directly into computers, and these kinds of documents are seldom used. *Manuscript* now refers to the author's word processing file, which usually is input directly to the production process.

Double-Check Your Spelling and Grammar Checkers

Perhaps an obvious first step in preparing a written draft for publication is to check its spelling, grammar, and punctuation.

What's wrong with this sentence?

```
I no you love me to.
```

Apparently, nothing. That is, if you pass this curious piece of prose to a computer spelling checker in an application such as Word or Excel, no errors will be found.

And you might or might not get a clue that something is wrong from a grammar-checker such as Grammatik. Is this the correct interpretation?

```
I know you love me, too.
```

Or, is it something more suggestive?

```
I know you love me to (mysterious verb omitted but
perhaps understood).
```

Alas, your computer won't know the answer. The point of this example is that there has yet to be found any automated substitute for old-fashioned, low-tech copyediting and proofreading.

Copyediting Isn't Proofreading

Traditionally, copyediting was done on a manuscript before it was set in type. The subsequent task of proofreading involved reading the typeset proofs of printed pages. Even though both of these quality-control steps focus on finding errors, they occur at different places in the production process—one before and the other after type has been set.

Further evidence that these are separate disciplines is that copy editors and proofreaders use different techniques for marking manuscripts for correction, as shown in Figures 5.1 and 5.2. Copy editors mark corrections within the body of the text, and authors' manuscripts are usually required to be double-spaced for this reason (Figure 5.1). On the other hand,

FIGURE 5.1

Copy editors make most of their marks on manuscripts inside the text area.

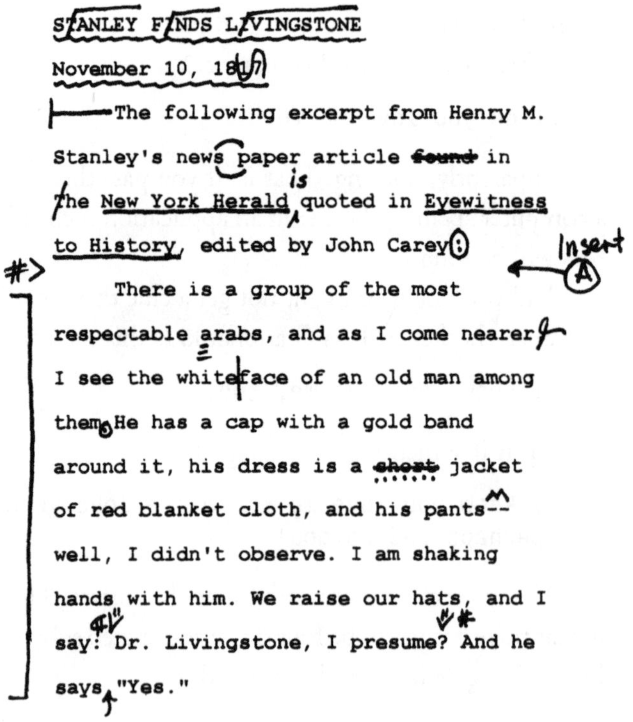

STANLEY FINDS LIVINGSTONE

November 10, 1871

The following excerpt from Henry M. Stanley's news paper article found in the New York Herald is quoted in Eyewitness to History, edited by John Carey:

Insert A

There is a group of the most respectable arabs, and as I come nearer I see the white face of an old man among them. He has a cap with a gold band around it, his dress is a short jacket of red blanket cloth, and his pants-- well, I didn't observe. I am shaking hands with him. We raise our hats, and I say: Dr. Livingstone, I presume? And he says, "Yes."

150

proofreaders make their marks mostly in the margins of typeset page proofs, and the marks themselves differ from the copy editor's marks (Figure 5.2).

In general, the copy editor will focus on correcting the author's errors of spelling, punctuation, and grammatical style—as described in some detail in this chapter. Although the proofreader must catch these types of errors also, the main concern is with the appearance of the page, including any errors that might have been introduced by the typesetter.

The most meticulous proofreading involves *two* people at the same time—one to read aloud the editor's marked-up copy of the manuscript and

FIGURE 5.2

Proofreaders mark typeset page proofs in the margins, using a small caret in the text or circling an item to point to the location of the change.

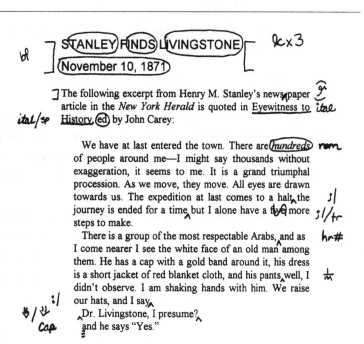

the other to listen while silently reading the typeset proof (traditionally called a *printer's galley*). The purpose is to correct errors before printing (traditionally, before the expense of making printing plates was incurred).

Besides speaking the original words, the first reader announces the punctuation and special capitalization, and spells out proper names:

```
In the words of initial cap President Franklin in-
itial cap f-r-a-n-k-l-i-n initial cap D period
Roosevelt initial cap r-o-o-s-e-v-e-l-t comma quote
initial cap We have nothing to fear but fear itself
period close quote.
```

This copy should be set as:

```
In the words of President Franklin D. Roosevelt, "We
have nothing to fear but fear itself."
```

Using two pairs of eyes assures a word-for-word comparison of the typeset version with the original. Two-person proofreading was necessary when an author's typewritten (or handwritten) manuscript had to be recomposed by a typesetter. Otherwise, with just one reader checking just the galley, reasonable-looking errors could go unnoticed—such as inadvertent paraphrasing, misspellings of unusual proper names, and omission or transposition of numbers.

Computer technology has reduced the possibility of errors in translating words into type, because the material need only be typed once. If the author is working at a word processor, those keystrokes are captured in a disk file and are the same characters from which the final typeset text is composed. So, if there are any errors of spelling or punctuation, they are more likely to be the author's than the typesetter's.

Perhaps because today's keystrokes need never die, the labor-intensive two-person approach to proofreading is rarely done. (It's still used for preparing some types of formal legal documents.)

Furthermore, as both manuscript development and production are being done within systems such as Windows, the distinctions between copy editing and proofreading are beginning to become blurred. It is possible, for example, for authors to work directly with typeset text and to preview the appearance of printed pages, all within the word processing application. Copyediting and proofreading, then, tend to merge into a single quality-control inspection of a near-finished product.

Whether these steps are handled separately or together, the need for assuring accuracy remains. Whether you are publishing your own inspired words or assembling a company newsletter from several contributors, you might think of publishing as manufacturing: You must design quality-control steps into the process.

Do You Know the Two-Step?

Again, if your writing and publishing operations occur entirely within a Windows system, you probably won't even notice the translation of the keystrokes to typeset printing. The Windows environment is set up so that what you see on the screen is supposed to be what you get on paper. (That's the WYSIWYG catch-phrase: What You See Is What You Get.) The translation of your keystrokes into the fonts produced by the printer is handled invisibly by the printer-driver software.

However, even in this high-tech age, most publishing remains at least a two-step process. The division is between the people who write and edit the words and the people who compose the printed pages.

The reasons for this separation of responsibilities include:

¶ As rapidly as WYSIWYG technology has emerged, most authors have not been trained to design finished columns or pages.

¶ Especially for periodicals, publishing usually involves gathering written material from many different authors. Although you can set standards for manuscripts and for the word processing files by which the manuscripts will be submitted, an editorial step is usually required to prepare the copy for production.

❡ The people who worry about the words have traditionally been different people from those who worry about the look of the words on the page.

In fact, until Windows became popular, it was common in large and small publishing operations alike to find two parallel standards for desktop computers: The writers and editorial staff used PCs, and the typesetters and graphic artists used Macs. Nowadays, the Windows environment combines PC compatibility with WYSIWYG type and graphics in the same system. The separation is also beginning to blur because PCs and Macs are becoming increasingly similar in both their manner of operation and the results they produce.

However, even if all steps of your writing and production process are done under Windows, you may encounter some technical difficulties in attempting to merge the work of multiple authors on a single typeset page. Some of these issues are covered later in this chapter. (See *Are We Compatible, or What?*)

The Right Way, the Wrong Way, and My Way

The copy editor bridges the gap between authors and the special requirements of production. The essential job of copyediting is to review the manuscript and to correct it so that it adheres to the publication's *house style.*

I once worked for an editor who said, "We don't have a house style around here. We just do it the right way." Confused, I asked what the right way was. He glared back and replied, "My way!"

A house style is usually published in its own volume as a manual for authors, editors, and production staff. Policies on style usually cover:

- Spelling, punctuation, and grammatical style
- Word processing formats
- Typesetting codes

If You Don't Have a Style, Steal One

If your publication involves anyone besides yourself as author or editor, you probably need a house style manual. If you don't have one, call up another publication and request a copy of theirs. Keep what you like, change what you don't—but consult an authority such as *The Chicago Manual of Style* before you lay down your own law. In developing your own guidelines, pay particular attention to terms and conventions that might be unique to your field or industry. (Incidentally, *The Chicago Manual* was developed initially as an internal style manual for a publisher—the University of Chicago Press.)

Spelling, Punctuation, and Grammatical Style

It might seem that the rules of English spelling, punctuation, and grammar are engraved in stone, which was probably the impression your teachers gave you in school. However, scholars and publications differ widely in their opinions about what is "correct," and the rest of us are busy changing the language daily (intentionally or otherwise). That's why house style manuals exist.

Word Processing Formats

You will simplify your life greatly if your style manual also specifies submission formats for word processing files. Among Windows formats, Microsoft Word 2.0 is probably the most common. You might also specify a particular template and a limited set of fonts.

Specifying fonts is not absolutely necessary, since TrueType fonts can be embedded in application files. In a document that was created on another Windows system, the text will be displayed on another Windows system just as it appeared originally—even if those fonts don't reside on the second computer. (Both computers should be running the same version of the application, though.)

However, making sure that everyone uses the same margins, spacing, and fonts will remove some of the uncertainty from handling multiple submissions—particularly in the face of critical publication deadlines.

You might also want to include standards for file compression, particularly if documents will be transmitted to you by modem or over a network. For example, PKZIP is a widely used DOS file-compression utility program that can reduce the size of document and picture files, creating a compact .ZIP file. Compressed files generally require much less time to transmit (and less space on disk). But to restore the original file, you need the same or a later version of the complementary program PKUNZIP. So, both the preferred compression program and the required version number of that program should be spelled out in your style manual.

Even more complex than document files are pictures and graphics, which might be included in authors' submissions—or even embedded in their Windows documents. If everyone is working in Windows, you might specify its .BMP file format for bitmaps and the .WMF Windows Metafile format for vector graphics, or line art. Indicate also whether you expect 16 (VGA) or 256 (Super VGA) levels of monochrome or color. File formats that can be used more readily if Macs as well as PCs are involved are Tag Image File Format, or TIFF (.TIF extension) for bitmaps and Encapsulated PostScript (.EPS) for line art.

Typesetting Codes

If you do all steps of your publishing process—from keystroke input to output of printed pages—within the Windows environment, you probably need not worry about developing special typesetting codes. The formatting of the word processing application can be translated by the printer driver software to produce output that closely resembles the page-layout displays you see on the screen.

Special typesetting codes are required when:

❡ Authors use a variety of word processors.

❡ Output will be to a non-Windows printer or platemaker.

Large-scale publishing operations generally face both these situations. Far from sharing the same computing environment, authors might not even share the same character set! For example, an article written on an Italian keyboard—even if the text is in English—might include a different set of character codes.

The output side creates other challenges. Most laser printers supported by Windows have a resolution of 300 dots per inch (dpi). Some newer models provide 600 dpi. However, the usual requirement for newspapers, magazines, and books is 1200 dpi. Machines at this level of resolution include phototypesetters, which produce printed pages on photographic film, and electronic platemakers, which create page images directly on printing plates.

These output machines have their own proprietary typesetting codes. Although Windows drivers are becoming available for some of these devices, publishers have preferred to develop coding schemes that are independent of specific output devices. If all authors and editors can be encouraged to use the same set of codes, it can be straightforward to do search-and-replace in a later computer-based production step to translate the files for a specific typesetting system.

In Windows word-processing applications, the computer codes that control the appearance of the page are usually hidden. That is, you see their effects rather than the codes themselves.

In contrast, publishers' typesetting codes are visible in the document. The codes are usually standard characters in unique combinations that would not ordinarily occur in a manuscript. For example, the required coding of a first-level headline might be:

```
#1:This Is a First-Level Head:1#
```

In this example, the code **#1:** turns the headline effect on and **:1#** turns it off, indicating a shift back to normal text. The headline effect usually would involve changing the font and increasing its point size, as well as justifying the headline according to the margins and the page design.

Although there is now an ANSI standard for typesetting codes, many publishers still follow the rules they have already developed internally—and I've never seen two the same! Here are the requirements for such a proprietary set of codes:

- Each code must be a combination of characters that is unusual enough not to occur in normal text.

- To assure compatibility with the widest variety of word processing systems—old and new—the characters that comprise the codes should be restricted to ASCII characters with decimal values 33–126. (See *Asky or Antsy—Who Cares?* in this chapter.) This is the only set of characters that will be standard on most systems and in most fonts.

¶ Codes must be used consistently. Transposing or omitting characters in a code will make it invalid. Also, for every code that turns an effect on, there must be a matching code to turn it off.

¶ Word-processing files should not contain any formatting other than these printable ASCII codes. Any formatting that is unique to the word-processing application—such as boldface or italics—should be shown in the corresponding typesetting code instead.

Hey, why reinvent the wheel? A study committee of the Association of American Publishers (AAP) has developed recommendations for electronic annotation of manuscripts and typesetting codes for the book and magazine industries. These recommendations are now included in National Information Standard Z39.59-1988 Electronic Manuscript Preparation and Markup. This document describes the Standard Generalized Markup Language (SGML). For a copy of the standard, contact Transaction Publishers in New Brunswick, New Jersey, at (908) 932-2280.

Just Your Style (Short Version)

Here are some of the generally accepted style points that most often make work for copy editors, typesetters, and proofreaders. Feel free to incorporate them in your own style manual. The main categories usually include the following:

¶ Punctuation

¶ Use of italics

¶ Capitalization

¶ Numbers and fractions

❡ Alternate spellings

❡ Person and voice

❡ Reading level

Punctuation

These aren't all the rules—just the ones that get missed most often:

Apostrophe Generally, use *'s* to indicate the possessive form of a noun or indefinite pronoun, or add just the ' to a plural form that ends in *s*. However, if the word ends in an *s* or *z* sound but is singular, add *'s* if this last syllable will be pronounced, but just the ' if the possessive part isn't pronounced:

```
the box's shape
for goodness' sake
Keats' poetry
Loch Ness's monster
```

Colon You can use a *:* instead of *and* to join a compound sentence. However, the second clause should amplify or clarify the first. Style books differ on whether to capitalize the first word of the second clause:

```
This is certain: the sun will come up tomorrow.
or
This is certain: The sun will come up tomorrow.
```

There is more reason to capitalize the second clause if it is lengthy.

Comma The *serial comma* is often a point of contention. Is this sentence punctuated correctly?

```
I bought apples, oranges, and grapes.
```

Or do you hold that the *and* takes the place of that last comma in a series:

```
I bought apples, oranges and grapes.
```

I'd say publications are split about 50-50 on this one. Personally, I'm in favor of more serial commas, especially when the *and*'s start to proliferate:

```
We're having apples, oranges, bagels and cream
cheese, and grapes.
```

Another use of commas is to set off dates and geographic locations when they appear in the middle of a sentence:

```
I now live in Boulder, Colorado, but I moved there
recently from Sioux City, Iowa.
On June 6, 1999, the note will become due.
```

However, if the reference includes *only the month and year*, the commas are omitted:

```
The note will come due in June 1999.
```

Dash If an *em dash* is used to separate two clauses, the comma that would otherwise go there is omitted:

```
I don't want you to make a mistake—and I'll be
careful, too.
```

Ellipsis This one is tricky. Use three dots (…) to indicate words that have been omitted from a quotation if the omission is *within* a sentence. If the omission is at the end, you need *four* dots—three for the ellipsis and one for the period! (As I pointed out in Chapter 1, it is better to use a font's … character rather than type a string of periods.)

Hyphen Use hyphens in compound words (self-examination) or to divide broken words at the ends of lines. (Remember that the hyphen is being dropped increasingly from compound words, even if it means joining two vowels: *reenter.*) Use an *en dash* (slightly longer) instead of a hyphen to indicate a range (0–60 mph). Also, don't use a hyphen for a minus sign (−).

Parentheses If an entire sentence is enclosed within parentheses, capitalize the first word and put the period inside the closing parenthesis:

```
(This comment is definitely parenthetical.)
```

But if the parenthetical sentence appears inside another sentence, omit the initial cap and the period, although a question mark or exclamation point is permitted:

```
This fact is obvious (don't you think?), but I'd
double-check it.
```

If the parenthetical expression is a fragment and it comes at the end of the sentence, put the period outside of the closing parenthesis:

```
This much is obvious (or maybe not).
```

Period Style books vary in requirements for periods after some abbreviations. In general, use periods if the abbreviation is not an accepted acronym, but don't expect that rule to apply in all cases.

```
born in the USA
Meet me at 10 A.M. EST.
the Hon. Thurgood Marshall
```

Question mark Here are two different ways of posing a series of questions:

```
I want to know which font will you use? what size
will you want? do you prefer serif or sans serif?
```

```
I want to know (1) which font will you use, (2)
what size will you want, (3) do you prefer serif
or sans serif?
```

Quotation marks Here's another item that gives editors fits. Periods and commas go inside the closing quotation mark—even if not part of the quoted material. Colons and semicolons go outside. Dashes, question marks, and exclamation points go inside if part of the quotation, outside if part of the sentence as a whole.

If quotation contains another quotation, enclose the embedded quotation in single quotation marks (' '). If the embedded quotation comes at the end of the sentence, put the period first, then the single quotation mark, then the double:

```
He said, "I said, 'Don't even think about it.'"
```

As I mention in Chapter 1, it is better to use the curly opening and closing quotation marks in the Windows font than ditto marks with quoted materials.

Semicolon You can use a semicolon in place of *and* to join a compound sentence, omitting the comma. But use the semicolon in place of the comma and keep the *and* if either clause contains commas:

```
Great Britain, France, and the United States were
allies in both world wars; and, in the midst of in-
tense economic competition, those ties still hold.
```

The formal style books also say to use a semicolon to separate compound items in a series:

```
The color schemes are red, white, and blue; orange,
green, and brown; and blue, blue-green, and yellow.
```

However, some writers, especially popular journalists and novelists, are doing away with using semicolons in place of commas (omitting some of the commas, as well), with the idea perhaps that the flow of the sentence can be improved:

```
Great Britain, France, and the United States were
allies in both world wars, and in the midst of in-
tense economic competition those ties still hold.
```

Use of Italics

Use italics for emphasis, to highlight letters, words, and phrases referred to as such, in foreign words and phrases, and for titles of longer works such as books, manuals, and names of periodicals.

Use double quotation marks rather than italics for titles of articles within periodicals, as well as for chapters or sections within books.

Style books vary on which words are considered foreign and therefore should be italicized. A good working rule is that if you can find it in the A–Z part of an English dictionary, it need not be italicized. Examples are the Latin words *versus* and *de facto*, which are in everyday speech. But you might italicize a term if you think your readers won't know it:

```
She spoke of the zeitgeist of that exuberant age.
```

A common area of confusion is whether to put special words or phrases in italics or to enclose them in quotation marks. In the cases just cited, italics are correct. Use quotation marks (sparingly) to enclose words that are used in unusual ways. Avoid using quotation marks to give special emphasis to words that are used conventionally.

Capitalization

There are lots of capitalization pitfalls. Here are just a few of them:

Quoted material Capitalize the first word in a quotation *unless* the quotation completes the sentence:

```
He said, "You made the whole thing up."
```
but
```
He insisted that you "made the whole thing up."
```

Bulleted items The first word of a bulleted item should be capitalized, whether or not the item is a sentence.

Headlines and titles This is an important one for publications and a point of some confusion. Capitalize each word in a headline or title except for internal conjunctions (*and*, unless it's the first word), prepositions (*in, with*), and articles (*a, the*). But—depending on the style book—longer prepositions are also capitalized:

```
Choosing Between These Two Alternatives
```

One rule is that if a preposition has more than five letters, capitalize it.

Titles of persons Government and corporate titles are capitalized only if used with the proper name of the person:

```
President T. J. Mackenzie spoke.
The president spoke.
```

Some government officials can be addressed by their titles in place of their names:

```
Mr. President, take a look at the polls!
Thank you, Mr. Speaker.
```

> ## Dealing with Those Windy Quotations
>
> If a quoted passage is lengthy, drop down and indent the entire quotation, omitting the opening and closing quotation marks, and setting the type in a smaller point size from normal text. If you don't use footnotes or otherwise identify the source in the text, the citation can follow, enclosed in parentheses. Let's say that you had this sentence, followed by a quotation:
>
> Just before encountering the great man for whom he was searching, the intrepid traveler remembered
>
>> We have at last entered the town. There are hundreds of people around me—I might say thousands without exaggeration, it seems to me. It is a grand triumphal procession. As we move, they move. All eyes are drawn toward us. The expedition at last comes to a halt; the journey is ended for a time; but I alone have a few more steps to make. (H.M. Stanley, *New York Herald*, November 10, 1871.)

Numbers and Fractions

Spell out numbers from *one* to *nine* unless they are used with units of measure:

```
You have two, perhaps three, choices.
The machined part will require a taper of 3 cm.
```

Spell out the commonly used fractions *one-quarter* and *one-half*, unless the fraction is preceded by a whole-number digit or followed by a unit of measure. Omit the endings *st, rd, nd, th*, or *ths* after numeric digits or fractions. Do not use *of a* or *of an* between a fraction and its unit of measure ($^1\!/_2$ inch).

As discussed in Chapter 1, use the typeset fractions included in a font rather than constructing them from two digits separated by a slash ($^1\!/_2$ rather than 1/2). And don't put a space between a whole number and the fraction that follows it ($5\frac{1}{4}$). If you frequently need fractions that are not included in a font, consider constructing them as custom characters with a font utility such as Fontographer (see Chapter 11).

Alternate Spellings

Some careful editors have specific preferences about alternate spellings, hoping perhaps to revolutionize the language single-handedly. For example, both of these spellings are correct, but a publication should enforce the use of only one of them:

```
judgment
judgement
```

Where there are two correct spellings of a word, the preferred spelling is listed first in the dictionary. (But which dictionary? And preferred by whom?)

Less obvious choices involve technical terms and jargon that are just starting to be accepted in general usage. To pick an example close to home, here are two versions of a familiar term that are now considered equally correct:

```
file name
filename
```

Just a few years ago, you had other options for *workstation—work-station* and *work station*. Both are now considered incorrect.

A house style manual will usually include a list of preferred spellings—especially for the technical terms and jargon of the readership—and will also cite a specific edition of a dictionary to be consulted for anything else. A commonly cited authority in the United States is *Merriam-Webster's Collegiate Dictionary, Tenth Edition*.

If you have to go to an unabridged dictionary to find a word, many of your readers might not know it. Consider using a more common synonym or even several simpler words that describe the concept.

In general, abbreviations should be avoided within sentences, but exceptions might be permitted for units (MHz for megahertz), geographic names (Calif.), forms of address (Ms. with or Ms without the period), and so on. A style manual should list the preferred forms of abbreviations and acronyms that are used commonly in the publication.

Person and Voice

This category has little to do with typesetting but is nevertheless an important section of any style manual.

Depending on the formality of the publication, there may be rules about direct references to the author or to the reader. Some publications permit *I* and *you*, although many discourage *we* as condescending or confusing (who are *we*, anyway?). The "editorial *we*," by which the author attempts to hide in an anonymous group (with the editorial staff? with fellow wizards?), has all but disappeared.

Lest they appear condescending, presumptuous, or even adversarial, internal corporate publications must be particularly careful about the use of we. It is often a matter of strict policy that we cannot be used unless it is clear from the context that the reader is included!

Some more formal publications recommend avoiding personal pronouns except for the third person—*he, she, it,* and *they.* However, this rule can force the author into stuffy formalisms such as

```
The reader will discover that...
```

A poor alternative is the cold impersonality—and vagueness—of the passive voice:

```
It will be discovered that...
```

Using the passive voice is all the more undesirable because most style manuals encourage writers to use the active voice wherever possible:

```
You will discover that...
```

Reading Level

Also related to style is the educational level that is assumed of the audience. Major-market newspapers assume a tenth grade reading level—which is also the standard for most undergraduate college textbooks!

Some grammar-checking software will analyze word-processing files and report the reading level as a score called the *readability index*. Microsoft Word will report on readability after it has performed grammar checking by way of the Tools ➤ Grammar command. Here are some general guidelines, for which you don't need a grammar-checker:

- ¶ Avoid words having more than three syllables.

- ¶ Keep sentences to fewer than 20 words.

- ¶ Don't include more than two clauses in most sentences.

More to the point of composing typeset pages, shorter words and sentences will make it easier to justify and rejustify paragraphs, especially in relatively narrow columnar layouts.

Want to Be Even More Stylish?

If you want to get serious about this style business, here are some of the most frequently consulted sources:

Bernstein, Theodore M., *The Careful Writer: A Modern Guide to English Usage* (Macmillan, 1977) ISBN 0-689-10038-8.

Chicago Editorial Staff, *The Chicago Manual of Style* (Fourteenth edition; University of Chicago Press, 1993) ISBN 0-226-10389-7.

Fowler, Henry W., *A Dictionary of Modern English Usage*, (Second edition; Ohio University Press, 1987) ISBN 0-19-869115-7.

"Handbook of Style" in *Merriam-Webster's Collegiate Dictionary* (Tenth Edition; Merriam Webster, 1993) ISBN 0-87779-709-9.

Strunk, William Jr. and E.B. White, *Elements of Style* (Third edition; Macmillan, 1979) ISBN 0-02-418220-6.

Warren, Thomas L., *Words into Type* (Fourth edition; Prentice-Hall, 1992) ISBN 0-13-966060-7.

Other Quality-Control Steps

In addition to enforcing these standards, the copy editor also should read the material for *sense* (as in, "Will this make sense to most of our readers?").

Although the content of the material usually has been approved in a prior editorial step, the copy editor may also be responsible for assuring its accuracy. For example, copy editors often do *fact-checking*, looking up statistics in reference books or calling people who are quoted in an article to confirm the accuracy of the quotations.

It's Not Just Polite, It's the Law

Requirements for obtaining permission to reproduce quoted material and drawings is an essential part of any editorial policy. The relevant law in the United States is the 1976 revision of the U.S. Copyright Act.

Editorial policies differ in their interpretation of the doctrine of *fair use*, or quotation of small excerpts from a longer work without explicit permission. If you get formal permission, you should set the *credit line*, or the citation of the source, exactly as specified by the permission grantor. If you use a short quotation under fair use, the source should still be cited.

Credit lines for photographs and illustrations are generally set in the figure captions. Permissions to quote may be included on the copyright page, which in a book should be on the back of the title page. Permissions might also be included in the book's acknowledgments. In more formal documents, such as scholarly articles and books, citations are included in footnotes at the bottom of the page or numbered by chapter in an appendix titled "Notes" or "References." (Note that a Bibliography is not a list of specific citations, but a separate listing of research sources.)

Related to the subject of permissions is the question of plagiarism. Don't assume that you can get around the need to obtain permission simply by paraphrasing, or rewording, a quotation. The revision to the copyright act uses the standard of *substantial similarity* to define plagiarism—and leaves it to the courts decide what that means in each case.

Some material is so old that it is out of copyright, or in the *public domain*. This material might not require permission for quotation. But be careful! For example, no one holds a copyright on the words of Shakespeare. However, the *typesetting* of his words in a new book edition might be protected by copyright law—so you can't just go reproducing the pages. Also protected would be a new translation into another language, scholarly comments or references included in the text, illustrations, and so on.

Don't look here for an interpretation of the law. I'm not a lawyer, but I reserve the right to play one on TV.

Preparing Copy for Production

With all of these style issues in mind—and usually under the pressure of an imminent deadline—the copy editor assumes the task of revising the writers' material to both follow the publication's house style and to code the manuscript properly for typesetting and production.

Don't Be Afraid to Make Your Mark

In this era of all-electronic work methods, marking up manuscripts by hand might seem as old-fashioned as two-person proofreading. But there are still some excellent reasons for using manually corrected drafts. Specifically, a marked up manuscript

- Preserves the original text on disk until changes are authorized.

- Provides a working document by which authors, editors, and designers can agree on changes.

- Highlights the proposed changes so that the author can see and learn from them. Having seen the editor's detailed comments and corrections, the author can make the next submission conform more closely to the house style, potentially saving work for the editorial staff.

Workgroups Are Electronic Pen Pals

Despite the usefulness of marked-up hard copy, this manual editorial step is also beginning to be replaced by electronic work methods. This change is particularly evident in workgroups that can share data files over a network under a system such as Windows for Workgroups or Lotus Notes.

One of the effects of automation in publishing is a compression of time between submission of manuscripts and printing. In newspaper journalism, for example, it is now possible to insert the text of a breaking story just moments before printing plates are created by electronic imaging. The effect on the relationship between authors and editors is that there may be little or no time for review and approval of changes.

Indeed, some editors—and some authors, too—advocate a process of "transparent editing," in which the copy editor makes changes directly to the author's word processing file. The author then receives only the clean, or proposed final, copy for review. Its proponents argue that this approach makes it easier to agree on the finished product, since it focuses attention on what's right rather than on what's wrong. It should also be easier to meet close deadlines because the steps of marking the changes and capturing them to disk have been merged.

If you're tempted to adopt a policy of transparent editing, consider a similar circumstance in the legal profession. When an attorney sends a new draft of an agreement to the client for review, any changes are highlighted so that the client can see how the terms have been affected by negotiations with the other parties. Traditionally, manual copies were marked up in red ink, whence derives the term *red-lined* for this version of the document. Today, now that computer-based word processing has almost entirely replaced manual typing in law offices, an electronic analog of red-lining is still used. The draft agreement in the word-processing file shows all deletions and insertions until the final document is printed. As shown in Figure 5.3, deletions are shown in strikethrough font, and insertions are shown underlined.

Most Windows word-processing applications such as Word support both strikethrough and underline effects. So, here's one time you can steal from your lawyer and get away with it. Annotate the changes in your shared electronic text files by at least highlighting the deletions and insertions.

FIGURE 5.3

Strikethrough and underline effects high-light deletions and insertions.

5. Author ~~stipulates~~ <u>represents</u> that the book <u>(hereinafter</u> <u>referred to as "the Work")</u> is original and does not infringe on the ~~works~~ <u>rights</u> of any third person.

With these annotations, it might also be helpful to add explanatory notes. In a Word document, for example, you might use the command Insert ➤ Footnote to add your comments to the document file. A handy tool for doing this in workgroup applications is Lotus Annotator. This program is included with some Lotus applications for Windows. Its icon appears in the application toolbar. To launch Lotus Annotator from within the application that holds your document, you simply click its icon:

A document window will open, as shown in Figure 5.4, into which you can type the text of a note. You can also insert other types of Windows objects, such as sound recordings.

FIGURE 5.4

The Lotus Annotator document window permits you to embed text and other types of Windows objects in the document files of Windows applications.

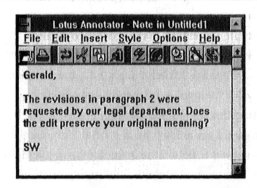

When you do File ➤ Exit in this window, the note appears as an embedded object in the application document.

People with whom you share the document will be able to retrieve the note by double-clicking on the note icon. Although the icon appears on the screen, it will not appear in screen shows (electronic slide shows) or in printouts.

Are We Compatible, or What?

Perhaps unfortunately for peace and harmony among authors and editors, all word-processing file formats are not alike.

Some degree of compatibility is assured if everyone is working in either Windows or in Apple System 7, since applications that run under these systems can use and exchange TrueType or PostScript Type 1 fonts.

Also, applications that run under Windows and System 7 generally are equipped with file translation *filters*, or utility programs that can convert among word processing formats. However, such translations are rarely perfect. If a filter is available for the format you want to read, chances are that the text will be translated correctly. But the appearance formatting won't always be interpreted correctly.

Unless you can impose strict standards on authors so that they all use the same applications and styles, you're better off requiring files to have no appearance formatting at all—just plain ASCII or ANSI text. This is the approach taken by most publishers who must deal with large numbers of submissions from authors who are not under their direct control. As I mention earlier in this chapter, these publishers may require authors to follow a style manual that includes human-readable typesetting codes that are composed of unique strings of ASCII characters.

A possible alternative is to require authors to submit word processing files in *rich text format (RTF)*. This is a standard that includes codes for both ASCII text and appearance formatting. It is perhaps the most widely supported file type for formatted text among non-Windows word processing applications.

Letting Foreigners in Your Windows

You can generally use one of three methods to bring text in a foreign file format into a Windows word-processing application:

❡ Open the file.

❡ Import the file.

❡ Convert the file externally.

Let's look at these in detail:

Open Many Windows applications permit you to access foreign files with the File ➤ Open command. In Word, for example, the Open dialog box will appear, as shown in Figure 5.5. You can change the type of files in the listing in the List Files Of Type drop-down box. (Notice that rich text format .RTF and ASCII .TXT files can be read directly, without a subsequent conversion selection.) To display any type of file, select All Files (*.*). Then enter the path and file name in the Files text box, or navigate the Drives and Directories boxes to select a file from the listing.

When you select OK (or double-click the file name), the Convert File dialog box will appear, as shown in Figure 5.6. (If you have selected a Word .DOC file or an .RTF or .TXT file, this dialog box will not appear and the file will simply be opened as the current Word document window.)

FIGURE 5.5

Foreign file types as well as .DOC files can be accessed through this dialog box when you do File ➤ Open in Word.

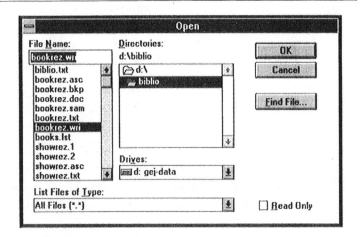

FIGURE 5.6

The Convert File dialog box displays a list of file conversion filters.

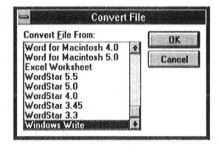

The listing in the Convert File dialog box shows the conversion filters that were selected when Word was installed. If you don't see the filter you need and if it is supported by Word, exit the program and run Word Setup to install the filter. If you need a filter that is not supported, you must handle the conversion externally, as described below, then open the converted file in Word.

For a supported filter, select it in the Convert File dialog box, then choose OK. The file will be opened in a Word document window. If

177

the source file has no font information, the text will appear in the font and size specified for Normal style. The amount of appearance formatting that will also be displayed varies depending on the formatting information in the source file and the capabilities of the conversion filter.

In most cases, it will be necessary to adjust the appearance formatting in Word. For example, to change the font globally, do Edit ➤ Select All, then specify a font name from the Font drop-down box.

Import Some Windows applications have a separate menu command—usually File ➤ Import—for accessing foreign file types, particularly for non-Windows types. The procedure is much the same as just described for File ➤ Open. In some applications, you do File ➤ Import, specify the file type and name, then choose a conversion filter. In others you select the filter before selecting the file.

As a trend in later versions of Windows applications, the File ➤ Import command is disappearing, being replaced with the more general File ➤ Open command, much as it is implemented in Word.

Convert externally As an alternative, a foreign file can be translated first by an external conversion program, then opened in or imported to a Windows application. This might be a necessary first step in accessing some non-Windows file types. For example, WordPerfect versions for DOS include the utility CONVERT.EXE, which can convert foreign files—including ASCII and RTF formats—to and from WordPerfect document formats for DOS. Conversions from Digital Equipment Corporation DECmate II word processing files (a popular office system) to DOS can be handled by the WPS utility, which is available from the following address:

Exceptional Business Solutions, Inc.
10811 Washington Blvd.
Suite 240
Culver City, CA 90232
(310) 558-3435

Asky or Antsy—Who Cares?

When you see a reference to ASCII or ANSI, it means "plain vanilla" text—with no formatting and only a few standardized special characters. The American Standard Code for Information Interchange includes the characters Alt-000 to Alt-127. (The three-digit codes are called *decimal ASCII*. To insert a character, hold down the Alt key while you press the three-digit code on the numeric keypad.)

The American National Standards Institute (ANSI) text format includes the characters Alt-0000 to Alt-0255, extending the ASCII set with international and special characters. The ANSI set is the Windows standard. If your computer is set up for U.S. English and you are exchanging files only with other computers so configured, you will notice no difference between ASCII and ANSI files.

As a general rule, specify ASCII if you must work with files from older U.S. machines. Otherwise, always specify ANSI.

Pick Your Translator Carefully

The translation of text files by your computer is controlled by Code Page settings in DOS (in versions 3.3 and later). A *code page* is a lookup table by which keystrokes and file character data are translated into binary computer code. Two commonly used tables are

```
Code Page 437 U.S. English (ASCII)
Code Page 850 Multilingual
```

Some Windows applications such as Harvard Graphics permit you to reset the Code Page specifically for the purpose of reading foreign files. In Harvard Graphics, you can do File ➤ Preferences and reset the option Import/Export ASCII Character Set.

You can select a different code page in Word with the command Format ▶ Language. The Language dialog box will open, as shown in Figure 5.7. Select a language (code page) from the listing, then select the Use As Default button. If you respond Yes to the notice that appears, the language you selected will become the default *for the current template only,* usually Normal style. (If you selected a block of text before doing this command and did not select the Use As Default button, the language you choose will apply only to that block in the current document.)

You can also perform spelling checks on foreign language text in Word by installing the appropriate dictionary obtained from Microsoft Customer Service. (To inspect the current dictionary setting, do Tools ▶ Options ▶ WIN.INI and select MS Proofing Tools in the Application drop-down box.)

If the correct dictionary is installed for the language you select, you can run a spelling check and Word will format the text correctly with the required special characters from the current font. However, fonts vary in their support for international characters, and you must make sure that the font contains the required characters. To inspect the character set of any font, you can open the Windows Accessories program group, run Character Map, and select the name of the font from the Font drop-down box.

FIGURE 5.7

You can reset the language code page in Word for a selected text block or as the default for the current template.

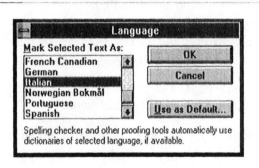

CHAPTER 6

Publishing Newsletters and Books

OR

Ink in Your Veins

HAPTER 5 FOCUSES mainly on preparing a manuscript for publication. In a publishing organization, the lucky person who has to worry about this stuff is the copy editor, whose job is basically one of quality control. This chapter moves on to explain the continuation of this process as you design and produce printed pages. Although publishing formats may look different, the essential task of *page makeup* is much the same whether you are doing a newsletter, a magazine, a booklet, a manual, or a full-length bound book or textbook.

Words into Print: The Big Picture

An overview of the publication process for a magazine or a book is diagrammed in Figure 6.1.

According to the numbered steps in the diagram, Chapter 5 is concerned mainly with step 3, Copyediting, including the development of a house style

FIGURE 6.1

Steps in the publica-
tion process

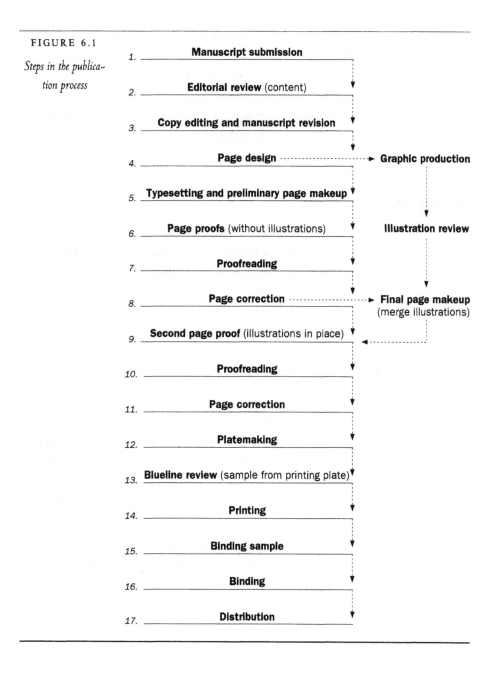

1. Manuscript submission
2. Editorial review (content)
3. Copy editing and manuscript revision
4. Page design ·····> Graphic production
5. Typesetting and preliminary page makeup
6. Page proofs (without illustrations) — Illustration review
7. Proofreading
8. Page correction ·····> Final page makeup (merge illustrations)
9. Second page proof (illustrations in place)
10. Proofreading
11. Page correction
12. Platemaking
13. Blueline review (sample from printing plate)
14. Printing
15. Binding sample
16. Binding
17. Distribution

manual as a guide. These rules of style also apply and are enforced in Steps 7 and 10, Proofreading, which is a close inspection of typeset samples of pages before the costs of printing get out of hand.

This chapter goes in for a close look at step 4, Page Design, as well as step 5, Page Makeup. More than any other part of the publication process, these steps involve detailed work with typography.

Designing the Page

Once upon a time in the not-so-distant past, setting words into type involved a serious expenditure of money. Marked-up typescript was sent to an outside typesetting house, which sent back galleys, or proofs, of the typeset copy. Conventional galleys were long strips of paper to permit editing of the copy before it was broken into separate pages. Revised galleys were then literally cut and pasted to make up the pages that became photographic masters for platemaking.

Copyfitting Means Tailoring Your Words

To avoid wasting money on incorrectly set type, the designer of a publication had to be very careful about typesetting *specs*, or specifications. This involved a lot of measuring and calculating in a process called *copyfitting*. The purpose of copyfitting is mainly to determine as carefully as possible the best choice of type size and leading to *fit* a given amount of text, or *copy*, onto a limited number of pages. The choice ultimately must be a compromise—a font that is large enough to be attractive and readable, but small enough to keep the publication within its budgeted number of pages.

WYSIWYG to the Rescue!

With WYSIWYG word-processing tools like Microsoft Word for Windows, the outside expenses of composing typeset-quality copy have been eliminated. These services will still be needed, however, if you require resolution, or print quality, higher than can be produced on the typical office-model laser printer. Most laser printers reproduce type and graphics at 300 dots per inch (dpi), some at 600 dpi. The requirement for publication-quality output is about 1200 dpi.

Although it still might be necessary to send out for high-quality typography, WYSIWYG technology has revolutionized the process of specifying type. Since you can compose and preview typeset pages on your PC, there's no more guesswork or mystery as you wait for the typeset result. If you send the finished word-processing file to an outside service, the result will simply be a much sharper image of the pages you have already inspected on your own computer screen.

What's more, with a program like Word, many of the arduous tasks of copyfitting can now be done easily and interactively—or with a little trial and error as you inspect the results of each of your choices.

Many outside typesetting services support PostScript Type 1 fonts; fewer of them can handle TrueType as yet, although the number is growing. So, find out which fonts are supported before you send in your order. It may also be necessary to convert document files to a format such as Encapsulated PostScript (EPS). Although you can generally mix Type 1 with TrueType fonts in Windows applications, don't try this when you're sending out for type.

It's a Paper Problem

Despite WYSIWYG, the need for copyfitting remains. Until the long-awaited paperless revolution (if it ever comes), publishing still must be faced with the physical limitations of using paper to manufacture newsletters, magazines, and books. Factors such as paper and printing costs, binding methods, the ratio of paid advertising space to the editorial space it supports—and even the costs of distributing the finished product in bulk—all contribute to serious concerns about the number of pages to be produced.

For example, the printing and binding methods to be used for a magazine or book are major factors in determining how many pages the publication can have. Glossy magazines and hard-bound books usually are printed in multiple-paged *signatures*, as shown in Figure 6.2.

Commercial offset printing presses print both sides of large-sized sheets which are then folded to form signatures. Depending on the size of the press and the number of folds, a signature can have 8, 16, or 32 pages. (Each printed page of a signature is called a *folio.*) Signatures are stitched, or sewn together, and then glued to the spine, or edge, of the publication's cover.

Signatures and Copyfitting

Printing a magazine or a book in signatures can affect copyfitting, including your choice of type size because

- ❡ You can adjust length only by whole signatures, or by a minimum of eight-page increments (16 on most large-volume commercial presses). This places strict requirements on manuscript length and imposes the need for accurate copyfitting.

- ❡ If you don't do your copyfitting homework, you could end up with blank pages (not pretty and downright embarrassing).

- ❡ If you don't estimate the page count (number of signatures) properly, you (or whoever gets stuck with the job) will order either too much or too little paper. These days, the costs of buying and

FIGURE 6.2

Folding an 11"×17" page twice produces a signature with 8 pages, each measuring 5 1/2 "×8 1/2 ". The book trim size (with the folds cut off) might be 5 3/8 " × 8 3/8 ".

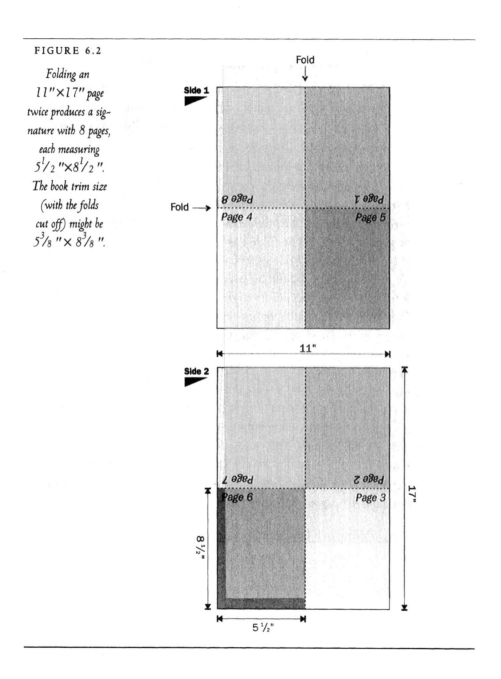

When Is the Page Size Not the Trim Size?

When you are composing pages on your PC, you usually set one of the standard paper sizes that can be handled by your printer. You can also set custom page sizes so that the dimensions of the WYSIWYG printable area on the screen match this page size setting.

If you are actually producing masters on your printer, you must be concerned with *two* dimensions: the page size and a smaller trim size. The page size is the overall dimensions of the sheet that will hold the master. The trim size is the finished dimensions of the pages in the publication. If the printed sheet will be folded as a signature, the trim size is what's left after the folds have been cut off.

A printing master should be larger than the page trim size, with an extra margin, or *bleed*, around its edges. The borders of the printed page are indicated on the master by *registration marks*, as shown in Figure 6.3, which are in the bleed area so that they will not be reproduced on the plate.

To make up a signature for printing, pages must be placed out of sequential order on the sheet so that the numbering will be correct once the sheet is folded. If you are sending masters to a commercial printer, you need not be concerned about composing pages as signatures. Instead, you should compose your masters as two-page spreads (use the Facing Pages option in Word), just as they would appear in an open book. Include the correct amount of bleed and registration marks. The printer will take care of arranging the pages on the plate for signatures.

FIGURE 6.3

A master for plate-making has an inch or more of bleed all around, with registration marks in the bleed area to indicate the trim lines, or page borders.

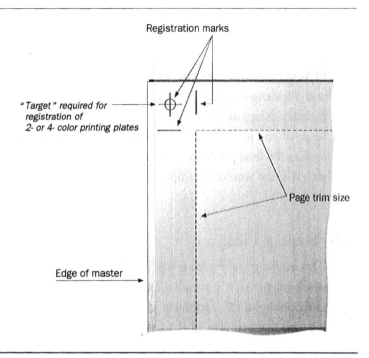

Registration marks

"Target" required for registration of 2- or 4- color printing plates

Page trim size

Edge of master

storing paper in bulk are so significant that printing plants are stocked on a just-in-time basis—receiving just the right quantity of paper, just prior to the job run. Being wrong about the paper requirement by even one signature can be an expensive error, considering that press runs for even limited-circulation publications such as company newsletters might number in the thousands of copies, for commercial publications, in the hundreds of thousands.

Copyfitting remains a problem even in low-volume production. For example, if you are producing a company newsletter or bulletin on folded 11"×17" sheets, you have exactly four pages per sheet to work with. If you run over, you could insert a single $8\frac{1}{2}$"×11" sheet; but you will then have to fill both sides of it, and you will complicate printing by mixing page sizes.

The WYSIWYG Approach to Page Design

Having cautioned you with some of the things that can go seriously wrong with the design of a publication, I should reassure you that developing a preliminary design in Windows on your PC can be painless, involving no measurement and just a bit of arithmetic. If you know a few basic requirements, such as the final page size, you can quickly develop several page designs and pick the one you (or an influential someone else) like best.

Baby Steps at First!

This might go without saying, but don't do this trial-and-error thing on a whole manuscript, especially if you're doing book-length stuff. Even with a fairly powerful PC, formatting the whole manuscript will be time consuming, and that can take all the fun out of experimenting with page designs!

Instead, make a copy of the text file for a few sample pages, and work with that. Choose pages that have both text and display type, such as heads and subheads. If illustrations will be included, do at least one of those pages.

In Which We Meet Mr. Twain

Look at the example manuscript in Figure 6.4. This plain-looking text (at least, from the standpoint of typography) is shown in the default style that Word users call Normal. (My apologies to Samuel Clemens, alias Mark Twain, for cribbing his stuff.)

This sample copy has one headline and enough text to fill a page. Here's what can be done experimenting with designs to compose this stuff to make an attractive page.

FIGURE 6.4

*Here's some elegant
prose that isn't
so pretty in
appearance—yet.*

My Début as a Literary Person

In those early days I had already published one little thing ("The Jumping Frog") in an Eastern paper, but I did not consider that that counted. In my view, a person who published things in a mere newspaper could not properly claim recognition as a Literary Person: he must rise away above that; he must appear in a magazine. He would then be a Literary Person; also, he would be famous—right away. These two ambitions were strong upon me. This was in 1866. I prepared my contribution, and looked around for the best magazine to go up to glory in. I selected the most important one in New York. The contribution was accepted. I signed it "MARK TWAIN"; for that name had some currency on the Pacific coast, and it was my idea to spread it all over the world, now, at this one jump. The article appeared in the December number, and I sat up a month waiting for the January number; for that one would contain the year's list of contributors, my name would be in it, and I should be famous and could give the banquet I was meditating.

I did not give the banquet. I had not written the "MARK TWAIN" distinctly; it was a fresh name to Eastern printers, and they put it "Mike Swain" or "MacSwain," I do not remember which. At any rate, I was not celebrated, and I did not give the banquet. I was a Literary Person, but that was all—a buried one; buried alive.

*There's more about page setup, paragraph formatting, columnar composition,
and runarounds in Chapter 2.*

Setting Up the Page

First off, you need to establish the boundaries of the printed page. In Word, you would do Format ➤ Page Setup. The Page Setup dialog box will appear. When you select the Size And Orientation option button, the content of the dialog box will change as shown in Figure 6.5.

Assume that you will be producing a book with a trim size of 6×9". For purposes of design (but not for output), the page size and the trim size are the same. So in this dialog box, you would set Page Size to Custom Size, Width to 6, and Height to 9. (The default unit of measure is inches unless you reset it.)

The next important design setting is the margins, which will also affect the length of text lines. Before you exit the Page Setup dialog box, select the

FIGURE 6.5

*Page Size settings for
a book trim size of
6"×9"*

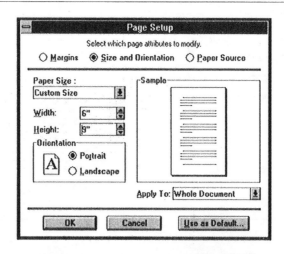

Margins option button, and the content of the dialog box will change back to its initial set of options, as shown in Figure 6.6. A traditional design for this page size might put a margin of 5/8" all around the page, or 0.625". Word rounds this setting to 0.63.

For books and magazines that are bound in signatures, the left margin of odd-numbered pages and the right margin of even-numbered pages should be a bit wider to allow for the binding. You can provide for this in Word by marking the Facing Pages check box and then entering a value for the gutter, or the amount of *extra* margin at the binding.

When you select OK to close the Page Setup dialog box, the copy is re-composed within the new dimensions. However, it is still a long way from looking like a finished page.

FIGURE 6.6

Typical margin and gutter settings for a book with 6" × 9" page size

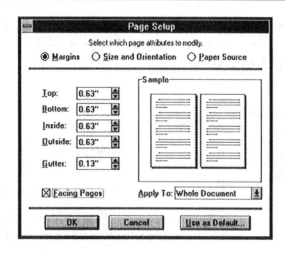

Style Selections

My initial choice for the headlines in this example is the Bitstream True-Type font Tiffany Light BT in 18-point size. Because I've begun the examples with a more conventional design, I centered the headline over the text.

For the text, I chose Goudy Old Style BT, also a Bitstream TrueType font, in the 10-point size.

Other style options in Word can be set by selecting the sample paragraphs and doing Format ➤ Paragraph. Also consistent with a more traditional design, I decided to justify the text both left and right, setting the Alignment option to Justified. All the Indentation options for the paragraphs are set to 0 inch. For a bit more space between paragraphs, I've set the Spacing options to 0.5 line Before and 0.5 line After to add a half-line of space before and after each paragraph. This gives one *extra* line height between paragraphs—the equivalent of *two* blank lines.

For the time being, until I preview the page composition with these settings, I've left Line setting at Auto, the default setting.

The consequences of my choices are shown in Figure 6.7 in Word's Page Layout view.

FIGURE 6.7

My initial design efforts produced some problems.

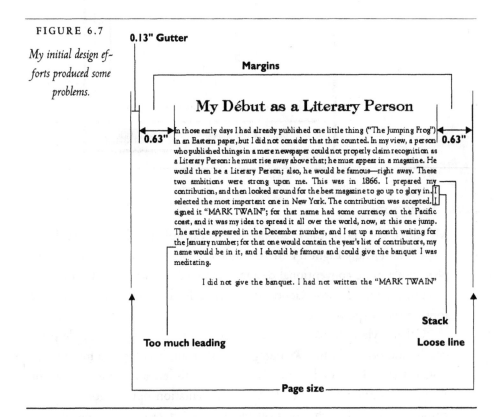

What's Wrong with This Picture?

There are several problems with the result. It's premature to worry about some of these, but I want you to get a real sense of how a nicely composed paragraph might look. Among other things, an attractive preliminary design should provide some "ideal" settings for type size and leading. So, here are some of those problems:

Loose lines Several of the lines have too much white space between words. Recall from Chapter 2 that this is a typical problem of fully justified lines and columns, a problem that gets worse at shorter line lengths.

Rivers The extra white spaces between words tend to flow together to form what typesetters call *rivers*. You want people to focus on the words, not on the gaps between them.

Stacks The same word or phrase occurring at the margin of two or more successive lines is called a *stack*. Stacks are unsightly, chance occurrences. You can usually find a way to recompose the paragraph to eliminate them.

Leading There appears to be a bit too much white space between lines, an unfortunate consequence of letting the program make the big decisions.

Hyphenation—the All-Purpose Fix-It Tool

Problems involving horizontal spacing can often be fixed by permitting hyphenation, breaking words between syllables at the ends of some offending lines. This gives the program more places at which lines can be broken and makes the horizontal spacing more even. Hyphenation almost always improves the appearance of fully justified columns.

To get hyphenation help in Word, do Tools ➤ Hyphenation. Make sure the Confirm check box is marked, and select OK.

When I did this with my sample paragraph, Word suggested hyphenating the words *contribution* and *appeared* in the first paragraph. The happy result, shown in Figure 6.8, is a considerable improvement, eliminating most of the

195

FIGURE 6.8

This is more like it!
All I did was let
Word help with the
hyphenation.

Another stack!

My Début as a Literary Person

In those early days I had already published one little thing ("The Jumping Frog") in an Eastern paper, but I did not consider that that counted. In my view, a person who published things in a mere newspaper could not properly claim recognition as a Literary Person; he must rise away above that; he must appear in a magazine. He would then be a Literary Person; also, he would be famous—right away. These two ambitions were strong upon me. This was in 1866. I prepared my contribution, and then looked around for the best magazine to go up to glory in. I selected the most important one in New York. The contribution was accepted. I signed it "MARK TWAIN"; for that name had some currency on the Pacific coast, and it was my idea to spread it all over the world, now, at this one jump. The article appeared in the December number, and I sat up a month waiting for the January number; for that one would contain the year's list of contributors, my name would be in it, and I should be famous and could give the banquet I was meditating.

I did not give the banquet. I had not written the "MARK TWAIN" distinctly; it was a fresh name to Eastern printers, and they put it "Mike Swain" or

Hyphenation suggested by Word

problems just discussed except for the extra leading—but introducing an annoying new stacked *it*.

Fixing one problem often gives rise to new ones. It's a good lesson to learn before you're really under the gun.

Get the Lead Out!

The next step is to get rid of the extra leading. For the time being, I'm not concerned with the impact of the leading on copyfitting and book length. I just want to see what an attractive and readable vertical spacing might be. My feeling is that the initial result is too loose. I'd like a tighter, more coherent paragraph.

To reduce the leading in the example, I selected both of the sample text paragraphs and did Format ➤ Paragraph. I changed the Line Spacing option to Exactly and the At setting to 10.5 points. (Since the default setting is in lines (li), you must drag the contents of the At text box and type **10.5 pt** to make this entry.) This setting means that each line is 10 points high (the height of the text font I chose), with an extra 0.5 point of leading. The result is shown in Figure 6.9.

Notice that my new composition is not free of flaws. The stacked *it* is still there, but I'll ignore it for now—first because it doesn't affect overall design decisions and second because I'm planning some other changes for this paragraph.

FIGURE 6.9

Here is the result of setting the Line Spacing paragraph option to exactly 10.5 pt, or a half-point taller than the text.

My Début as a Literary Person

In those early days I had already published one little thing ("The Jumping Frog") in an Eastern paper, but I did not consider that that counted. In my view, a person who published things in a mere newspaper could not properly claim recognition as a Literary Person: he must rise away above that; he must appear in a magazine. He would then be a Literary Person; also, he would be famous—right away. These two ambitions were strong upon me. This was in 1866. I prepared my contribution, and then looked around for the best magazine to go up to glory in. I selected the most important one in New York. The contribution was accepted. I signed it "MARK TWAIN"; for that name had some currency on the Pacific coast, and it was my idea to spread it all over the world, now, at this one jump. The article appeared in the December number, and I sat up a month waiting for the January number; for that one would contain the year's list of contributors, my name would be in it, and I should be famous and could give the banquet I was meditating.

I did not give the banquet. I had not written the "MARK TWAIN" distinctly; it was a fresh name to Eastern printers, and they put it "Mike Swain" or "MacSwain," I do not remember which. At any rate, I was not celebrated, and I did not give the banquet. I was a Literary Person, but that was all—a buried one; buried alive.

Three more line fit on this part of the page (See Figure 6.8)

Playing with the Design

Although not essential to the task of copyfitting, some other elements of design can be considered for this sample.

Paragraph Indentation

It's standard practice, although by no means mandatory, to start the first paragraph after a headline flush to the left margin instead of indenting its first line.

Another consideration—which *does* affect copyfitting—is the amount of indentation you use for subsequent paragraphs. The default indentation for the first tab stop of the first line of a paragraph in Word is 0.5 inch. However, that's generally too much for tightly set copy. Many book designs use just two or three *em* spaces for the paragraph indent. In general, you want to balance the first-line indent with the spacing between paragraphs: A larger indent will look better with more white space above it.

To adjust the paragraph indent in Word, select the paragraph (or all the paragraphs) and do Format ➤ Paragraph. The Paragraph dialog box will appear. To create a first-line indent, enter a value (usually, in inches) in the First Line box of Indentation options, then select OK.

There are other ways of accomplishing this. As alternatives, with the paragraphs selected, you could drag the top portion of the left margin indicator in the ruler. Or, you could create a tab stop for the indent and insert a Tab character at the beginning of each paragraph to be indented. An advantage of using a Tab for first-line indents is that you can easily control which paragraphs will be flush left simply by omitting the Tab character.

Adding Some Nice Little Touches

As it is, this first paragraph in the example looks rather plain. Here are a couple of ways of dressing it up:

Lead-ins Set the first few words or lines at the beginning of a chapter or section in a larger type size. A technique used by some book designers is to capitalize the first few words. The idea is to lead the eye into the paragraph with the more attention-getting type.

Dropped caps Refer to the practice of enlarging the first letter of the first word in a chapter or section—usually making it as large as the headline—in a display font. This is a downright ancient technique—going back at least as far as medieval illuminated manuscripts in which the first letter was an ornate drawing.

Here's my example done with an all-caps lead-in.

My Début as a Literary Person

IN THOSE early days I had already published one little thing ("The Jumping Frog") in an Eastern paper, but I did not consider that that counted. In my view, a person who published things in a mere newspaper could not properly claim

Doing a dropped cap in Word is a bit more involved. You can't necessarily select the first letter of the paragraph and change its point size. If you have Line Spacing set to anything but Exactly, the program will use that character to adjust the height of the entire line. Also, the letter will extend above instead of below the first line.

If you have installed Microsoft Draw along with Word, you can add the dropped cap in a *frame*. Place the insertion point at the beginning of the paragraph and delete the first letter (the one you will replace with a dropped capital). Then do Insert ➤ Frame. The cursor will change to small crosshairs. Drag the cross down and to the right to create a square that is two or three lines tall. When you release the mouse button, a vertical insertion point will appear inside the frame. Type the letter of the dropped capital. Select the letter, change its font and point size, then choose Center alignment. Figure 6.10 shows the result when I did this with the sample paragraph and chose Bitstream Shelly Allegro BT for the dropped cap.

As a nice bonus for my creativity, Word rejustified the paragraph to make room for the frame, and the stacked *it* went away!

199

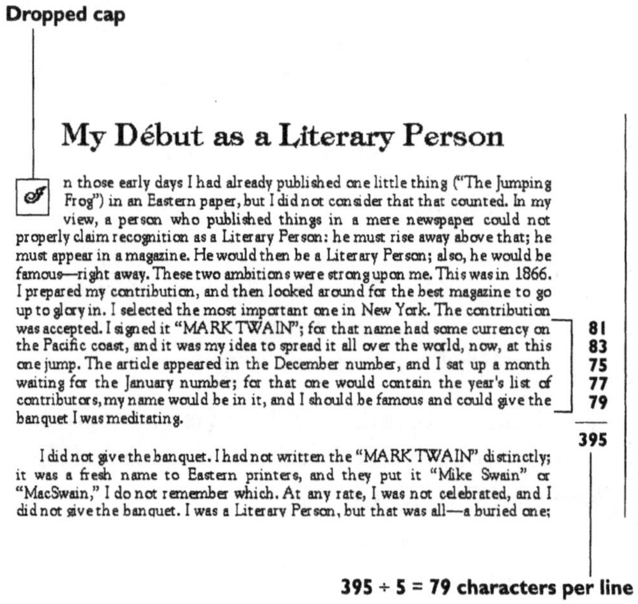

FIGURE 6.10

You can use the Draw utility in Word to create a frame, or graphic box, that contains a dropped cap.

Dropped cap

My Début as a Literary Person

n those early days I had already published one little thing ("The Jumping Frog") in an Eastern paper, but I did not consider that that counted. In my view, a person who published things in a mere newspaper could not properly claim recognition as a Literary Person: he must rise away above that; he must appear in a magazine. He would then be a Literary Person; also, he would be famous—right away. These two ambitions were strong upon me. This was in 1866. I prepared my contribution, and then looked around for the best magazine to go up to glory in. I selected the most important one in New York. The contribution was accepted. I signed it "MARK TWAIN"; for that name had some currency on the Pacific coast, and it was my idea to spread it all over the world, now, at this one jump. The article appeared in the December number, and I sat up a month waiting for the January number; for that one would contain the year's list of contributors, my name would be in it, and I should be famous and could give the banquet I was meditating.

I did not give the banquet. I had not written the "MARK TWAIN" distinctly; it was a fresh name to Eastern printers, and they put it "Mike Swain" or "MacSwain," I do not remember which. At any rate, I was not celebrated, and I did not give the banquet. I was a Literary Person, but that was all—a buried one;

81
83
75
77
79

395

395 ÷ 5 = 79 characters per line

Preliminary Design Specs

From this preliminary design of the sample page, I can derive some design specifications:

Page size: 6×9"

Margins: 0.63" all around

Gutter: 0.13"

Headlines: 18-point Tiffany Light, centered over text

Text: 10-point Goudy Old Style BT (Bitstream TrueType)

Justification: Full, single column

First paragraph after head: Flush left

Dropped cap: 14-point Shelley Allegro BT

First-line indent of internal paragraphs: 0.2"

Line height: 10.5 points (or, leading of 0.5 point)

Paragraph spacing: Two lines (21 points)

I have still not provided for headers and footers, which might include page numbering, but these will be put in the top and bottom margin areas and therefore won't affect the amount of text that can fit on a page with this design.

Summary of Preliminary Design Steps

The steps involved in achieving this first look at the printed page are summarized in the diagram in Figure 6.11.

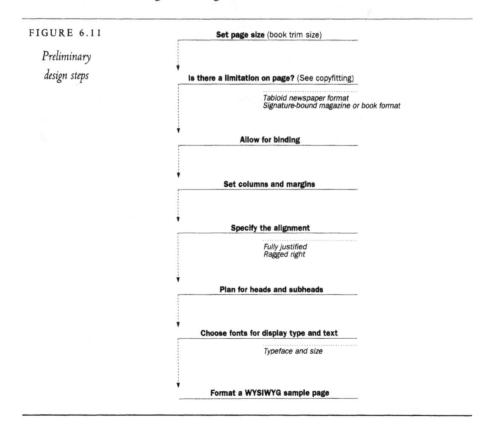

FIGURE 6.11

Preliminary design steps

Set page size (book trim size)

Is there a limitation on page? (See copyfitting)
Tabloid newspaper format
Signature-bound magazine or book format

Allow for binding

Set columns and margins

Specify the alignment
Fully justified
Ragged right

Plan for heads and subheads

Choose fonts for display type and text
Typeface and size

Format a WYSIWYG sample page

There at two good reasons for laying out the page this way:

❡ You want to achieve an attractive and readable design.

❡ From the type size, spacing, and other specs of the design, you want to be able to project the number of pages required to set the manuscript. In short, you want data for copyfitting.

Traditional Rules for Copyfitting

In the days before slick word processing, you had to calculate the manuscript character count. This is the main reason why manuscripts had to be typed in a monospace font such as Courier. If margins and line spacing were specified also, editors and designers could develop guidelines for the number of characters on a typical page. Then, given the parameters of the page design, an estimate of the ratio between manuscript pages and printed pages, or folios, could be calculated. If the publication stuck to the same design, it would be possible to estimate, for example, that it usually takes two manuscript pages to make up one book page. Illustrations and tables might be factored into the page count by allowing one-half page for each.

Copyfitting the Easy Way

The traditional steps of copyfitting are shown here. However, if you start with a preliminary WYSIWYG design as just described, much of the calculating and guesswork can be eliminated.

✔ Count the characters in the manuscript! (Word will do this for you.)

✔ Pick a text font (typeface and size).

✓ Cast off: calculate the number of characters per line or just count them on your design.

✓ Calculate the number of lines.

✓ Set the leading, or vertical spacing between lines.

✓ Determine the number of text lines per page.

✓ Calculate the number of pages.

✓ Make allowance for inserted material: illustrations, display type (heads and subheads), sidebars, teasers, and so on. Add these to the estimated book length as fractions of pages.

✓ Determine the trial page count.

✓ Adjust type size, leading, and space for inserted material by repeating previous steps.

✓ Determine the final page count.

Here's how to proceed at each step in more detail.

1. Count the Characters in the Manuscript

Most word processing programs, including Word, will do this step for you. When you open or save a document file, Word reports the character count in the status bar in the bottom-left corner of the document window. Or, more detailed information can be seen for the current document by doing File ➤ Summary Info ➤ Statistics. The length of the manuscript file in pages, words, and characters will be reported at the bottom of the Document Statistics dialog box, as shown in Figure 6.12. Note that the program counts each blank space as one character. (The page count shown here won't mean much at this stage unless you've formatted the entire document for printing.)

FIGURE 6.12

This dialog box reports the length of the manuscript in pages, in words, and in characters.

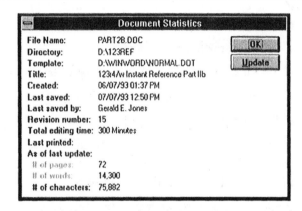

2. Pick a Text Font (Typeface and Size)

If you did a preliminary design, you've already selected a type size that appears attractive and readable, but you have no idea what impact your choice will have on page length. Typical sizes for text are 8–12 points. The smaller sizes often are used to set the relatively narrow columns of magazines and newspapers. Remember that if you use a small text size, you might have to increase the leading to improve readability.

3. Cast Off (Calculate Characters per Line)

If you did a preliminary design, you can count the number of characters in several lines and then divide by the number of lines to get an average. Since you are probably using a proportional font for the text, there will be some variation in line lengths. In the sample I did (refer back to Figure 6.10), I counted 81, 83, 75, 77, and 79 characters on five lines *including spaces*, or an average of:

```
395 characters ÷ 5 lines ~= 79 characters/line
```

 *WYSIWYG technology really helps you in the casting-off step. By the old methods, you'd have to calculate the line length in picas (1 pica $= \frac{1}{6}$ inch) then consult a table provided by the font vendor (in its type spec book) for a numeric index of the average number of set characters in a given face and point size that will fit in one pica. This numeric index is called characters fit per pica, or CPP. For example, a particular face in the 9-point size might have an index of 2.85, meaning that an average of 2.85 of those characters will fit in a horizontal space one pica wide. You would then multiply the line length in picas by this index to get the number of typeset characters per line.*

4. Calculate the Number of Lines in the Manuscript

Divide the manuscript character count (result of step 1) by the number of characters per typeset line (step 3). For example, if the manuscript is 854,630 characters, and my sample design fits 79 characters per line, then the following is true:

```
854,630 characters ÷ 79 char./line = 10,818 lines
```

(Rounding off your answers is okay. Copyfitting is more of an art than an exact science.)

5. Set Leading, or Vertical Spacing between Lines

You already know what your preliminary WYSIWYG design requires. In my sample, each line is 10 points tall for the type, with an additional 0.5 point of blank vertical space, or leading.

6. Determine the Number of Text Lines per Page

You can count them on your design, or you can calculate them. To calculate the lines per page, subtract the distances of the top and bottom margins from the page height. In my sample, there's a 9" page height minus 0.63" at top and bottom (1.26"), or 7.74" of *page depth*. In points, that is

```
7.74" × 72 points/inch = 557.28 points deep
```

If each line is 10.5 points tall, I can fit

```
557.28 points ÷ 10.5 points/line = 53 lines/page
```

Notice that this calculation does not allow for headlines or any inserted material, including the extra space between paragraphs. If your manuscript uses heads and subheads liberally, it's probably better to include them on the sample pages and then get an actual count of the number of text lines, including the heads. If instead you calculated the maximum number of text lines without inserted material, you'd have to make an additional allowance for that in the step 8.

7. Calculate the Number of Pages

The number of pages required to set the manuscript is the number of text lines (step 4) divided by the lines per page (step 6). In my estimate, I'll use 50 lines per page instead of 53 to allow for the extra spacing between paragraphs. For the sample, that is

```
10,818 lines ÷ 50 lines/page = 216.4 pages
```

8. Make Allowance for Inserted Material

To the page estimate must be added space for illustrations, display type (heads and subheads), sidebars, and other inserted material. It's easiest to figure these as fractions of pages for each category of inserted material, then add them. A good rule of thumb for illustrations is one-half page for each, unless you know that full pages or even two-page spreads are required for the larger ones. (If you insert illustrations in the text with runarounds, you should set some sample pages and get actual character and line counts to use in your copyfitting calculations.) Vertical space needed for headlines can be calculated in points, then converted to fractional pages. The headline I used is 18 points tall, with two lines of space above and one below. That's 72 points, or 1 inch, per headline:

```
72 pt/headline ÷ 557.28 pt/pg = 0.13 pg/headline
```

If there are 18 headlines in the manuscript, that's

```
0.13 page/headline × 18 headlines = 2.3 pages
```

So, figure about 2.5 pages to allow for the headlines. Now, if each headline starts a new section or chapter, you must also allow for *sinkage*, or the fractional parts of pages that will be blank at the beginning and end of each section. As with illustrations, you can figure sinkage at an average of one-half page per section.

9. Determine the Trial Page Count

The specifications for my sample are shown in Table 6.1. In my estimate, I've included manuscript text, illustrations, and headlines. I've also added 8 pages for a title page, a table of contents, and an index, or *frontmatter* and *endmatter*. The trial page count is 239 pages.

ITEM	CALCULATION	PAGES[1]
Text	10,818 lines ÷ 50 lines/page	216.5
Headlines	18 heads × 0.13 page/headline	2.5
Sinkage	18 heads × 0.5 page/head	9
Illustrations	6 illustrations × 0.5 page each	3
Title page	1	2
Table of contents		4
Index		2
Total		**239**

[1]Rounded to the nearest half-page

TABLE 6.1: *A Summary of Our Trial Page Count*

If this book is to be printed and bound in 16-page signatures, the number of signatures will be

```
239 pages ÷ 16 pages/signature = 14.9 signatures
```

So the trial page count for setting the sample manuscript gives the result that the book is going to be just one page short of a 15-signature book.

10. Adjust Type Size, Leading, and Space for Inserted Material

A book of 15 signatures would have 15 × 16, or 240, pages. The trial page count I've calculated is just one page less. An easy way to make up the difference is to increase the sinkage by dropping down further from the top margin at the beginning of each section or chapter. If instead my estimate had gone just over a whole number of signatures, it would be necessary to eliminate some space. Besides adjusting the sinkage, the easiest and most obvious choice is to reduce the size of or even eliminate some illustrations. It would also be possible to reduce the size of headlines. A last resort, but one that must be considered if the trial count is as much as a half-signature too much, is to reduce the type size, the leading, the paragraph spacing—or all three—and repeat Steps 2–9 to get a revised estimate.

11. Determine Final Page Count

Remember after all this estimation effort that copyfitting amounts to a good guess. The objective is to arrive at a design that can be reasonably expected to fit within the page constraints. As you begin to compose and assemble the actual pages, you will find that some last-minute adjustments are almost unavoidable.

Can We Show You Something in a New Design?

In general, the preliminary page design comes first, copyfitting second. But an alternative to revising the specs of the design can be simply to try something altogether different. Figures 6.13 and 6.14 show two alternatives for the sample manuscript.

Figure 6.13 is a two-column layout that might be used to run the material on a newspaper page. Notice that the text is broken up with a *pull-quote*, a quotation culled from it to grab the interest of people who might be skimming the paper. Pull-quotes can also be used to increase length.

The headline in this example is 12-point Garamand bold condensed. The Bold and Condensed attributes were added in Word with the command Format ➤ Character.

209

FIGURE 6.13

The sample has been reset in columnar format to run in a newspaper. Pull-quotes are used to draw the reader's attention.

My Début as a Literary Person

In those early days I had already published one little thing ("The Jumping Frog") in an Eastern paper, but I did not consider that that counted. In my view, a person who published things in a mere newspaper could not properly claim recognition as a Literary Person: he must rise away above that; he must appear in a magazine. He would then be a Literary Person; also, he would be famous—right away. These two ambitions were strong upon me. This was in 1866. I prepared my contribution, and then looked around for the best magazine to go up to glory in. I selected the most important one in New York. The contribution was accepted. I signed it

would have been no survivors. He was a New Englander of the best sea-going stock and of the old capable times —Captain Josiah Mitchell.

"I was a Literary Person, but that was all—a buried one; buried alive"

I was in the islands to write letters for the weekly edition of the Sacramento *Union*, a rich and influential daily journal which hadn't any use for them, but could afford to spend twenty dollars a week for nothing. The proprietors were lovable and well-beloved men: long ago dead, no doubt, but in me there is at least one person who still holds them in

---

FIGURE 6.14

The sample is set here in a modern book layout with hanging indents and ragged-right composition.

My Début as a Literary Person

In those early days I had already published one little thing ("The Jumping Frog") in an Eastern paper, but I did not consider that that counted. In my view, a person who published things in a mere newspaper could not properly claim recognition as a Literary Person: he must rise away above that; he must appear in a magazine. He would then be a Literary Person; also, he would be famous—right away. These two ambitions were strong upon me. This was in 1866. I prepared my contribution, and then looked around for the best magazine to go up to glory in. I selected the most important one in New York. The contribution was accepted. I signed it "MARK TWAIN"; for that name had some currency on the Pacific coast, and it was my idea to spread it all over the world, now, at this one jump. The article appeared in the December number, and I sat up a month waiting for the January number; for that one would contain the year's list of contributors, my name would be in it, and I should be famous and could give the banquet I was meditating.

I did not give the banquet. I had not written the "MARK TWAIN" dis-

---

The first letter is an *initial cap*, a variation on the dropped-cap idea. The character is 12 points tall and bold to match the headline.

The text of the article is set in 8-point Lucida Bright, a good choice for the smaller type required by columnar newspaper formats. (Garamand can be found in the Typecase selection from Swfte, and Lucida family of fonts is available in the TrueType Font Pack from Microsoft.)

The pull-quote is set in 16-point Times New Roman—bold, italic, and centered. I started by creating a frame with the Insert ➤ Frame command, then typed the text into the frame and formatted it. I changed the border and shading of the frame with the Format ➤ Border command.

Figure 6.14 is typical of more contemporary book layouts. The headlines are sans-serif, set flush left. All of the text is indented (called a *hanging indent*). Text is left-aligned with a ragged-right margin, making the composition look less formal and also making the letterspacing within paragraphs much more uniform.

The headline is 16-point GillSans, a sans serif Type 1 font from Monotype, supplied with ATM. This attractive font is found on much of the signage in Great Britain, including the signs in the London Underground. (Remember that it's okay to mix Type 1 and TrueType fonts, but only if you stay in Windows.)

The text is 9-point Garamand. The lead-in is 11-point Garamand italic.

Breaking Up the Page with Inserted Material

Although it adds some complexity to the task of copyfitting, inserting other material within text helps add visual interest to printed pages. Types of inserted material already covered in this chapter include

- Headlines
- Lead-ins
- Dropped and initial caps
- Illustrations
- Pull-quotes

Here are some other design elements that you might want to consider:

Subheads Help to show the logical organization of the text. As many as four levels of heads and subheads might be used, which correspond with the levels of the material as it might be shown in outline form. Subheads are commonly used in magazine articles, reports, and in books like this one.

Graphics Are like illustrations, but smaller. A graphic is a "thumbnail" illustration that can be inserted within the text (called *in-line* composition), often combined with runarounds, making the text flow around it. A dropped cap created within a frame is an example of an inserted graphic. In Word, you can embed graphics by the commands Insert ➤ File (to retrieve external formatted text files), Insert ➤ Frame (to add a drawing or text box using Microsoft Draw), Insert ➤ Picture (to add a bitmap or drawing file), and Insert ➤ Object (to embed a Windows object, including graphics and equations).

Teasers Are similar to pull-quotes but are usually placed on the cover of the magazine or at the beginning of an article. A teaser is a summary of topics, benefits, or other reasons to read the item. A teaser for the sample might read as follows:

Mark Twain confesses how he

- ❡ Tried *and failed* to make his literary reputation

- ❡ Took favors from an influential diplomat

- ❡ And much, much more!

Sidebars Particularly in magazines and newsletters, explanatory or background material can be boxed and set apart from the body of an article. The purpose is to segregate optional material from the main topic, making both easier to read and understand. The boxed material *Traditional Rules for Copyfitting* in this chapter is a sidebar.

Pagination with Imagination

A major challenge of the publishing process is *pagination,* or dividing up the text and illustrations into pages.

The topic of composing attractive pages is larger than this modest chapter can handle, but here are a few further typesetting concerns that arise when you're doing page makeup:

- Running heads and folios
- Widows and orphans
- Jumplines

Watch Those Running Heads and Folios

The terms *running heads* and *folios* typically refer to the headers of book pages or the footers of magazine pages. On even-numbered (left-hand) pages of a book, the running head is usually the title of the book, part, or chapter. The folio is simply the page number. On odd-numbered (right-hand) pages, the running head is the chapter or section title. (No illustration necessary—look at the running heads on these pages!)

In a magazine, the running head on the left is usually the title of the publication, possibly also the volume number, and the running head on the right might be the date and the year. Again, magazines usually put the running heads and folios in footers rather than headers. (Some magazine designers just put the title and date on *both* sides.)

Headers and footers need not be considered in copyfitting because they are printed in the top or bottom margin areas. To set headers and footers in Word, do View ➤ Header/Footer. The Header/Footer dialog box will appear, as shown in Figure 6.15. The distance from the edge of the page can

FIGURE 6.15

*Set options for run-
ning heads and folios
in this dialog box.*

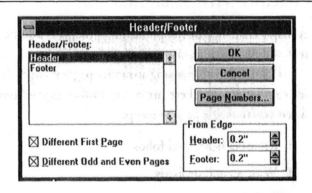

be set in the From Edge options. Separate sets of options can be selected for headers and for footers.

In a publication with facing pages, the first page is always on the right so that right-hand pages are always odd-numbered. By convention, the first page is not numbered. To provide for this, mark the Different First Page check box.

To set headers and footers that alternate the publication title on the left with the date or chapter title on the right, mark the Different Odd And Even Pages check box.

To set pages numbers as alphabetic letters (a, b, c...) or Roman numerals (i, ii, iii...) instead of as Arabic numbers (1, 2, 3...), select the Page Numbers button and change the settings in the Page Number Format dialog box. Also in this dialog box, you can specify whether the numbering in the current document continues from another document section or starts with a specific number.

When you select OK to close the Header/Footer dialog box, Word formats the header or footer entries you type according to these options. If you are working in Normal view, the Header or Footer window will open. Type the header or footer that should appear on the current page. To insert the page number, or folio, click the icon with the # symbol in the window title bar:

Click the Close button to accept the entry and return to Normal view. If you marked none of the check boxes in the Header/Footer dialog box, Word will use your entry here on all pages. If you marked the Different First Page check box, you can type a different header or footer on Page 1 or simply leave it blank. If you marked Different Odd And Even Pages, type a header or footer on Page 2 and a different one on Page 3. If you used the page numbering icon to insert the page number, Word will number all of the pages in the document and will readjust the numbering to keep up with your edits.

Care for Widows and Orphans

Page makeup often causes unsightly divisions of lines called *bad breaks.* Among these are the colorful terms *widow* and *orphan.* A widow is a short line—or especially a fragment of a divided word—that appears at the end of a paragraph. An orphan is such a fragment that gets stranded as the first line on a page. (Some people use *widow* to refer to both types of bad break.)

The solution for compassionately getting rid of widows and orphans is to recompose their paragraphs. Re-hyphenating sometimes helps. It might also be possible to expand or condense a line (an option with the Format ➤ Character command) to force a break at a different point. In general, a loose or expanded line might be tolerated in preference to a suffering widow.

The solution of last resort is to reword the paragraph. This choice is often preferred by editors, shunned by writers. (Don't try this if you're setting the Bible or the literary work of anyone who can sue you.) Other types of bad breaks include:

¶ A head or subhead on the last line of a page

¶ Only one line of indented or quoted material appearing as the first or last line of a page

¶ A footnote that is not referenced on the same page

Jumplines for Textual Acrobatics

In magazines and newsletters, longer articles often must be continued on nonsequential pages. A *jumpline* is the copy at the end of a page that instructs the reader to

(Turn to page 35)

Another jumpline must go at the head of the continued material:

(Continued from page 1)

As a courtesy to your readers—and also as a nice design element—use a unique symbol (such as a Wingdings character) to mark the end of each article. Especially if the article had to be cut abruptly for length, the reader won't think that a jumpline was omitted by mistake.

Don't Keep Those
Footnotes in Your Shoes

Footnotes are used to insert citations of sources and other explanatory material in the text of reports, technical articles, and textbooks.

The form of a footnote usually requires a superscripted number after the sentence in the text to which the note refers.[1] In the most common format, the numbered footnote appears at the bottom of the same page:

```
1. Word adds the superscripted number for you when
you do Insert ➤ Footnote. Otherwise, to set a super-
script, select the character and do Format ➤
Character ➤ Superscript.
```

Setting footnotes manually is a real composition and copyfitting chore, especially if the notes grow lengthy and cut significantly into the page depth. Lengthy notes also can be continued on following pages, which is not only a compositional problem, but also can be confusing to the reader.

Let Word Do It!

Fortunately, Word automatically handles many of the otherwise annoying aspects of generating footnotes. To put a footnote in a document, do Insert ➤ Footnote. The Footnote dialog box will appear. For sequentially num-bered footnotes, accept the Auto-Numbered Footnote option. (Otherwise, select Custom Footnote Mark and type an ANSI character, which can be an Alt-key decimal code.)

Select the Options button to control the placement of footnotes. The Footnote Options dialog box will appear, as shown in Figure 6.16. Place-ment options are End Of Section (as a list, usually at the end of a chapter), Bottom Of Page (same page as the reference, the default), Beneath Text (at the next paragraph break after the reference), or End Of Document (as a numbered list).

Mark the Restart Each Section check box if you want to start the num-bering with 1 with each new section of the document, as usually is done for each book chapter.

FIGURE 6.16

Word will handle footnotes automatically according to the options you set here.

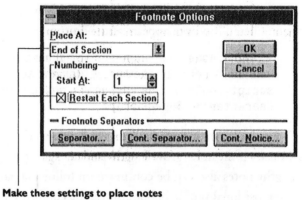

**Make these settings to place notes
at the end of each book chapter**

The Footnote Separators buttons control the appearance of an optional heading and dividing line (Separator options) just above the notes. Continuation options provide for notes that are spread across two or more pages.

Footnote Rules

Style rules for references to research sources vary by type of source. For the form of footnote references and citation of sources, see Chapter 15 of *The Chicago Manual of Style*, Fourteenth Edition, (Chicago: University of Chicago Press, 1993).

Once you have a page design you can live with, make your life easier the next time by saving your work as a template (Word .DOT) file. Do File ➤ Save As and select Document Template as the file type. You can then retrieve your named template any time you begin a new document with the File ➤ New command.

CHAPTER 7

Selling at the Point of Purchase

or

Listen to the Talking Sign

I N 1939, SO THE STORY GOES, a Chicago printing equipment salesman started to encourage retail stores to print price tags that showed not only the price of a product but also a few good reasons to buy it. These "talking price tags" rapidly became a widely-used merchandising technique, and the format has evolved to become the "talking sign." Today's stores are full of these talking signs, which solicit customers to make a purchase on the spot. The talking sign has become one of the most important tools in *point-of-purchase* (P-O-P) retail merchandising.

Making persuasive signs has developed into something of a science in the world of retailing. The format and composition of a talking sign are very specific, following merchandising principles that have been proven effective since the appearance of those verbose price tags in 1939.

This chapter covers signmaking techniques mainly from the viewpoint of retailing. However, the basic principles apply any time you need to make a sign that must persuade people to do something—to buy a product, to take a specific action, or just to pay attention to a message. (A no-nonsense term for the talking sign is the *benefit-oriented sign.*)

Composing a Talking Sign

Samples of talking signs are shown in Figures 7.1–7.4.

A sign can include several of the following elements, although any one sign would not normally include all of them:

> **Theme** In retail merchandising, a theme is a slogan, logo, or other design element that applies to all the signs—indeed to all the displays—in a store. The display theme is usually tied to an event (a sale, a fashion show, or a holiday), and themes are often seasonal. For example, a late-summer display theme might be BACK-TO-SCHOOL SALE, combining the seasonal beginning of the school year with a sales event that will last several weeks.

FIGURE 7.1

This talking (or bene-fit-oriented) retail sign uses the theme of a special event—a sale, in this case.

221

FIGURE 7.2

This talking sign combines a marked-down price with a reason to buy now—the limited duration of the sale event.

Reason to buy now

One Day Only!

Men's Cotton Dress Shirts

Famous Maker
Oxford Cloth
Never Need Ironing!

~~$34.99~~ **15.99**

Strikethrough regular price

FIGURE 7.3

Product benefits are the focus of this talking sign.

SALE

Sport Socks

Cool Orlon-Wool Blend
Extra Comfort Heels and Toes

$9.99

FIGURE 7.4

A lifestyle pitch about summer leisure activities leads off this talking sign.

Lifestyle pitch

Lifestyle pitch Particularly since the 1950s, the top-line message on retail signs has been an appeal to the customer's personal viewpoint. The lifestyle pitch relates the customer's personal lifestyle needs to the display theme or to the event. A lifestyle pitch is related to the theme but is more personalized. For example, if the display theme were BACK-TO-SCHOOL SALE, a lifestyle pitch might be GET THEM READY FOR SCHOOL!, an obvious appeal to parental responsibility.

Logo or art A display theme can be enhanced and combined with the store's logo, a logo that has been designed specifically for the event, or the logo of a well-known manufacturer of the product being advertised. The logo or art is put in the top (or *theme*) position of the sign because people's attention will be drawn to the familiar name.

Reason to buy now Particularly for a sale item, this part of the sign message reminds the customer that the opportunity to purchase is limited and therefore requires immediate action. Reasons to buy now might be TODAY ONLY! or LIMITED QUANTITY.

Product identification Any sign that advertises a product must identify it in the most quickly recognizable way—whether a product or brand name such as LEVI'S JEANS or a generic description such as MEN'S WORK PANTS. For some types of products, a well-known model number tells the story: LEVI'S 501 JEANS. Especially in the electronics and computer marketplace, the model number is the most meaningful identification: HP LJIV (Hewlett-Packard LaserJet IV printer).

Benefits The main reasons to buy are the product's benefits to the customer. Benefits are usually presented as a list of bulleted points:

- Waterproof and shockproof
- 5-year warranty
- Free carrying case!

Strikethrough full price For sale or promotional items, the regular price usually is shown in a strikethrough font or with a big × through the price.

Sale price The sale price is always shown big and bold, often in a point size that is at least three times larger than any other type on the sign.

Bar code Because a sign usually identifies a specific product, it can be convenient to include a machine-readable version of the product identification on the sign. The purpose is usually to assist store personnel who are taking inventory as they count the number of unsold items on shelves and product displays. Common examples of bar codes are the *universal product code* (UPC) on grocery products, the *International Standard Book Number* (ISBN) on books (see the back cover of this one), and the *International Standard Serial Number* (ISSN) on magazines. In the grocery industry, UPC codes are usually put on *shelf labels* just below the product location or on *endcaps* (product identification signs at the ends of aisles). For more information on bar codes, see the section *I See Bar Codes in Your Future* later in this chapter.

Where Does Sign Copy Come From?

In retail operations, the people who are usually responsible for initiating new signs and deciding what they will say are the product *buyers,* who purchase products from wholesale distributors. In a large chain of stores, each buyer usually deals with a particular type of product, perhaps also for a specific region of the country.

It makes sense for buyers to initiate the production of new signs because they know

- Which new products will be coming into the store

- When the products will arrive, requiring a change in signing

- Key product benefits

- Particularly competitive features of the product

- Suggested retail price

Based on this information, the buyer fills out a *sign requisition.* Examples of sign requisitions used in retail operations are shown in Figures 7.5 and 7.6. In some retail chains, the buyer initiates a sign requisition by typing the data into a computer terminal, and the record is transmitted to an automated sign-composition facility. In other operations, the paper sign request is forwarded to a sign shop that acts as a graphic arts service department for the store or for the chain of stores.

225

FIGURE 7.5

Sign requisition forms trigger the production of signs in response to changing market conditions or product features. (Courtesy The Reynolds Group)

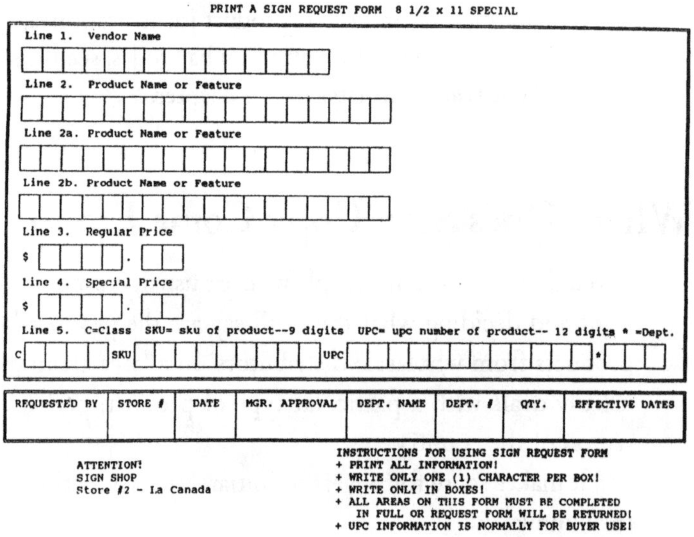

PRINT A SIGN REQUEST FORM 8 1/2 x 11 SPECIAL

Line 1. Vendor Name

Line 2. Product Name or Feature

Line 2a. Product Name or Feature

Line 2b. Product Name or Feature

Line 3. Regular Price

$

Line 4. Special Price

$

Line 5. C=Class SKU= sku of product--9 digits UPC= upc number of product-- 12 digits * =Dept.

C   SKU   UPC   *

REQUESTED BY	STORE #	DATE	MGR. APPROVAL	DEPT. NAME	DEPT. #	QTY.	EFFECTIVE DATES

ATTENTION!
SIGN SHOP
Store #2 - La Canada

INSTRUCTIONS FOR USING SIGN REQUEST FORM
+ PRINT ALL INFORMATION!
+ WRITE ONLY ONE (1) CHARACTER PER BOX!
+ WRITE ONLY IN BOXES!
+ ALL AREAS ON THIS FORM MUST BE COMPLETED
  IN FULL OR REQUEST FORM WILL BE RETURNED!
+ UPC INFORMATION IS NORMALLY FOR BUYER USE!

FIGURE 7.6

Sign requisitions should be composed to gather all data needed for the sign, even to restricting sign copy to a specific number of characters. (Courtesy The Reynolds Group)

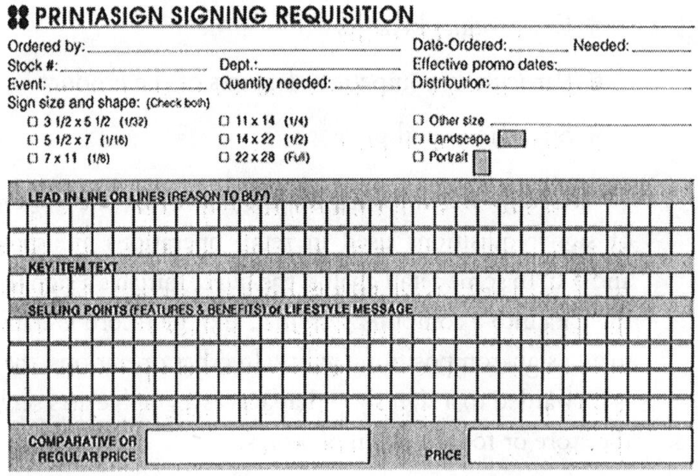

PRINTASIGN SIGNING REQUISITION

Ordered by:_____ Date-Ordered:_____ Needed:_____
Stock #:_____ Dept.:_____ Effective promo dates:_____
Event:_____ Quantity needed:_____ Distribution:_____

Sign size and shape: (Check both)
- 3 1/2 x 5 1/2 (1/32)
- 5 1/2 x 7 (1/16)
- 7 x 11 (1/8)
- 11 x 14 (1/4)
- 14 x 22 (1/2)
- 22 x 28 (Full)
- Other size_____
- Landscape
- Portrait

LEAD IN LINE OR LINES (REASON TO BUY)

KEY ITEM TEXT

SELLING POINTS (FEATURES & BENEFITS) or LIFESTYLE MESSAGE

COMPARATIVE OR REGULAR PRICE   PRICE

The buyer may also know the store's selling price or promotional price, but in this age of rapidly fluctuating competitive pricing, the price that goes on the sign usually is retrieved electronically from *price lookup tables* in the store's computer system. These are the same price tables that return the price to the clerk's point-of-sale terminal when the product's UPC is scanned. Verification of the price with the store's database is crucial because it is not uncommon for the prices to be updated daily.

Writing Effective Sign Copy

Here are a few tips on writing the text for a benefit-oriented sign:

- Be concise. Know the specific size of the printed sign and remember that smaller formats cannot hold as much text.

- Stay away from small-sized signs and text. Don't expect shoppers to wear eyeglasses just to read your signs.

- Answer customer questions, such as "How do I care for this item? Is the product color-fast? Pre-shrunk? Permanently pressed? Of what material is the product made or constructed? What sizes and colors are available? Is there a guarantee or warranty?"

- Use descriptive words, such as *advanced, convenient, durable, easy, innovative, money-saving, quick, safe,* and *versatile.*

Making a Sign in Microsoft Word

Signs can be created in almost any Windows application that can produce text and graphics, including Microsoft Word, Harvard Graphics, and CorelDRAW. This section contains tips for preparing benefit-oriented product signs in Word. The following Word features are especially useful for making signs:

- Templates
- Printing method
- Page size and orientation
- Margins
- Choice of fonts
- Font scaling
- Database links
- Borders
- Art
- Colors

Let's look at each of these features in more detail.

Templates Product signs can adhere to fairly strict sign formats, such as the example in Figure 7.7. Even if you make signs only occasionally, you should make several templates for this purpose. Modify a Normal document in Word according to the specifications described here, then save it as a document template (.DOT) file by doing File ➤ Save As ➤ Document Template. You can then retrieve the named template any time in Word by choosing File ➤ New.

Printing method Because the type is very big and bold, signs have large areas of solid printing. Laser printers produce excellent black-and-white output, and color signs can be produced with color laser or thermal printers. In general, dot-matrix and ink-jet printers, whether monochrome or color, will produce less than satisfactory results. The cloth ribbons of dot-matrix printers loose color saturation quickly as large areas are laid down, and the flow of ink through ink jets is not

FIGURE 7.7

*Sign template created
in Microsoft Word*

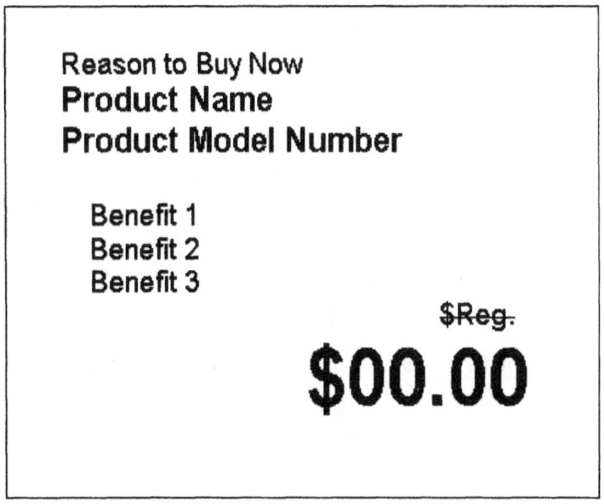

> **Reason to Buy Now**
> **Product Name**
> **Product Model Number**
>
> **Benefit 1**
> **Benefit 2**
> **Benefit 3**
>
> ~~$Reg.~~
> **$00.00**

always consistent. In either case, the result is visible *banding*, or striped variations in tone, in the solid areas. This problem will become quickly apparent if you try to produce signs in quantity. High-quality signs and banners can be produced in limited quantities on special purpose plotters called *vinyl cutters*, which use small knives instead of pens to trace the outlines of letters on pressure-sensitive, colored vinyl. Select a printer in Word by choosing File ➤ Print Setup.

Page size and orientation Product signs are typically printed on card stock in landscape orientation. For store displays, the page size is dictated by the dimensions of standard sign holders. Some of the more common sizes are given in Table 7.1. In the sign shops of large retail operations, multiple signs are printed on larger sheets of card stock, which are then cut down. Some specialized signmaking software packages include predesigned formats for composing and printing signs on these sheets. In Word, set the page size and orientation by doing

Format ► Page Setup ► Size And Orientation. To adjust for the card-stock sizes in Table 7.1, select the Custom Size setting for Paper Size and enter the dimensions for Width and Height.

Margins For smaller-sized signs, be careful about the margin setting. Typically, a printed sign card is inserted into a sign holder from the top. The sides and bottom of the holder are grooved to hold the card in place. Provide some extra margin to allow for the depths of the grooves, which can range from $\frac{1}{8}$"–$\frac{1}{2}$". (Default margins of 1" all around will be much too large for most signs. Remember that you want to fit as much text as you can attractively in a small area.)

DESIGNATION	PRINTED SHEET SIZE (W × H in)	PAGES PER SHEET	CUT PAGE SIZE (W × H in)
S13	11 × 8.5	1	11 × 8.5
S14	8.5 × 11	1	8.5 × 11
S51	14 × 11	1	14 × 11
Nametent	11 × 7	2	3.5 × 11
S3	7 × 11	1	7 × 11
S15	14 × 8.5	1	14 × 8.5
S16	8.5 × 14	1	8.5 × 14
S21	7 × 11	8	3.5 × 2.75
S22	11 × 7	8	2.75 × 3.5
S25	11 × 7	4	2.75 × 7

TABLE 7.1: *Some Typical Sheet and Page Sizes for Sign Printing*

Choice of fonts Most retail signs use simple sans serif fonts such as Arial or Helvetica, often in boldface, especially for the larger sizes used for product names and prices. In general, use text fonts for all the sign copy, and pick a font that scales well in the larger sizes, especially when you add boldface. Again, use a font with strikethrough to show the regular price when you are featuring a discounted price on the same sign. Use display fonts only for designer, store, or theme logos. Fonts and attributes in Word can be set by selecting the text and doing Format ➤ Character. Table 7.2 shows sign elements and some typical point sizes.

FIELD NAME	POINT SIZE	ATTRIBUTE
Reason to Buy Now	36	Normal
Product Name/Number	42	Bold
Benefits	36	Normal
Regular Price	36	Strikethrough
Sale Price	100	Bold

T A B L E 7 . 2 : *Suggested Point Sizes for Sign Text (Arial)*

Font scaling In theory, font scaling to large sizes for signs and banners shouldn't be a problem in Windows, since both TrueType and Adobe PostScript Type 1 fonts can be scaled continuously. However, some applications, such as Microsoft Word, restrict the point sizes by default. In Word, the permitted range is 4–127 points, for a maximum character height of about 1.75 inches. In CorelDRAW 4, the permissible range is from 0.7–2160 points.

Database links In the Windows environment, even the owner of a small business can use the latest technology to link sign copy to pricing tables, just as the big chains do. If you keep prices in a database or spreadsheet application in Windows, you can use the DDE feature to link the price data to the price copy on the sign. Use the Edit ➤ Copy command to copy the price from the database field or sheet cell, then do Edit ➤ Paste Special ➤ Paste Link to insert a linked copy into the sign in Word. If you want to get really fancy, you can link the product names and model numbers, as well, so that any time you edit your inventory listing, your signs will be updated automatically in Word.

Borders Lines and shading are nice graphic touches to signs, as long as you use them consistently for all the signs in a display or in a store. Use the Format ➤ Border command to add borders and shading in Word.

Art You can add line art to a sign in Word with the Insert ➤ Frame command, then use the drawing tools to create the object. Or, use the Insert ➤ Picture command to import a bitmap or other graphic. This command is useful for inserting scanned bitmaps of product photos in signs.

Colors Colorful signs can be produced by printing colored type on a coated card stock with a color laser or color thermal printer. The command for specifying the color of a selected character string in Word is Format ➤ Character ➤ Color. When selecting colors, be guided by the legibility chart in Table 7.3.

Despite the ability to produce signs in color, many designers of store displays prefer black text on a white background for all the signs in the store. Their reasoning is that black-and-white signs actually stand out better against the wide variety of colors in store displays.

RANK	TYPE COLOR	BACKGROUND COLOR
1	Black	Yellow
2	Green	White
3	Red	White
4	Blue	White
5	White	Blue
6	Black	White
7	Yellow	White
8	White	Red
9	White	Green
10	White	Black
11	Red	Yellow
12	Green	Red

TABLE 7.3: *Order of Legibility for Color Display Signs (ranked best to worst)*

It's Not Just a Sign, It's a Merchandising Strategy

A retail sign should be more than a price tag. It should be a well-coordinated part of an overall merchandising strategy. From the standpoint of graphics design, this simply means that the themes, logos, colors, and designs used on signs and particularly on sign toppers should match the artwork and fonts used in the store's event-oriented displays. Graphics and text in signs should also tie in with the elements of advertising campaign themes—print ads, television commercials, promotional catalogs, and direct mailings to customers.

Looking for Signmaking Software?

Here are some Windows application packages that are designed specifically for making signs:

Announcements (Parsons Technology)

Banners on Windows (Boomerang Software)

Instant Artist (Autodesk)

New Print Shop (Broderbund Sofware)

Ready Flow SignPro (Ready Flow)

To find out about Windows software for commercial sign shops and retail information systems, see *Are You Seriously into Signmaking?* in this chapter.

Put another way, repeating these graphic themes on the signs in a store reinforces the message of the advertising campaign at the place where it matters most—at the point of sale.

Other Signs You Can't Ignore

Specialized sign formats that have been developed for uses other than product display advertising include the following:

Name tents Much in demand for corporate meetings and seminars, these folding cardboard signs tell everyone who is sitting where. As shown in Figure 7.8, if a name tent is to be printed so that it reads both from the front and from the back, the name must be printed in an inverted position on the second side so that it reads right-side-up when folded. To produce such a name tent, you need a Windows graphics

FIGURE 7.8

A folded name tent or a product topper that can be read from either side requires text to be flipped vertically.

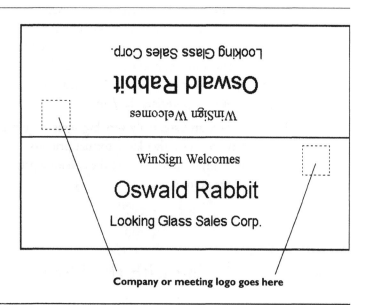

Company or meeting logo goes here

application that can mirror, or flip, the text object. A name tent that shows a product name or promotional slogan and sits atop a store display is called a *product topper*.

Category signs Rather than advertising a specific product, a *category* sign in a story points to the location of a department or type of product. An example would be a sign that marks the displays for JUNIOR SPORTSWEAR. The purpose of category signs is to guide shoppers through a store so that they need not rely on salespeople to find the products they are looking for. The design of category signs should adhere to a corporate *sign manual*, or style book, that specifies fonts and layouts that will be consistent throughout the store.

Informational signs Road signs and other direction-finders are examples of *informational signs*. The guideline here is *the simpler the better*. Readability is most important, with the minimum copy required to deliver the message. The annoyingly familiar OUT OF ORDER sign on

235

the door of an elevator or restroom is an example. Opinions vary on this, but my advice would be to omit cute designs intended to embellish—or worse, to excuse—an unpleasant message. For example, adding a shrugging cartoon character to the OUT OF ORDER message is a tempting and clever touch, but the customer who is being inconvenienced might not appreciate the humor.

Banners These are essentially very big signs, requiring not so much special software, but rather large-format printers, including thermal printers and vinyl cutters. Be sure the software permits text to be scaled to large point sizes.

Volume Sign Production: Coping with the Flow

In a typical chain of retail stores, sign production is a large-scale operation. During a given week, price changes, new products, and new promotions require perhaps hundreds of signs in a single store to be changed. Compounding the size of the chore is the number of store locations, each of which might have a different mix of products or be subject to different price or discount structures.

As if high volume weren't a big problem in itself, there is further pressure to produce updated signs quickly. If the chain must respond to a competitor by initiating a last-minute promotion, the signs for the promotion must be produced and set up throughout the store literally overnight.

The need for high-volume sign production with fast turnaround creates some special requirements for signmaking software. It should be capable of

❡ Data-driven formatting

❡ Printing in sheets

❡ Printing in batches

❡ Distributed signing

Let's look closely at each of these requirements.

Data-driven formatting To produce many signs quickly, templates should be stored on disk for each sign format that is used regularly. The signmaking system should be linked to the store's pricing database so that price and product changes in the database can be imported to the templates for automatic production of updated signs.

Printing in sheets Production speed can be increased by printing multiple-sign sheets on large-format printers. Not only must sign templates be sized correctly for standard sign holders, but they must also provide for positioning several such signs on large sheets. The sheet sizes must be matched to the large-format printers that can produce them, as well as be correct multiples of the sign-holder sizes.

Printing in batches When you start to print signs in volume, you run up against another problem, that of collating printed signs by store, by department, by promotion, or by whatever sets are easiest to distribute in bulk and to set up in the store. For this purpose, you should be able to group signs for printing in batches, or *stacks*. In Windows, a logical way to group signs in stacks is to organize the document files in different subdirectories, one for each stack.

Distributed signing Commercial signmaking systems must be flexible enough to support different patterns of sign production and distribution, depending on the requirements of the store or chain. The physical separation of sign composition from printing is called *distributed signing*, and it can take several forms. For example, department stores typically print signs in volume centrally, at corporate headquarters, then ship collated stacks of signs along with their regular deliveries of merchandise to the stores. Many discount chains use a different approach: The database of inventory and pricing is maintained on a central computer system, but only the data for composing the signs is transmitted over a network to stores around the country. The data drives sign templates in PC systems in each store, and the signs are printed locally. In many specialty stores, the pricing and inventories vary so much from one store location to another that all sign production is handled at the store level on PC-based systems.

A growing practice in large chain-store operations is to print most signs centrally on high-volume laser printers that can produce 30–135 pages per minute (ppm), then ship the signs in bulk to the stores. However, at the store level, low-volume laser printing is done for local promotion and for signs that were damaged in transit.

Are You Seriously into Signmaking?

The requirements described above for high-volume distributed signmaking are beyond the capabilities of most general-purpose graphics applications for Windows. A commercial software package for Windows that is specifically designed to interface with retail information systems is WinSign. (I used WinSign to produce all of the sample signs shown in this chapter with the exception of the Word template in Figure 7.7.) For information on this product contact

Reynolds Printasign

2301 N. San Fernando Blvd.

Burbank , CA 91504-3352

800 446-5050

The WinSign Operator desktop is shown in Figure 7.9. Clicking the icons along the left side of the screen initiates signmaking commands, including retrieval of printing sheets in specific sizes, retrieval of predefined sign formats, sign composition, placement of formats onto sheets, and arrangement of sign documents in stacks for queued printing runs.

FIGURE 7.9

Shown on the Win-Sign desktop are operator selections for various standard sheet sizes.

Select a sign format
  Select a sheet size and orientation
    Access files
      Text-entry mode
        Design a new format

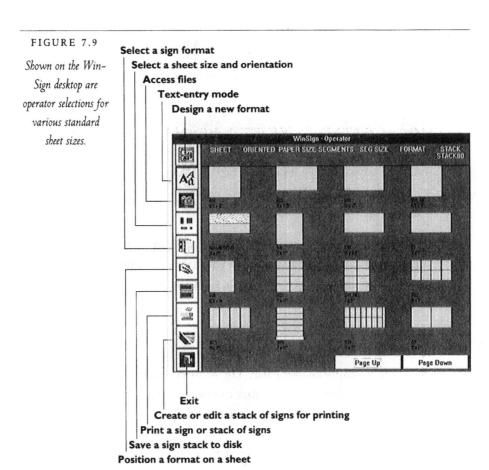

Exit
Create or edit a stack of signs for printing
Print a sign or stack of signs
Save a sign stack to disk
Position a format on a sheet

I See Bar Codes in Your Future

The topic of bar codes is so complex that it deserves a book all to itself. There are literally scores of different formats (Figure 7.10), most of which have been developed for specific applications in specific industries. A single, all-encompassing standard—if such a thing were desirable or feasible—is nowhere in sight. Even the UPCs used by the retail and grocery industries

239

> ## Who's Doing It Already?
>
> Lest you think I exaggerate, the following retail chains have integrated their retail information systems with automated sign production:
>
> ¶ P.A. Bergner & Co., Milwaukee, Wisconsin
>
> ¶ Venture Stores, O'Fallon, Missouri
>
> ¶ Woodward & Lothrup, Washington, D.C.

have many variations, typically by industry or by product line.

If you need to include bar codes in your signs, here are some preliminary answers and pointers to get you on the right track.

What's in a Bar Code?

A bar code is simply an identifier. The most common format is a series of vertical bars of different widths that can be scanned optically. The pattern of bars is interpreted in software as a series of alphanumeric characters, usually numeric digits.

Perhaps the most important point about bar codes is that *actual product information is not stored in the bar code;* instead, the pattern of bars represents a unique code (usually a number) for each particular product. The descriptive data, such as the make, model, size, and unit price, are stored in a lookup table in the store's computer system. When the bar code is scanned optically, the system looks up that numeric identifier in the lookup table. If the scanning is done at the sales terminal, the product name and price are retrieved. If the scanning is done by the wand of an inventory clerk's palmtop computer, the product stock number, or *stocking unit* (SKU), and the number of units that are supposed to be on hand might be retrieved.

FIGURE 7.10

Here are just a few of the many bar code formats that are available as Windows fonts (Courtesy Precision Type, Inc.).

241

One conclusion you can draw from this is that errors in retrieving information from a scanned bar code usually aren't the result of errors in the printing of the code or even of problems with the scanning process. Rather, the error is usually in the lookup table, which might not have been updated properly or might be otherwise corrupted.

How Are Bar Codes Generated?

Depending on the bar code format, of which there are many, the character string that the bars represent might not be just the SKU. It can also include other data that the computer system needs to process the code, including characters for error checking. Bar code processing can use *checksums,* as is done in some types of modem transmission, to verify the accuracy of the scanned code.

Generation of the bar code within the store database usually begins with entering the SKU number. A mathematical formula is then applied to the SKU to translate it into the alphanumeric characters that will be represented by the bar code. (These characters will include the exact number of characters required by the bar code format, plus any characters used for error checking.) The alphanumeric result is then translated into a pattern of bars by special software.

Bar patterns vary considerably by format; for example, some are tall and some are short. Some contain one group of bars, some two or more. Even within the same bar code format, the spacing of the bars (or *bar code density*) can vary between low (widely spaced), medium, or high (closely spaced).

How Can Bar Codes Be Generated
by Windows Applications?

Windows applications can produce bar code output either as bar code fonts or as graphics. Here's how each works.

Bar code fonts Bar codes in various formats are available as TrueType or Adobe PostScript Type 1 fonts. You type the character-code equivalent into the application as text and choose the bar code format name as the font for that text object.

Using bar code fonts will work well in some cases, but the drawbacks include the following:

- Bar code fonts generally can't be rotated. You must therefore install separate fonts for printing in portrait or landscape page orientations.

- The bars in a bar code font are spaced with fixed density. You must specify high, medium, or low bar density when you order the font.

- Even though a laser printer might be rated at 300 or even 600 dots per inch (dpi), the actual size and density of the printed dots can vary depending on printer model, type of toner, toner level in the machine, and type of paper. Although the dot size isn't apparent when reproducing type, any variation can become critical to the actual density and machine readability of a bar code. Since bar code fonts are fixed in density, there is no way to compensate for these variations.

Bar codes may be available for your printer as a plug-in font cartridge. For example, a cartridge for the Hewlett-Packard LaserJet II is designated *HP:Bar Codes & More*. The printer driver file required to use this cartridge with Microsoft Works is HPBAR.PRD.

Graphics Applications that are designed specifically to generate bar codes produce them as bitmapped graphics. When you input the character string for the code, the software applies the bar code algorithm, a mathematical formula, for the format you select. Because the bar code image is being generated from scratch, in effect, the software can calculate all aspects of the image, including rotation and variations in bar density. Since the bar density can be adjusted by fine increments, even the variation in dot size among printers can be compensated for. For example, you might output a bar code in the highest density that your scanning equipment is specified to accept, then try to scan the result. If the scan weren't successful, you could decrease the density by small increments until the scanner recognized the code correctly.

Find Yourself behind Bars?

Bar code fonts for Windows are available from Precision Type at the following address:

Precision Type, Inc.

47 Mall Drive

Commack, NY 11725

800 248-3668

To find out about application software that generates bar codes as graphics, contact Applause Identification Systems at the following address:

Applause Identification Systems, Inc.

7533 Tyler Boulevard, Unit C

Mentor, OH 44060

800 878-6833

CHAPTER 8

Designing
a Screen Show

Surviving in the
War Room

N TODAY'S TECHNICAL JARGON, an executive conference room equipped for presenting computer-generated screen shows is called a *war room*. The display is usually on a large monitor or on a wall screen lit by a video projector and controlled by a PC or server, and perhaps also connected to a network for interaction with computers at remote sites.

This chapter should help you create a screen show, especially the text elements, so that you can make a good impression the next time you are summoned to the dreaded war room!

Screen Shows, Slide Shows, and Your Show of Shows

In a business setting, a screen show generally follows the format of a traditional slide presentation to management—a sequence of charts that report performance data, interspersed with text slides showing the main topics and message points of the presenter's live speech. The speech usually interprets the graphics for the audience and solicits a conclusion, decision, or action based on the new information.

This chapter and the two following it present tips on designing text frames for shows in different presentation media. This chapter covers shows on the computer screen. Chapter 9 deals with aspect ratios and other technical requirements for video and broadcast television, and chapter 10 describes the special considerations involved in composing text graphics for output as color slides and overhead transparencies.

The sequence of a screen show is much more flexible than a slide presentation, which must follow a predetermined, linear sequence. A computer-generated screen show can be interactive, its sequence controlled "on the fly" as selections are made by the presenter or operator while the show is running. Furthermore, the *transition effects* between screens (visual frames) are much more varied on a computer than those on conventional slide-projection equipment. Effects such as wipes and dissolves, once available only using multiple slide projectors with special controllers or on videotape with professional editing equipment, are easy to produce in Windows.

Many Windows applications that generate graphics, such as Harvard Graphics, Freelance Graphics, and PowerPoint, have built-in capabilities for creating screen shows. You can also use Excel to organize spreadsheets, charts, and graphics in screen-show sequences. The family of applications shipped with CorelDRAW includes CorelSHOW, which can be used to organize graphics from multiple sources into electronic show sequences. Hollywood is a self-contained package designed specifically for building screen shows in Windows from multiple source files. Now that newer PC models are being equipped for multimedia, screen shows in Windows can also include digital audio, animation, and live-action digital video.

The increased flexibility of screen shows as compared to presentations on slides offers both good news and bad news: The good news is that screen shows are easier and more economical to produce and edit than similar material done with conventional audiovisual media such as film or videotape. The bad news is that this flexibility not only can increase the complexity of a show (permitting many different possible interactive sequences), but also makes revisions so easy that last-minute changes can be demanded by picky managers.

You see, once a set of slides is locked into a projector tray, there are only two choices—forward or backward, one slide at a time. For many presenters, there's a certain comfort in that static organization: Your bosses know you can't easily rearrange your presentation at the last minute, and certainly wouldn't expect you to reorganize your talk while it is in progress!

But there's no such comfortable assurance when you are presenting a computer-generated show. Its flexibility and ease of access to the data allow an audience to ask questions about alternatives and to demand different scenarios. That may be the power of technology, but put yourself in the place of a middle manager who goes into a meeting prepared to present a set of conclusions and ends up playing what-if games with the top executives!

Interactive screen shows can stimulate what-if analysis. If you are brainstorming with your peers, all of you gathered breathlessly around the monitor of your PC late into the night, this may be exciting stuff. But you don't necessarily want to encourage such open-ended discussions with management when you are making a formal presentation. If the stakes are high, play it safe and stick to slides.

So, how do you avoid the panic of having your supervisors rewrite your speech, in effect, as you are giving it? There is no guarantee, but your chances of surviving the experience will be improved if your presentation has a *visible structure.* And unlike some other types of visual presentation, that structure must be rooted in words. (Yes, I'm getting around to fonts!) The better organized your presentation is, the less prone your audience may be to reorganize it for you.

Business Presentations Aren't Movies

I'll admit that a good picture, such as a well-conceived chart, is worth a thousand words. But a business presentation can't be (or at least shouldn't be) all pictures. The audio portion, whether live or prerecorded, must explain and interpret the pictures for the audience. You will be asking for trouble if you throw a chart of last quarter's sales results on the screen and then pause in silent meditation, awaiting the wisdom of the viewers. You must tell your audience what conclusions *you* draw from the data; as the presenter, the agenda should be yours. If your objectives aren't clear, if your conclusions aren't specific, you will lose control of the agenda, as well as your influence over the management decision you seek.

A time-honored technique for giving your presentation visual structure is to put the outline of your speech on the screen.

Sounds dull, you say?

Don't Sit at This Table!

A third type of text screen—the dreary table—is to be avoided. If you are tempted to show data in a table (or worse, if you try to put a whole spreadsheet on the screen), consider converting the numbers to a graph, which will almost always show the relationships better. For tips on creating charts (as well as tables, if you must) see Chapter 3.

I don't mean the whole outline, and not all at once. Instead, break up the points of a topic outline into text screens. Two types of text screens give structure to a presentation: titles and lists.

Titles Are Topics

A title screen shows the text of a main topic or title, sometimes with a subtopic or subtitle, as shown in Figure 8.1. Insert a title screen before each section of charts in your presentation, just as you would introduce the paragraphs of a report with headings and subheadings.

Speechwriters call title screens *signposts*, for the obvious reason that a title points the way to what's ahead. This reinforces the structure of your presentation so that the audience is with you at every step.

FIGURE 8.1

A title screen tells the audience what to expect and follows the structure of main topics in your presentation outline.

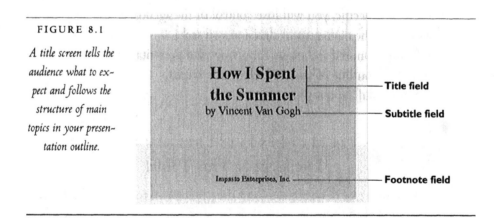

Put Your Agenda in a List

A set of related subtopics can be presented as a list, with the items bulleted or numbered, as shown in Figure 8.2. A list should recap the subordinate points of one main topic in your presentation outline.

FIGURE 8.2

A list recaps the details of one main topic in your speech outline.

Subjects of My Paintings

In Southern France

- Landscapes
- Still life
- Live models
- My room

However, showing a naked list (all items on the screen at once) encourages the so-called "read-ahead" problem. The audience can read faster than you can talk. They can see the whole list at a glance and will have a natural tendency not only to read ahead, but also to think ahead—perhaps anticipating your conclusions, perhaps wrongly!

The solution to the read-ahead problem is to subdivide a list into several separate screens as a *build-up sequence*, as shown in Figure 8.3.

Consider subduing, or dimming, the previously presented items and highlighting the current item. The subdued color might be a lighter shade of the background, and the highlight color should contrast sharply with dimmed items. For example, if the background is dark blue, the subdued color could be light blue, with white or yellow as the highlight color.

There's more about creating build-up sequences with Harvard Graphics Version 1 for Windows later in this chapter.

FIGURE 8.3

A build-up sequence presents a list in stages to avoid the "read-ahead" problem.

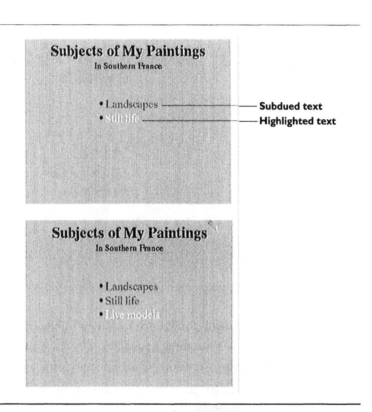

Take Your Cue from Your Text

If you put words on the screen, you'd better say them. And you've got to say them right when the audience *sees* them. This synchronization of video with audio is called *visual cueing.* Any picture should be cued (should appear on the screen) at the moment that you begin to talk about it. If the screen contains text, you should start by saying those words.

Careful speechwriters even make sure that the syntax, or word order, of the spoken words matches the text on the screen. For example, the audience might be distracted needlessly if they see INCREASE MARKET AWARENESS on the screen but hear you say, "Recognition of our product in the marketplace should be enhanced in the coming months." For the most effective reinforcement of your message, you should say, "We want to *increase market awareness* of our product in the months ahead."

Creating Title and Bullet Charts in Harvard Graphics

In a Harvard Graphics ScreenShow, each screen is called a *slide*, even though it need not be recorded on film. The procedure for creating text slides, including titles and bulleted lists, involves little more than typing the text.

After starting Harvard Graphics, do File ➤ New Presentation to create a presentation. The Add Slide dialog box will open. Select the option button for the type of slide you wish to create, in this case, a Title or a Bullet. Then select OK, and the Data Form (a document window for data input) for the selected chart type appears. The Data Form for the Bullet chart type is shown in Figure 8.4.

Type the text into each field of the form, pressing ↵ after each entry. To add levels of indentation to the bulleted items, press Tab before typing an indented entry. Press Shift-Tab to move the pointer left before typing a continuation of the first-level list.

FIGURE 8.4

*The Data Form for
a Bullet chart, with
sample typed entries.*

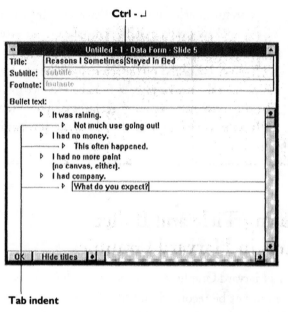

Ctrl · ⅃

Tab indent

When you select OK to close the Data Form, a WYSIWYG view of
the text slide will appear in the Slide Editor, the default view of Harvard
Graphics in which most editing and drawing functions can be done. (See
Figure 8.5)

Changing Text
Appearance in Harvard Graphics

You can change the appearance (or *attributes*) of text in Harvard Graphics by
selecting the text object in the Slide Editor and then choosing commands
from the Text pull-down menu. However, that isn't the most efficient way
to work.

FIGURE 8.5

Here's the Slide Editor view of the text data in Figure 8.4.

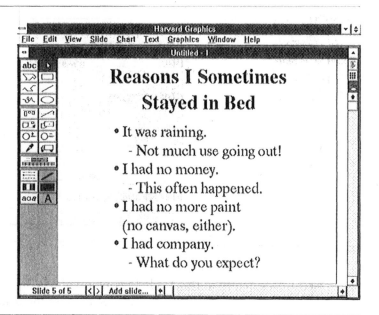

Harvard Graphics includes a set of predefined *styles* by which you can change the look of an entire presentation, including text attributes such as fonts. Each style also refers to a color palette, a design-coordinated set of numbered Chart colors (which are pre-assigned to specific types of objects) and Custom colors (used for drawings). Chart colors can be regarded as relative: The color number assigned to an object stays the same, and when you change palettes, the object assumes the color at that number location in the new palette. By contrast, a Custom color can be considered absolute: An object with a Custom color will not change when you change palettes.

To change the look of an entire presentation in the Slide Editor, even including the fonts if you wish, do Slide ➤ Presentation Style ➤ Apply. The Apply Presentation Style dialog box will appear, as shown in Figure 8.6.

Select the name of a predefined style from the Files list. To see a sample, select the Preview button, then the chart type you wish to see previewed.

255

FIGURE 8.6

You can change options for an entire presentation by applying a different style.

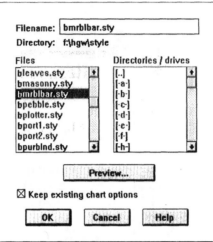

Select OK to return to the Apply Presentation Style dialog box, where you can reselect a named style or select OK to close the dialog box and apply the style you chose.

To change only the font for the entire presentation in the Slide Editor, do Slide ➤ Change Presentation Font, select a font name from the list that appears, and select OK. To change the attributes of selected characters, words, or lines of text in a slide, follow the procedures described later in this chapter under Adding the Build-and-Subdue Effect.

Putting Your Words on the Screen—the Easy Way

Some Windows charting applications, including Harvard Graphics, have married the process of outlining neatly to the generation of graphics that contain titles and lists. If you type or import the text of your speech outline into the application, it will generate the title and list screens of your presentation automatically. (The process also works in reverse: If you create title and list screens in graphics mode, you can view the text in outline form at the click of a button.)

Entering Text in the Outliner View of Harvard Graphics

In Harvard Graphics, the feature that creates this alternate, text-based view of the data in a presentation file is called the Outliner. You can open the Outliner window after you have begun a presentation with the commands File ➤ New Presentation or File ➤ Open. In the Slide Editor view (the default document window), do View ➤ Outliner or click this button in the top right corner of the desktop:

The Outliner window will open, as shown in Figure 8.7. As you type your speech outline into this window, the levels of indentation determine how the program will render each line of text as a graphic.

Entries that are flush left are treated as titles. If a slide has only a title with no subordinate items below it, the Title chart format is used. If there are indented items also, the Bullet chart format is used, with the title at the heading of a list. (However, the first slide of a presentation is assumed to be a Title chart, regardless of the number of indentation levels.)

When you type the first text line of a slide in the Outliner and press ↵, the pointer drops down to the next line and is indented, ready for your entry of the first bulleted item in a list. If, instead, you make no subordinate entry and press ↵ again, the pointer moves back flush left for you to enter the title of the next slide.

FIGURE 8.7

The Outliner view in Harvard Graphics shows the text in a presentation file (excluding labels of data charts and drawn text).

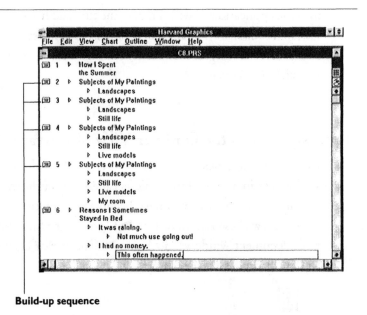

Build-up sequence

To enter two lines on the same level of indentation, whether for a title or a bulleted item, press Ctrl-↵ at the end of the first line. To add subtitle and footnote fields to a title slide in the Outliner, do Outline ➤ Show Subtitle & Footnote, then type text into the new fields that appear in the outline.

When you type a bulleted item and press ↵, the pointer drops down to the next line but does not indent. You can then continue the outline by typing the next item in the list.

As many as nine levels of indentation are permitted (not including the title) in any slide of the outline. The indents will appear in the list of a Bullet chart just as they appear in the outline. To change the indentation level of a line of text, click the starting point of the string to move the insertion point to its left edge, then do Outline ➤ Indent or press Tab. The line will be indented one tab stop to the right. To move a text line up in the hierarchy (to the left), put the pointer at its left edge and do Outline ➤ Unindent or press Shift-Tab.

Indented text in the Outliner can be converted to a third chart type—the organization chart. To change a slide from Bullet to Organization chart format, click the slide number in the left margin of the Outliner to select the slide and do Chart ➤ Change Chart Type ➤ Organization. When you return to the Slide Editor view, you will see that the levels of indentation in the list have been translated into organizational levels in the chart. Each text entry will be the name label of one box in the chart. In the Outliner, an optional Job Title field will appear as another level of indentation beneath each name.

Importing an Outline

If you've already written your speech outline in a word processing application, you can do File ➤ Import in the Harvard Graphics Outliner view to read ASCII text into the document window. Or, if the outline is a Windows document, you can do Edit ➤ Copy in the source application and then Edit ➤ Paste in the Outliner.

Whether you import the text or paste it from the Clipboard, the levels of indentation in the data are preserved. Each Tab character is interpreted as an indent. Each time a text line begins flush left after a carriage return, a new slide is started. By this method, you can automatically generate one slide for each main topic in your outline.

Maybe you're the type of person who does the graphics first, then writes your speech. If you build your outline in the Outliner initially, you can do Edit ➤ Copy and then Edit ➤ Paste to insert it into a Windows word processing application, or do File ➤ Export to write the outline to an ASCII text file that can be loaded into a word processing program.

Creating Build-Up Sequences

So much for the Outliner. Here's how to create those nifty build-up sequences to emphasize your lists of topics. The conventional way to create a build-up sequence is in reverse order: You create the last slide (the complete list) first, then

1. Copy the slide.

2. Delete the last text line in the copy.

3. Repeat steps 1 and 2 for each of the remaining slides in the sequence.

To create a build-and-subdue effect, after step 2 you must recolor the last line to be the highlight color (yellow or white, if the background is dark).

If you create a build-up sequence in the Slide Editor of Harvard Graphics Version 1 using the procedure just described, the results will be unsatisfactory. Each time you delete a line of text, the program will recompose the slide. This will destroy the build-up effect, which requires the composition to match exactly from slide to slide. To stop the Slide Editor from recomposing the slide, you must change the list's Anchor Point to Top Left. The anchor point is the fixed point from which a text block grows. After selecting the text in the Slide Editor, use Text ➤ Set Anchor Point to change the anchor point from the default setting of Top Center. There's an easier way to achieve the same result: Copy and delete the text in the Outliner instead, as described below. (Composition will also remain unchanged if you delete text in the Data Form, the document window by which text chart data is entered if you don't use the Outliner.)

Creating Build-Up Sequences in the Outliner

To create a build-up sequence in Harvard Graphics Version 1, start by creating the last slide (the completed list), then duplicate that slide once for each of the other slides in the sequence. The duplication can be done easily in the Slide Sorter view. To open the Slide Sorter, do View ➤ Slide Sorter or click this button in the top right corner of the desktop:

The Slide Sorter document window will open, as shown in Figure 8.8. If it is not already highlighted, select the list slide by clicking on it. Do Edit ➤ Copy to copy it to the Clipboard and then do Edit ➤ Paste to duplicate the slide. Repeat this once for each additional slide in the sequence.

FIGURE 8.8

You can duplicate slides in the Slide Sorter view by doing Edit ➤ Copy and Edit ➤ Paste.

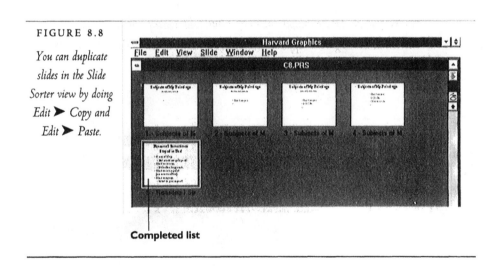

Completed list

For example, if your completed list slide has four bulleted items, do Edit ➤ Paste three times to end up with four copies of the same list:

The next step is to delete the text of bulleted items in stages. Switch back to the Outliner, where the same text entries will appear in all slides of the sequence. Select the text to be deleted in each slide by clicking to the left of the icon for that line or by drawing a box around a group of items. The selected text will be highlighted in a solid color (blue on color monitors), as shown in Figure 8.9. Then press Del to remove the text.

Some graphics applications offer an auto-build feature, which will automatically generate the component slides of a build-up sequence from the completed list slide. Among these applications are Harvard Graphics 3 for DOS and Freelance Graphics Release 2 for Windows.

FIGURE 8.9

Click to the left of an item or draw a box around a group of items to select them in the Outliner.

Adding the Build-and-Subdue Effect

To create the build-and-subdue effect, you must use the Slide Editor to recolor the text in the list of each slide so that the last item is shown in the highlight color and the preceding lines are dimmed. To switch to the Slide Editor view, do View ➤ Slide Editor or click this button in the top right corner of the desktop:

To select the text list for editing, click on it once. Handles (small squares) will surround it. Then, click the Text tool, which is located near the top left corner of the desktop:

abc

A text block window will open around the list. With the mouse, *drag* the line or lines of text that you want to recolor. Your selection will be highlighted in reverse color. Then do Text ➤ All Attributes or click the Text Attributes tool, which is located at the bottom of the toolbox on the left side of the desktop:

The Text Attributes dialog box will open, as shown in Figure 8.10.

When you click on the Color box, the Text Color dialog box will open, showing color selections from the current palette. Click a color to select it, then select OK to close the Text Attributes dialog box.

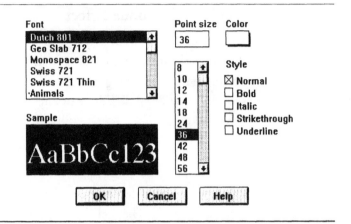

FIGURE 8.10

In the Slide Editor, you can change the appearance of a selected text object using the Text Attributes dialog box.

In Harvard Graphics Version 1, chart color 4 is normally assigned to Text and color 6 to Text Dim, or subdued text. A special text highlight is color 5, Text High. If you stick to these color numbers when creating a build-and-subdue sequence, the text colors in your slides will be coordinated correctly even if you change color palettes.

Generating Topic Slides from Lists (Slide Summaries)

Harvard Graphics can create a sequence of slides that you might consider the opposite of a build-up: A *slide summary* is a sequence of slides with the title of each having been generated from the subtopics in a master list slide, or *parent*.

Start by creating the parent slide (in the Outliner or in the Slide Editor). It might be a list of the main topics to be covered later in your presentation, as shown in Figure 8.11. Then make sure the pointer is on this entry and do Outline ➤ Make Slide Summary.

FIGURE 8.11

A set of summary slides can be generated automatically from a master list like this one.

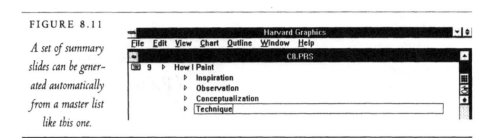

The result of the command in the Outliner is shown in Figure 8.12. One new *child* slide has been generated for each subtopic of the original list, each with the subtopic as its title under which another list can be entered.

FIGURE 8.12

Here's the result of creating a slide summary.

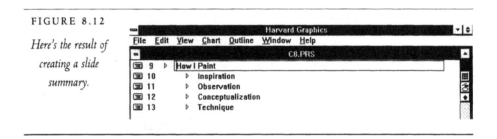

Notice in the figure that the parent entry in the Outliner no longer includes the list items, which have become the Title field entries of the new slides. However, the Slide Editor view of the parent slide has the complete list, as shown in Figure 8.13.

 OTE *The slides within a summary sequence are linked and can only be manipulated (for example, edited, moved within a presentation, or deleted) as a group. If you edit the text of a subtopic (bullet item) in the parent, the corresponding title of the child slide will be changed also.*

FIGURE 8.13

The Slide Editor view of the parent slide of a slide summary shows all the items in the original list, even though they do not appear in the parent entry in the Outliner.

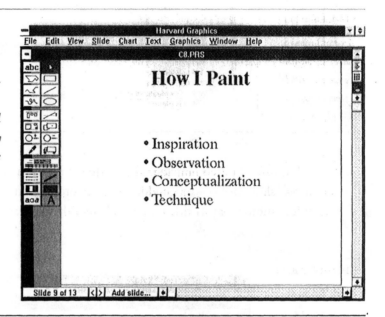

Creating a Harvard Graphics ScreenShow

If you have created a presentation or sequence of slides in Harvard Graphics, you already have everything you need to run a ScreenShow. With the presentation file open, simply do File ➤ ScreenShow ➤ From Beginning (or press Ctrl-F2). The first slide in the presentation will appear in full-screen mode. Click the *right* mouse button or press any key (except Esc) to advance to the next slide. When the last slide in the presentation file has been displayed, you will be returned to the view from which you started the show.

The order of slides in the show can be rearranged in the Slide Sorter. To move a slide to another position in the sequence, click its icon in the Slide Sorter to select it and drag it to the new position.

Adding Transition Effects

The actions and patterns with which a slide is "painted" onto the screen in a ScreenShow can be varied. To change the transitions, do File ➤ Screen-Show ➤ Edit ScreenShow Effects. The Edit ScreenShow Effects dialog box will appear, as shown in Figure 8.14.

The titles of the slides in the current presentation file are listed in numbered show order in the Slide List box. You can select a slide in the list for a custom effect, or select Default Transition Effect to change the effects for all slides in the show.

The Draw effect is used to bring the slide onto the screen; the Erase effect is used to remove it. (To see the results of these options, try resetting them and running your show.)

For text slides, use transition effects that match the direction in which the eye will read the words. For example, to introduce a list, you might use Blinds Down; to remove it, Blinds Up. If the list is a build-and-subdue sequence, use Fade and Fade Down. For a single-line title that the eye scans from left to right, consider Wipe Right to introduce it and Wipe Left to remove it.

FIGURE 8.14

Edit transition effects in this dialog box.

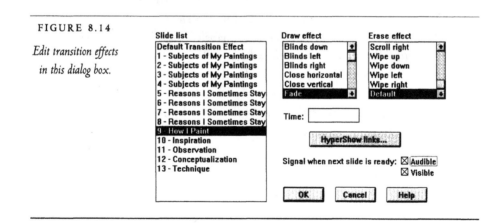

If you make no selections for transition effects, the Draw setting for Default Transition Effect (applied to all slides) is Replace with the Erase setting None, which causes a new slide to pop onto the screen, replacing the previous one.

If you type an entry from 0–9:59 (minutes:seconds) in the Time box, the show will automatically advance to the next slide after this length of time has elapsed. A setting of 0 will make the show advance as fast as possible.

Planning Any Delays?

There will always be some delay between slides in a screen show for the time required to load video memory (the display buffer) with the next image. The more complex the image, the more time it may require to load. Slides that contain bitmaps and gradient (shaded) backgrounds will take the longest. Take this time into account when you are setting the slide duration for an automatic show. Remember that any delay will be *in addition to* the duration you enter in the Time box. If you don't allow for this, the show might run slower than you expect.

If the show will be run manually (requiring a mouse click or key press to advance the slide), you can make things easier for the operator by marking one or both of the check boxes labeled Signal When Next Slide Is Ready. If you mark Audible, a beep will sound when the next image is loaded and ready. If you mark Visible, a small arrow will appear in the bottom right corner of the screen.

The delay between slides can be eliminated by using a special *double-buffered* (dual-memory) video controller in the computer.

Adding Special Effects to Text

The following special effects can be added to any text object in the Slide Editor of Harvard Graphics:

- Rotation

- Frame

- Drop shadow

- Sweep

Text can be created either by typing entries into a chart Data Form window or by using the Text tool to create a free-form text object.

To use the Text tool to create a free-form text object, click on the tool, drag to create a box that will contain the text, type the text, then click outside the box to accept the entry and close the box.

Rotating Text

To rotate text in Harvard Graphics, select the text object by clicking on it. Handles (small squares) should surround the object. Then do Graphics ➤ Rotate or click the Rotate tool:

Drag the rotation pointer to a new location.

 *Only the following Bitstream Speedo fonts supplied with Harvard Graphics Version 1 can be rotated: Dutch 801, Geo Slab 712, Monospace 821, Swiss 721, and Swiss 721 Thin. Text in other fonts, including TrueType and Adobe PostScript Type 1, can be rotated, but the rotated text will be rendered in one of the above bitmap fonts.*

269

Adding Frames, Drop Shadows, or Sweeps

To add any of the other special effects to text, select the text object by clicking on it, then do Graphics ➤ Special Effects. The Special Effects dialog box will appear, as shown in Figure 8.15.

Your selection from the Effect drop-down box will determine the other options displayed in the Special Effects dialog box. Choose Frame, Drop Shadow, or Sweep (or None to remove a previously created effect).

FIGURE 8.15

Settings in this box can add visual impact to text in ScreenShows.

How I Paint

Effect: Drop shadow

Color:

Transparency:

OK   Cancel   Help

Frame

For a *frame*, or box surrounding the text, you can specify its Color (for the fill inside the rectangular frame), Transparency (degree to which the background shows through the frame), Size (of the rectangle), and 3D Frame (dimensional effect on the edges of the rectangle). Here's an example of a 3D frame:

How I Paint

Drop Shadow

For a drop-shadow effect, you can specify the Color of the shadow (a second instance of the text just behind the first) and its Transparency. You can also adjust the position or offset of the shadow by dragging it in the sample box:

A drop shadow can improve the readability of text, particularly if the text color does not contrast well with the background color or the object over which the text is placed as a label.

Sweeps

A sweep is also called a *multiple drop shadow* because it can generate many over-lapping instances of a single text object:

271

The Sweep options are shown in the dialog box in Figure 8.16. The Rotation option, which can be Right or Left with respect to the original text object, can be adjusted in degrees by dragging the pointer on the circular indicator on the left.

You can also adjust the sweep by dragging the object in the sample box. If you do this, the Sweep Direction option is set to Custom.

FIGURE 8.16

Options for a Sweep effect include the number of steps (or instances) and the amount and direction of rotation.

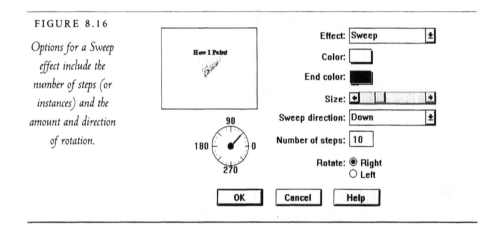

Sweeping Tips

Note particularly the Number Of Steps option for sweeps. Increasing the number of steps of the text object will make a smoother effect. However, a large number of steps can greatly increase the complexity of the slide and the delay before it appears in a ScreenShow.

You can produce a nice animated effect using a sweep in a ScreenShow. Precede the slide with the sweep by a slide with the same blank background, then use Overlay as the Draw effect. The sweep will be painted over the background, one step at a time.

And Now for Some Technical Stuff

Keep these technical considerations in mind when you are designing a screen show, whether in Harvard Graphics or in another Windows graphics application:

Viewing distance and text size Whether the show will be viewed on a monitor or projected on a wall screen, a typical viewing distance is at least *four times the height of the screen*. Therefore, don't use text smaller than can be read comfortably at this distance.

Color palettes Avoid large areas of white as a background. In general, use dark backgrounds with light-colored text for screen shows. Adjust these colors for the typical lighting conditions in the room. The more brightly the room is lit, the lighter the background color must be. In a highly lit room, you might need to use a light-colored background with dark text.

Standalone operation The procedures in this chapter for creating a ScreenShow require running Harvard Graphics Version 1 for Windows during the show. To create a show that will run on DOS machines that do not have Harvard Graphics installed, you must export the presentation file to a DOS format, then use the ScreenShow Projector utility (a separate program available from Software Publishing Corporation) to create a self-running (or *standalone*) show file. These standalone show files are specific to each type of video controller. You will need separate show files for VGA and for EGA monitors. (In Freelance Graphics Release 2 for Windows, the command for creating a standalone screen show is View ➤ Screen Show ➤ Prepare Standalone. You must select VGA or EGA format for the output file.)

Interactive show In Harvard Graphics, any object, including text, can be assigned the Button attribute by the Graphics ➤ Button Attributes command. When the operator of a show clicks a button object, the show sequence goes to the Destination specified when the button was created. By including buttons in a ScreenShow, you can create an interactive show (called a *HyperShow* in Harvard Graphics). In general, it is better to create an object that looks like a pushbutton control (such as a dimensional square with a text label) than to simply assign the Button attribute to a text object. Otherwise, the operator of the show might not know exactly where to click to activate the choice.

That's the short and sweet of producing business presentations that will be viewed on a computer screen. If your output medium will be something different, such as videotape or color slide film, be sure to review the tips in the next two chapters.

CHAPTER 9

Generating
Video Titles

or

Play One on TV!

ITH THE ADVENT of multimedia technology, inside your PC you can have all the tools you need to be a television producer. This chapter deals mainly with the technical requirements of the video medium as they affect titles that you create with Windows applications.

The procedures for creating title and list screens, including build-up sequences, are covered in the previous chapter, using Harvard Graphics for the application examples. My suggestion of visualizing the structure of your presentation should be just as useful whether the presentation will be shown on the computer screen, on videotape, or on a wall screen as projected slides. You can use the same basic design techniques in Chapter 8 for creating titles and lists that will be shown on television.

To keep things simple, I use the term television *in this chapter to mean any form of analog video, such as VHF and UHF broadcast television, commercial cable television, and closed circuit television (CCTV), as well as analog video recording on tape or disk. The term* video *can encompass these media, as well as computer-generated graphics and other forms of digital and digitized video.*

Special Requirements for Video

In some key respects, computer video and television are very different media. The main differences lie in

- Screen aspect ratio
- Resolution
- Signal format
- Color quality
- Video noise
- Video safe areas
- Minimum text size

Screen Aspect Ratio

The width of the screen divided by its height is its *aspect ratio*. For a computer display, these dimensions are measured in square *pixels*, or picture elements. A standard VGA display measures 640 pixels wide by 480 pixels high. Its aspect ratio is therefore 640:480, or 1.3333:1.

The aspect ratio of a television screen (of any size) is the same—1.3333:1—so, from the standpoint of screen dimensions, the two media, computers and television, would seem to be perfectly compatible. But take a look at your computer screen (with the machine turned on, please). Notice that the image does not fill the screen: There's a black border all around, and the corners of the image are sharp right angles. (See Figure 9.1.) On a television or broadcast video monitor, the image fills the entire screen, and the corners are rounded.

Comparing the screens in Figure 9.1, you might conclude that the television image is slightly larger than the same one on the computer because

FIGURE 9.1

*Comparison of
computer and
television screens*

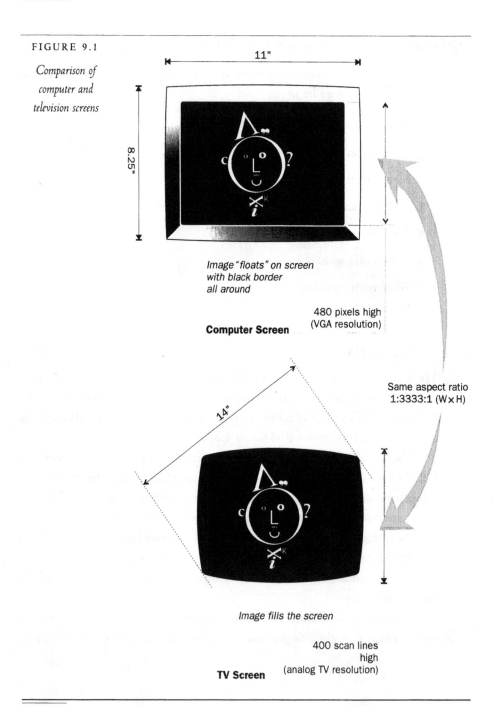

11"

8.25"

Image "floats" on screen
with black border
all around

Computer Screen

480 pixels high
(VGA resolution)

Same aspect ratio
1:3333:1 (W × H)

14"

Image fills the screen

400 scan lines
high
(analog TV resolution)

TV Screen

its screen is completely filled. That's true, but other factors make that image *less sharp* than the one you see on the computer monitor.

Remember that a television picture will usually look fuzzier than a computer graphic, depending on viewing distance. On screens of the same size viewed at the same distance, the television image will be both larger, filling the screen, and less sharp—both because there are fewer scan lines and because the scanning must cover a larger area. Since today's television screens are generally larger than computer screens, the fuzziness will be even more apparent. (For video projection, don't use television technology, if you can avoid it. Instead, use a high-resolution computer video projector, as described below.)

Resolution

In computer terms, screen resolution is the number of pixels that can be displayed. Again, a standard VGA display has 640 × 480 pixels. Some other display devices and monitors can produce 800 × 600 or 1024 × 768. However, the resolution of videotape is lower than any of these, and broadcast television is lower yet.

In technical terms, the height and width in pixels of a computer display is its spatial resolution, or image sharpness. Another factor is its chromatic resolution, or the number of colors it can reproduce. For example, a standard VGA display can show 16 colors; Super VGA can show 256. Although color television has less spatial resolution than computer displays, its chromatic resolution is theoretically better because analog television signals can show a continuous variation—hence, a finer blending—of colors. However, in practice, television color can look "washed out" by comparison with computer colors because the signal can lose quality in the processes of analog recording and broadcast.

Here's a basic difference: Computer video is digital and television is analog. Computer pictures are arrays of discrete dots, or pixels. Television pictures are composed of a series of horizontal *scan lines*, and the variations in color along a scan line are less well defined: If you think of a pixel as a nice, neat dot, an analog color burst on a video scan line is more of a smudge.

All these factors considered, the most direct comparison between the resolution of a computer display and a television picture is to compare the pixel height of the computer screen with the number of scan lines on the television. An analog video recording has just over 400 scan lines, so the image is considerably less sharp than standard VGA (480 pixels high). By the time a television signal has been broadcast over a cable or as radio-frequency waves to reach a home receiver, the picture can become so fuzzy that it appears to have about 335 lines, less than 70 percent of the resolution of the computer image.

 *You can improve the quality of computer-generated color on television by upgrading your computer display to greater chromatic resolution (from 16 to 256 colors, for example). However, upgrading the spatial resolution will do no good at all. No matter how sharp the original image, the final television picture will still have only about 400 scan lines, much fewer than even standard VGA.*

Signal Format

If you aspire to produce TV on your PC, you won't be able to connect the computer directly to an analog video recorder (such as a VCR) without a piece of extra equipment called a *video encoder*. Computers, as well as television cameras and monitors, handle color as separate red (R), green (G), and blue (B) components. A fourth component, synchronization pulses (or *Sync*) is required to generate RGB video. On some RGB devices, Sync is a separate signal; on others, Sync is combined with the G component.

In North America, video signals for recording or broadcast must be translated into a format called *NTSC* (an abbreviation for the National Television System Committee, which set the rules for color television in the early 1950s). The three components of NTSC signals are I, Q, and Y. The I and Q components (called *chrominance*) contain color information, and the Y signal (*luminance*) is monochrome, or information about light and dark areas of the picture. The purpose of the NTSC standard was originally to make color broadcast signals compatible with existing black-and-white television sets, which use only the Y component. The output of an NTSC encoder is one video line (or signal wire) in which I, Q, and Y have been encoded in a single *composite video* signal.

The process of converting computer video into television is diagrammed in Figure 9.2.

Similar, but not directly compatible, standards were developed for recording and broadcast in the United Kingdom (the PAL standard) and in France (SECAM).

Some computer video interface boards have built-in NTSC encoders so that composite video can be fed directly from a connector on the back of the computer to the video input jack of a VCR. One manufacturer of RGB/NTSC video cards is Willow Peripherals. You can reach them at the following address:

Willow Peripherals

A Division of A.B.V. Electronics, Ltd.

190 Willow Avenue

Bronx, NY 10454

800 444-1585

FIGURE 9.2

*Conversion of com-
puter RGB signals to
composite video*

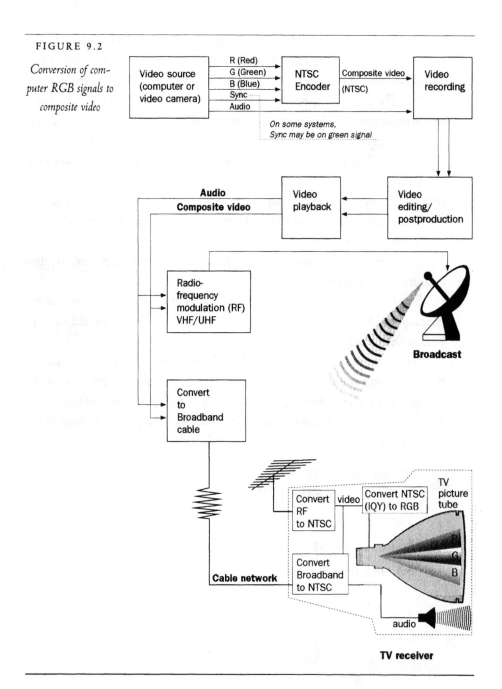

Try to avoid using an NTSC video projector for wall-sized computer displays. If the projector has both RGB and NTSC inputs, connect the three (or four if Sync is separate) monitor outputs on the computer to the RGB inputs on the projector. This way, you won't need an encoder at all. Ideally, use a high-resolution video projector that can accept RGB input from a video card that generates at least 1024 × 768 pixels.

Color Quality

You will also notice some difference in color between the computer image and the television picture. The television colors will appear less vivid because the color gets degraded by the NTSC encoding process. The picture starts out as RGB, gets translated to IQY, then must be translated *back* to RGB inside the television. The R, G, and B signals are then sent to three electron guns that paint red-, green-, and blue-glowing phosphors. These phosphors, which form a coating of dots on the inside of the picture tube, are caused to glow by the scanning beam of electrons from the gun.

If the signal is transmitted over a commercial cable network or broadcast as radio-frequency waves by a television station, the degradation of the signal in both resolution and color is even more pronounced.

Don't try to compensate for the washed-out colors on television by using more intense computer colors. The result will be more video noise, as explained in the following section.

Video Noise

To make matters worse, television sets are not designed to reproduce the intense, solid colors of computer-generated graphics. Television was designed primarily to carry pictures of live scenes, in which there are usually very many tiny areas of color, in a wide variety of hues and shades—but within a scene that is constantly changing and moving.

Again, think of those analog color bursts on a television scan line as smudges. That's a fine way to paint live scenes, especially scenes that are always moving, because the resolution doesn't have to be sharp. (Nothing stands still long enough for you to notice.) However, computer-generated graphics have none of these virtues. The colors are bright and comparatively pure, with no variations within relatively large areas of the screen.

Bright computer colors create problems for television sets, particularly at the edges of text characters and graphic objects. At any edge, such as the boundary between the background color and a bright object, there is an abrupt transition in contrast, from dark to light or from light to dark. There aren't these kinds of abrupt changes in most live scenes. The transitions are blended, partly by the analog process in the television camera that recorded the scene.

The circuits of most analog televisions can't handle edges or abrupt changes in contrast very well. The result is one kind of *video noise*, which shows up as a shimmering or vibrating effect around the object or text.

Two different approaches to reducing video noise are diagrammed in Figures 9.3 and 9.4.

FIGURE 9.3

Drop shadow and outline effects can reduce video noise by softening the transitions at edges.

Solutions for Video Noise

There are several remedies to the "creepy crawlies" that are produced by video noise on television screens:

Use less-saturated colors If your graphics application permits you to mix colors by *hue, saturation,* and *value,* or HSV, (the third component might be called *brightness (HSB)* or *luminance (HSL)*), keep the saturation value to 80 percent of maximum, particularly for the background and for other large areas of color. (HSV, HSB, and HSL are equivalent terms for the same color mixing scheme, which follows the *Munsell color model.* By this scheme, most people find it easier to match colors by eye, making separate adjustments in H, S, and V (or B), than to adjust red, green, and blue in the RGB model. For example, HSV mixing is supported in Harvard Graphics, HSB in CorelDRAW.)

Use drop shadows or outlines at edges For text, you can create an intermediate transition from the background by adding a drop shadow or an outline, the color of which lies between the background and the text face color. The scan proceeds from left to right, so the noise is most noticeable at the left edge of a character or object. You can remedy this by putting the drop shadow on the left side of the text, not on the right as is usually done, or by adding an outline that entirely surrounds the text. (See Figure 9.3.)

Insert comb filters Noise can also be diminished in video post-production, or after the image is generated but before it is recorded on tape or transmitted. As shown in Figure 9.4, a piece of special video noise-reduction equipment called a *comb filter* can be inserted between the RGB source and the encoder. (Some encoder models incorporate comb filters in their designs.)

FIGURE 9.4

Noise can sometimes be reduced electronically by inserting comb filters in each RGB input line to the encoder.

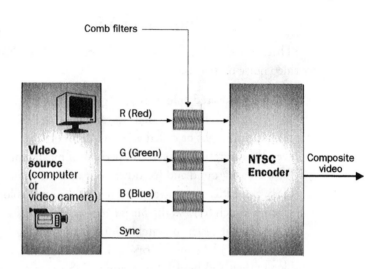

Another undesirable effect from video noise is called the *moiré effect*, which is a shimmering or vibrating appearance when two dissimilar patterns overlap. The television screen's scanning produces a horizontal pattern, so any pattern that is not strictly horizontal or vertical in an image can create the moiré effect. This is one reason you don't see more television announcers dressed in plaid! Such interference can be caused by any bold diagonal lines in the image.

To prevent the moiré effect in television pictures, avoid backgrounds and object fills that contain patterns, hatches, or gradients (blended-color bitmaps). Now, I know that you see bold text graphics and patterned backgrounds on television. How do they get away with it? The character generators *that produce these graphics are specially designed to compensate for the noise problems in analog video. There are no such features built into the typical PC.*

Video Safe Areas

The Society of Motion Picture and Television Engineers (SMPTE) has published recommendations for the format and dimension of television pictures, including graphics. The format and dimensions were used to construct the video *test pattern* shown in Figure 9.5.

The test pattern defines the *safe action area* in which "significant action," (including graphic objects) should be confined. The recommended area for text is bounded by the *safe title area*.

The safe action area is the center 90 percent of the screen. Typically, the size of a television screen is given as its diagonal measurement (the distance between opposite corners of the picture area). So, a 14-inch screen is about 11 inches wide by 8.25 inches high. The safe action area on this screen would be 90 percent of each dimension, or 9.9 × 7.425 inches.

FIGURE 9.5

SMPTE test pattern for video screens (Copyright © 1989 by the Society of Motion Picture and Television Engineers. Reproduced with permission.)

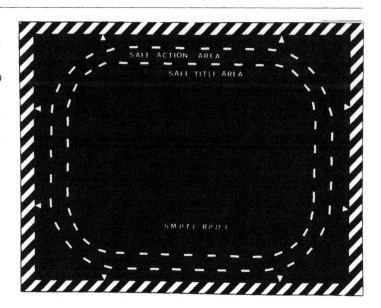

The safe title area is the center 80 percent of the screen. On the same 14-inch screen, the dimensions within which text must be composed would be 8.8 × 6.6 inches.

The corners of both safe areas are rounded to allow for the rounded shapes of older television picture tubes.

The SMPTE Recommended Practice described here is contained in document RP 27.3-1989, "Specifications for Safe Action and Safe Title Areas Test Pattern for Television Systems." It is available from the following address:

Society of Motion Picture and Television Engineers

595 West Hartsdale Avenue

White Plains, NY 10607

914 761-1100

Minimum Text Size

According to the SMPTE Recommended Practice, the height of characters used in titles should be at least 2.5 percent of the height of the screen. The height of a 14-inch screen is 8.25 inches, or 594 points (72 points per inch). So, the characters should be at least 2.5 percent of 594 points, or 14.85 points tall. However, remember that this measurement is *not* the type point size. The point size of a font is measured from the bottom of a lowercase descender to the top of an ascender, as shown in Figure 9.6. But the specification here is for the minimum height of any letter, such as a lowercase *a*. The actual point size of a font for which the lowercase *a* is about 14 points tall would be about 20–24 points, depending on the design of the font.

FIGURE 9.6

Don't confuse the minimum height of characters with the point size of the font.

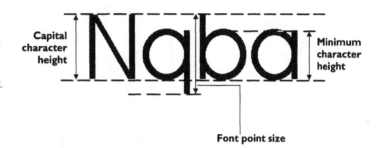

Capital character height

Minimum character height

Font point size

IP *You don't have to worry about variations in screen sizes. If you compose graphics to correct measurements for your computer display, allowing for safe action and safe title areas as well as minimum letter height, these elements will always be in the correct ratio. See the example below for creating television graphics in CorelDRAW.*

Creating Television Graphics in CorelDRAW

Here's how to put these tips into practice when creating graphics for television in CorelDRAW Release 4 for Windows. (The procedures in other graphics applications for Windows will be much the same.)

Setting the Image Size and Background Color

The first step is to set up the correct orientation and boundaries of the image area. After starting CorelDRAW, do Layout ➤ Page Setup. The Page Setup dialog box will appear, as shown in Figure 9.7.

FIGURE 9.7

Set up a custom page
that has the physical
dimensions of the tele-
vision screen.

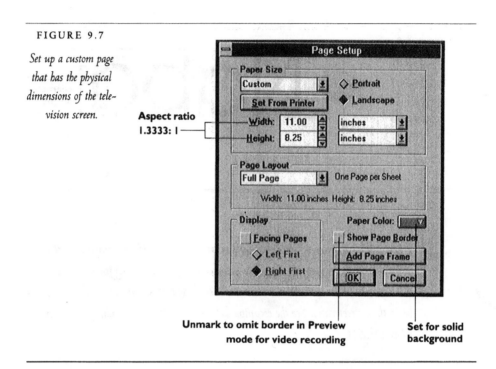

Aspect ratio
1.3333: 1

Unmark to omit border in Preview
mode for video recording

Set for solid
background

For the Paper Size option, select Custom. For orientation, select Landscape. The actual dimensions of the page are less important than the aspect
ratio, or ratio of width to height, which must be 1:3333:1. You can leave
the Width set to 11 (the default for letter-sized paper) and reduce the
Height setting from 8.5 to 8.25. (You will have to type the value into the text
box; the numeric incrementor buttons adjust the setting by 0.10 increments only.)

To specify a solid background color in CorelDRAW, you can set the
Paper Color option in the Page Setup dialog box. Click this option, then select a color from the menu that pops up.

Remember that colors should not exceed 80 percent saturation, whether for background or for titles. To mix a color, click the More button in the pop-up menu:

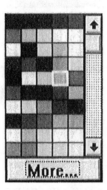

The Paper Color dialog box will appear, as shown in Figure 9.8. In the Show drop-down box, select the HSB Color Model option. There are two ways of adjusting the color here:

- Type numeric values for Hue (0–359), Saturation (normally 0–100, but do not exceed 80), and Brightness (0–100).

- Drag the small, square indicator in the color wheel counter-clockwise to increase or clockwise to decrease the Hue, from 0 (3 o'clock position on the wheel) to 359 degrees. Drag the same indicator outward from the center of the wheel to increase or toward the center to decrease the Saturation value. Watch the numeric indicator on the right to make sure it does not exceed 80 for video graphics. Drag the indicator in the vertical slider on the right up to increase or down to decrease the Brightness value.

After mixing the background color, select OK to close the Paper Color dialog box, then OK again to close the Page Setup dialog box. (Be sure the Show Page Border check box is unmarked to prevent the border from appearing on composite video output.)

FIGURE 9.8

You can mix a color in this dialog box by the HSB method to prevent oversaturation of video graphics.

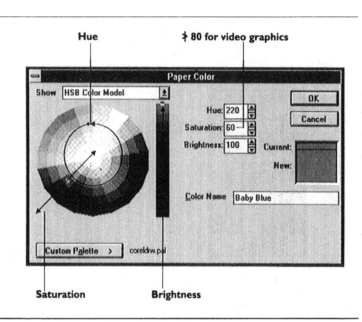

Marking the Safe Title Area

As a guide for composing text screens, you should mark the safe title area within the image size you have set. In CorelDRAW, the safe title area (and safe action area also, if you wish) can be marked by dotted horizontal and vertical lines called *guidelines*. Guidelines appear in the drawing area but not on screen previews or on printouts.

To mark the guidelines, do Layout ➤ Guidelines Setup. The Guidelines dialog box will appear, as shown in Figure 9.9.

The safe title area requires four guidelines. Specify a guideline by distances (in inches, in this case) as follows: For the two horizontal lines, enter the distances vertically from the lower left corner of the page border. For two vertical lines, enter the distances from the right of the same corner.

To mark a guideline, select Horizontal or Vertical for the Guideline type, enter a numeric value for its position in the Ruler Position text box,

FIGURE 9.9

Specify four guide-lines in this dialog box to mark the boundaries of the video safe title area.

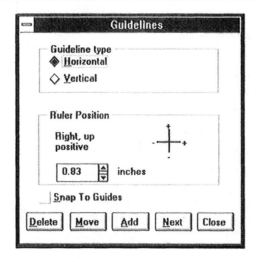

then select Add. Repeat the command three more times for the other three guidelines. Assuming that you've set a page size of 11 × 8.25 inches, the Guideline Type and Ruler Position Settings for the video safe title area are shown in the diagram in Figure 9.10.

Click the Zoom tool, then the Full Page option (rightmost icon) to see the whole page displayed with the guidelines in the drawing area, as it is shown in Figure 9.11.

Composing Text

In CorelDRAW, you can compose the text for video screens as either Artistic or Paragraph text. Use Artistic text, which can be kerned, for headlines and logos. Use Paragraph text for bulleted lists.

FIGURE 9.10

Guidelines must be specified by distances from the lower left corner of the image area (page border).

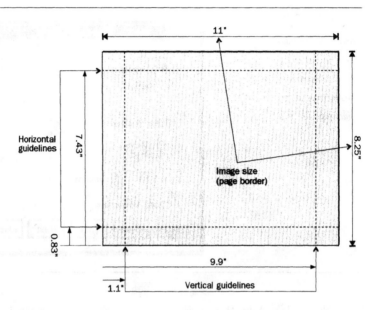

In general, sans serif faces will work better for video graphics. The relatively low resolution and tendency for noise in analog video argue against using serifs and unusual display fonts for anything other than logos.

 *For details on creating Artistic and Paragraph text objects in CorelDRAW, see Chapter 2, particularly the tips on adding drop shadows and floating drop shadows.*

Remember that to prevent video noise, the colors of text and other objects you create should not exceed 80 percent saturation. To mix the color of an object, select it, then select the color wheel icon from the Fill tool menu:

FIGURE 9.11

This full-page view of television graphic shows horizontal and vertical guidelines for the safe title area.

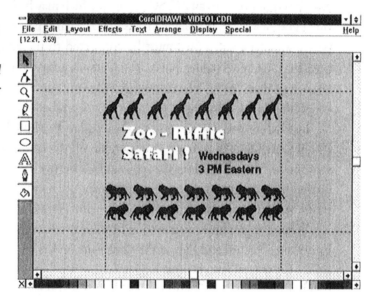

The Uniform Fill dialog box will appear. (Its options and controls are the same as the Paper Color dialog box; refer back to Figure 9.8.) Use the HSB Color Model option and make sure that the Saturation value is not greater than 80 percent.

Recording Graphics on Video

When you've finished composing your video graphic, save your work to a CorelDRAW drawing file by doing File ➤ Save and naming the .CDR file. If you will be doing more text screens, it will be handy to save the layout (along with the safe-title-area guidelines and your custom color selections) as a template. Do File ➤ Save As and choose CorelDRAW Template (.CDT) as the file type. You can then create drawings from this template by doing File ➤ New From Template and selecting the template file name.

To make an analog video recording of your graphic, your computer must be equipped with an NTSC encoder, which may be integrated with the video graphics card. If the encoder is an external type, the RGB output of your computer's video card must be connected to the RGB inputs on the encoder. (Again, to reduce noise, it may be necessary to insert comb filters on each of these lines.) The composite video output of the encoder must be connected to the video input jack on the video recorder.

Just before you start recording, do Display ➤ Show Preview (or press F9) in CorelDRAW to make your graphic fill the computer screen in Preview mode. You will still see the typical black border surrounding the image on the computer monitor, but the encoder should remove it so that the composite video image completely fills a television screen.

When the graphic is displayed in Preview mode, start recording (usually by pressing Record and Play at the same time on the recorder). Run the recorder for at least five seconds longer than you will want the graphic to appear in the finished production—even longer if you will use transitions such as dissolves before or after it. You need extra time at the beginning of the recording for the correct videotape speed to be reached, with some additional time at the head and tail (front and back of the recorded segment) for proper cueing during editing and to allow for transition effects.

For professional-quality results, record your graphics on a 1-inch Type C video recorder. This is the same tape format used in most professional video editing facilities. The $^3/_4$-inch U–matic and $^1/_2$-inch VHS formats in particular can be noisy when used for mastering video graphics.

To display a sequence of text screens, you can combine a series of .CDR files in a show (.SHW) file using the CorelSHOW application. You can then record the show on videotape as it runs. However, you will not be able to overcome the delays discussed in Chapter 8 that represent the time

Technology Watch!

Some multimedia PCs are equipped to handle digital video. However, the memory and disk-storage requirements are very high—something like 3 MB for each *second* of video running time. Video compression technology will no doubt reduce this requirement in the future, and high-density storage on magneto-optical or optical devices will make recording and playback on the PC more practical.

Also on the horizon is *high-definition television (HDTV)*, which has a resolution higher than Super VGA. Although standards for recording and producing HDTV have been established, at the time this book was written various competing methods of encoding it for broadcast to both existing and advanced television sets were still under review by the Federal Communications Commission. (Existing low-resolution sets would only process half the picture information, rather like receiving only one channel of a stereo radio broadcast.)

HDTV holds the prospect of merging digital computer and television technologies in single high-resolution video format. Aspect ratios and safe title areas for HDTV will be different from those for conventional TV.

required to load the next screen into the video memory of your computer (unless you have a video card that does double buffering). You will usually get better results if you record each graphic separately on videotape and then edit them together in video postproduction.

CHAPTER 10

Producing
Color Slides
and Transparencies

or

Breaking into

Film

HIS CHAPTER DESCRIBES how you can get your snazzy, computer-generated graphics output on color photographic film. You can create text screens in many Windows graphics applications, following more or less the same procedures outlined in Chapter 8 for designing screen shows. But as you might expect, the film medium has its own special, even downright picky, requirements when it comes to fonts, colors, aspect ratios, and so on. Images that look good on your computer screen won't necessarily look good (or even the same) on film. To understand why, you need a little background on digital film recording.

Computer Cameras and Film Recorders

There are two basic types of computer peripherals that produce color film output: the dumb kind and the smart kind (speaking only of the complexity of their electronics).

Computer Cameras

The dumb kind are called *computer cameras*. These are connected directly to the monitor output (RGB color signals) of the video card in your computer. As shown in Figure 10.1, a computer camera is little more than a light-sealed

FIGURE 10.1

A peek inside a computer camera.

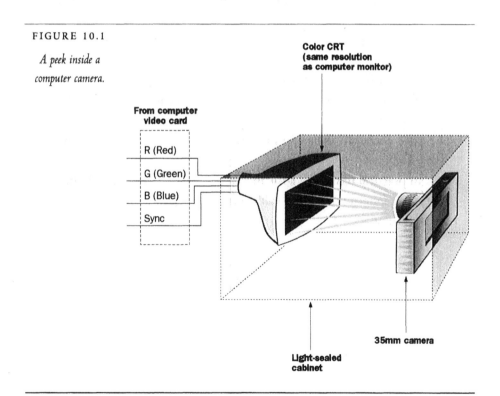

From computer video card

R (Red)
G (Green)
B (Blue)
Sync

Color CRT (same resolution as computer monitor)

35mm camera

Light-sealed cabinet

box (about the size of a shoe box) that contains a miniature color monitor aligned with a photographic camera (usually the 35mm variety). The color monitor in the computer camera is of the same type and has the same characteristics as the monitor of the average desktop PC, such as VGA. The image that the camera records is a close match to the computer display, with the same colors, fonts, and resolution. You would get a similar result by taking a timed exposure of your computer screen in a darkened room.

The virtue of computer cameras is that they are inexpensive. The drawbacks are poor color and fuzzy resolution.

Let's take resolution first. Since the computer camera has the same resolution as your desktop monitor, the sharpness of the photographic image falls far short of the best picture that the film can record. The resolution limit of 35mm color slide film, for example, is equivalent to about 2,000–3,000 horizontal scan lines.

The color problem actually arises from the fact that you're making a direct recording of the face of a color monitor. Color film (any brand from any manufacturer) is not directly compatible with computer RGB colors. The face of the monitor is a finely-deposited array of dots that glow red, green, and blue. But color film is coated with three layers of grainy, light-sensitive chemicals that, when processed, release colored dyes of magenta, blue, and cyan.

In practical terms, the basic incompatibilities between the monitor and the film can mean that a tan color on the computer screen looks more like pink on film.

Film Recorders

The smarter (and relatively more expensive) devices for producing color film output are called *film recorders*. In computer-whiz terminology, film recorders have *onboard intelligence* (their own private microprocessors and memories). Using a rough analogy to printers, a computer camera would be a dot-matrix—printing the graphics just the way you send them—and a film recorder would be a PostScript laser—translating instructions in a page-description language.

In Windows, all film recorders are set up as printers. Through a special printer driver, the recorder accepts instructions in high-level command language. Examples of high-level languages used with film recorders are color PostScript, Encapsulated PostScript, SCODL, and Binary Lasergraphics Language.

A so-called "intelligent" film recorder is connected to the computer by a parallel interface, such as Centronics or SCSI. However, since film recording is a big calculation job, the recorder often is connected to a separate workstation and accepts its inputs as files on diskette or as transmissions received over a network communications link.

As shown in Figure 10.2, inside the film recorder is a high-resolution black-and-white cathode ray tube (CRT), a type of video picture tube. The computer-generated image is built in three separate exposures while the film remains stationary in the camera. A color-filter wheel in front of the CRT is rotated to the corresponding red, green, or blue filter for each of the exposures.

The colors of the filters are designed to match closely the color-reproduction characteristics of the dyes in the color film. The *chromatic resolution* (or color depth) of these recorders is also very high. Most use 24-bit RGB

FIGURE 10.2

*What goes on inside
a film recorder.*

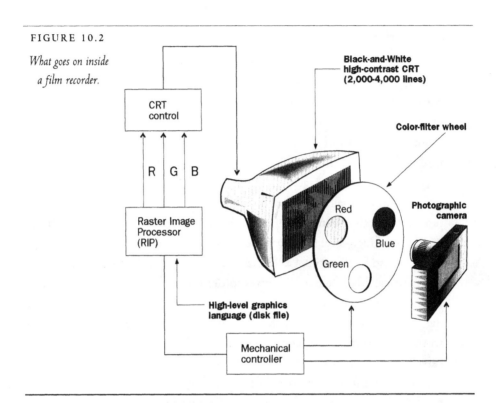

colors, for a palette of 16.7 million colors. You will be able to see these sub-tleties of color only on a computer monitor with a True Color video card. On other types of displays, including VGA and Super VGA, the intermediate colors will be dithered, the simulated colors composed of multicolored dot patterns. In practical terms, the color rendering of a film recorder is actually much better than can be produced on most PC monitors.

What's more, the black-and-white CRT is scanned at the rate of either 2,000 lines for 35mm film or 4,000 lines for 4" × 5" and 8" × 10" sheet film. These resolutions are close to the maximum amount of detail that the film can show, so the images are very sharp.

Film Recorders Are Not Printers

Two characteristics of film recorders make the procedures for using them different from those you would use to send output to a Windows printer:

❡ You don't print directly to a film recorder. Instead, you export the graphics file in its high-level language or print it to disk, specifying a file type that the recorder's *raster image processing* (RIP) software can accept.

❡ Although many film recorders can accept bitmaps as well as vector graphics, they are most efficient when fonts are processed as vectors. For this purpose, film recorders usually have their own resident hardware fonts, similar to the cartridge fonts that can be loaded into intelligent printers. These fonts might not always match the ones you've selected in the graphics application (more about this below).

Composing for Film Aspect Ratios

To make matters more complicated, the aspect ratios (width to height) of film formats differ from standard paper sizes and from the dimensions of the computer screen itself. Because Windows and its applications handle all output devices as printers, you usually must set the image area for slides and transparencies as a Paper Size setting in the application.

The aspect ratios of different media are shown in Figure 10.3. Notice particularly the difference between 35mm double-frame and 35mm motion picture (single-frame) formats. In photography of conventional color slides (sometimes called 2×2 slides because the mount measures 2" × 2"), film

FIGURE 10.3

*Aspect ratios for
different media*

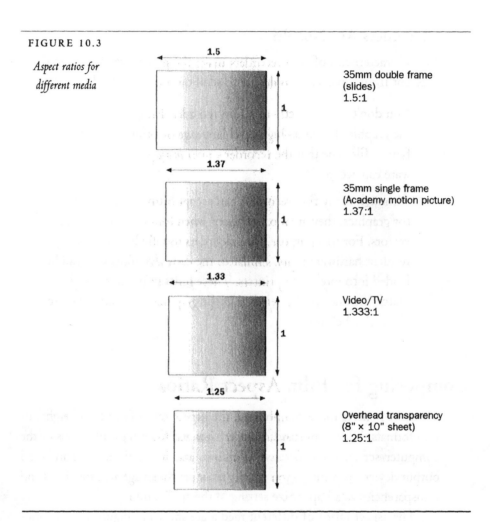

1.5

35mm double frame
(slides)
1.5:1

1

1.37

35mm single frame
(Academy motion picture)
1.37:1

1

1.33

Video/TV
1.333:1

1

1.25

Overhead transparency
(8" × 10" sheet)
1.25:1

1

passes through the camera horizontally. Each slide actually takes up the film area that would be used by two motion picture frames. (The film passes vertically through a motion picture camera.) Figure 10.4 shows how the two formats would look on the same strip of film.

In most Windows graphics applications, you must set the aspect ratio by the physical dimensions of a page, even if those are not the actual

FIGURE 10.4

Double-frame (slide)
and single-frame
(movie) 35mm
formats

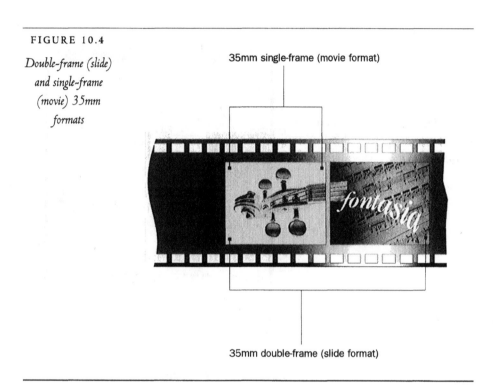

35mm single-frame (movie format)

35mm double-frame (slide format)

dimensions of the film on which the image will be recorded. For example, in CorelDRAW Release 4 for Windows, the command for setting up the page is Layout ➤ Page Setup. The Page Setup dialog box appears, as shown in Figure 10.5.

In CorelDRAW, as in some other Windows graphics applications, you have the Paper Size option Slide. Notice that when you select this option, the physical dimensions of the page are set automatically to 11 inches for width by 7.33 inches for height. The first dimension is the width of the image on a typical 14-inch (measured diagonally) computer screen. The ratio of 11:7.33 is 1.5:1, the correct aspect ratio for double-frame 35mm film.

FIGURE 10.5

*The image area must
be defined as a physi-
cal page size, even
though it is not the
actual dimensions of
the film output.*

Aspect ratio
1.5: 1

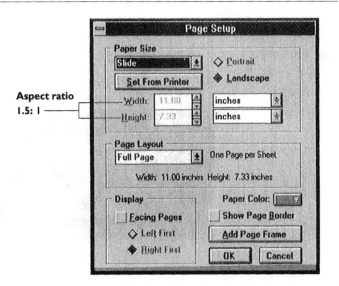

*As of Windows 3.1, the application can override any default printing options
that you set through the Windows Control Panel. Depending on the printer
driver you will be using to create the film recorder input file, the Page Setup
options might be the only settings you need to make. However, if you are using
the PostScript driver to create a file for Autographix, as described later in this
chapter, the Printer Setup option must be changed from the default Letter size
to Note, which also nominally measures 11" × 8.5" but defines a larger
printable area.*

If you are creating overhead transparencies, you would normally set the
Paper Size to 10 inches in width by 8 inches in height. The recommended
format for film recording is Landscape orientation.

Tips on Color Selection

For any projected media, including slides, overhead transparencies, or even video on a wall screen, the lighting conditions in the meeting room should be a key factor in your selection of colors. For example, bright room lights tend to decrease the apparent brightness of colors on the screen. In the HSB color model, turning up the room lights has the effect of reducing the B component. (There's more on HSB in Chapter 9.) So, in a bright room, a slide's royal blue background might appear black. Drop shadows tend to disappear unless they contrast well with both the background and the face color of the text.

The purpose of a presentation can determine both the amount of room light and the projection medium. For example, in a training session at which participants are expected to take notes, the room should be well lit. In a more formal presentation, you want all attention focused on the screen, so the room should be dark.

Referring to the HSB color model in CorelDRAW, here are some general rules for color selection:

- In a dark room, use dark backgrounds (B < 50) with light text (B > 80).

- In a bright room, use light backgrounds (B > 80) with dark text (B < 50).

- For build-and-subdue sequences on slides, the subdued (dim) color can be the same H and S values as the background, with the B value 30 units higher. (Do not use build-and-subdue sequences with overhead transparencies. Use a *slip card* instead to physically cover the items on the list you wish to hide, sliding the card downward to reveal them one at a time. This avoids needless juggling of transparencies.)

❡ Reduce the saturation of all colors if you are recording graphics on videotape or as slide masters for duplication (S < 80). Remember that the contrast (relative brightness between light and dark areas) will be increased by the process of copying a slide.

Submitting Files to a Slide Service

Many Windows graphics applications include software for creating files for film recording and for submitting them to an outside service. For example, Harvard Graphics, Freelance Graphics, and CorelDRAW are among the applications that come with software for submitting files to the Autographix Overnight Slide Service. Microsoft PowerPoint includes software for submitting files to Genigraphics service centers.

I'll describe here the procedures for creating film recorder files and submitting them to Autographix from CorelDRAW. The steps and guidelines are much the same for producing output from other Windows applications for many types of film recorders.

Adding the Printer Definition to the PostScript Driver

The preferred file format for submission to Autographix is color PostScript (.CPS). You can create such a file by using the Windows PostScript driver to print a file to disk. However, you must first configure the PostScript driver with a special Windows Printer Definition (.WPD) file supplied by Autographix.

The file name is AGX41.WPD, and it is supplied with applications that support Autographix output. The file must be copied to the WINDOWS\SYSTEM subdirectory. This file is normally copied automatically during installation of any Windows application that comes with Autographix support.

If the file is not present, you can install the PostScript driver and the printer definition file using the command Control Panel ➤ Printers. After installation, the following name will appear in the Installed Printers list:

```
Autographix 4.1 on <port>
```

Select the Connect button to reassign the port. The correct port selection is FILE, which configures the driver to print to disk. If you select FILE as the port, Windows will prompt you for a file name each time you request printing through this device. Other setup options for the PostScript driver for use with Autographix are given in Table 10.1.

APPLICATION	DIALOG BOX	OPTION NAME	OPTION SETTING
Control Panel	Printers ➤ Autographix ➤ Setup ➤ Options	Print To	Printer (if port is FILE)
Control Panel	Printers ➤ Autographix ➤ Setup ➤ Options	Margins	Default
Control Panel	Printers ➤ Autographix ➤ Setup ➤ Options	Scaling	100 percent
Control Panel	Printers ➤ Autographix ➤ Setup ➤ Options	Color	On
Control Panel	Printers ➤ Autographix ➤ Setup ➤ Options	Send Header with Each Job	On

TABLE 10.1: *Recommended Setup Options for the Autographix PostScript Printer Driver*

APPLICATION	DIALOG BOX	OPTION NAME	OPTION SETTING
Control Panel	Printer Setup Options (Advanced)	Halftone Frequency	60 (reset from 0)
Control Panel	Printer Setup Options (Advanced)	Halftone Angle	45 (reset from 0)
Control Panel	Printer Setup Options (Advanced)	TrueType Fonts Send to Printer As	Adobe Type 1
Control Panel	Printer Setup Options (Advanced)	Use Substitution Table	On (with defaults)
Control Panel	Printer Setup Options (Advanced)	Compress Bitmaps	On
Control Panel	Printer Setup Options (Advanced)	Print PostScript Error Information	On
Control Panel	Printer Setup Options (Advanced)	All other check boxes	Off
Corel	File ➤ Print Setup	Specific Printer	Autographix 4.1 on FILE
Corel	File ➤ Print Setup	Orientation	Landscape (recommended)
Corel	File ➤ Print Setup	Paper	Note (if Slide)
Corel	Layout ➤ Page Setup	Paper Size	Slide
Corel	File ➤ Print	Copies	1 (specify quantity in ToAGX Mix Instructions)

T A B L E 1 0 . 1 : *Recommended Setup Options for the Autographix PostScript Printer Driver (continued)*

Preparing to Print PostScript Files to Disk

A color PostScript print file can be created from any of the Corel applications. For example, to submit a single drawing, open a .CDR file in CorelDRAW and print it to disk. However, to submit a batch of drawings it will be more convenient to combine them in a show (.SHW) file in Corel-SHOW and initiate printing to disk with the file open in that application.

Harvard Graphics and Freelance Graphics do not use separate files for screen shows. The main file type is a presentation, which can contain a sequence of slides. In Harvard Graphics, the extension is .PRS; in Freelance Graphics, .PRE. To submit a sequence of slides to Autographix, print the presentation file to disk as described below.

Before issuing the print command, be sure that the Autographix driver is set up as the current printer by doing File ➤ Print Setup. If that driver is not selected, choose Specific Printer and select Autographix 4.1 On FILE. Assuming the printer setup options have been selected (refer back to Table 10.1), select OK to close the dialog box, and then OK again to close the Print Setup dialog box.

If you chose Slide as the paper size in the application, the Paper Size setting for the PostScript driver should be Note. If you composed an overhead transparency in the application with the paper size set to Letter, the printer driver should be set to Letter also.

Creating the Output File

With the graphics file open that you want to submit, initiate printing to disk with the File ➤ Print command, then choose OK. (It is not necessary to mark the Print To File check box if FILE was specified as the port when you set up the driver.) When prompted for the file name, type an optional

313

path and a name no longer than eight characters and *be sure to add the .CPS extension*, then choose OK.

Unless you preceded the file name with a path, it will be printed to the subdirectory COREL40\PROGRAMS. But it will be easier to find and work with these temporary print files if you create a separate directory for them. You should delete the files after you have received the processed slides. If you make changes to the graphics files in the application, you will have to create new print files, and you don't want to run the risk of using the outdated ones.

Submitting Files for Processing

The .CPS file you have created must be processed by the program ToAGX-Windows (Version 1.10), which is part of the Autographix software included with the application. (Some applications have a prior version called WinToAGX, which uses the printer driver AGX.WPD.)

To start ToAGX, do one of the following:

❡ Double-click the ToAGX icon in the application's program group.

Autographix
Slide Service

❡ In File Manager, double-click the name of a .CPS file you wish to submit.

❡ In File Manager, double-click the file name TOAGX.EXE, which in the Corel applications should be in the subdirectory COREL40\AGRAPHIX\TOAGX.

❡ In Program Manager, do File ➤ Run and then type the path and **TOAGX.EXE**, then choose OK.

The ToAGX-Windows application window will open, showing a listing of files, as shown in Figure 10.6. If the directory to which you wrote the .CPS files is not shown, do File ➤ Switch Directories, type a new path in the Directory Is box, and select OK.

If the file listing in ToAGX shows many different file extensions, start by doing File ➤ Switch File Type. Select Display PostScript Files (.CPS), then select OK. With this setting, only color PostScript files suitable for submission to the service will appear in file listings.

FIGURE 10.6

The ToAGX application window shows a listing of files that can be selected for film recording.

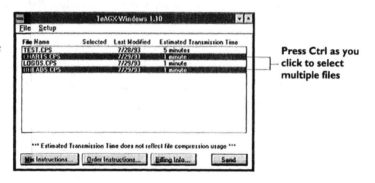

Press Ctrl as you click to select multiple files

From the list of files in the ToAGX window, click on the name of a .CPS file to be submitted. To select multiple files, hold down the Ctrl key as you click on each of them. After selecting the files, click on the Mix Instructions button.

The Autographix Mix Instructions dialog box will open, as shown in Figure 10.7. Type the number of copies you want of each type of output: 35mm slides, overhead transparencies, photographic color prints, and lasers (color laser photocopies). Other custom options, which vary by local service center, are numbered 1–3. Finish by selecting OK.

315

FIGURE 10.7

Specify the number of copies of each type of output.

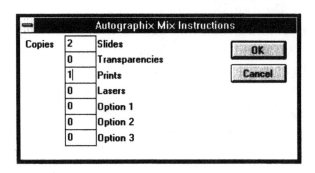

To specify different mix instructions for each of several files to be submitted, select each file name separately and follow the above procedure for each one.

Select the Order Instructions button, and in the dialog box that appears, specify whether your order will be submitted by Modem or by Diskette. (See Figure 10.8.) Enter the rest of the required information and select OK. (Select the Glass Mounts option for slides if precise slide-to-slide registration is required or if high-heat projector lamps will be used.)

You won't be able to go any further unless you select the Billing Information button and complete the required information. (Mandatory items are marked with an asterisk.) Then select OK.

If you selected Modem in the order instructions, you must do Setup ➤ Communications Setup to specify the characteristics of your modem and to enter the phone number for the data line of the service center you will be using. The dialog box that contains this information is shown in Figure 10.9. To enter the name and data phone number of a service center, select the Add button.

FIGURE 10.8

Select the submission method from this dialog box.

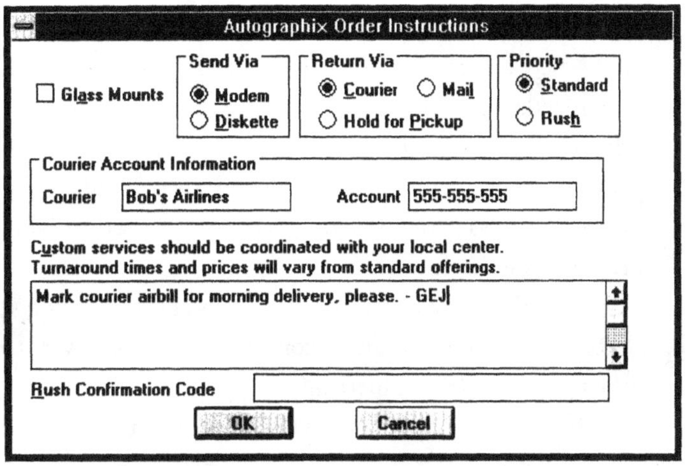

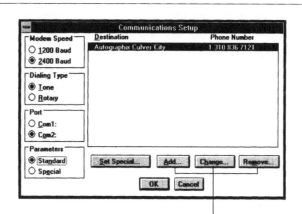

FIGURE 10.9

Enter the parameters of your communications hardware and the phone number of the data line at your local processing center.

Refer to Destination and Phone Number entries

If you need to enter a custom modem configuration, set Parameters to Special and select the Set Special button in the Communications Setup dialog box. For example, you might need to do this to configure the modem for speeds higher than 2400 bps (if the service center supports it), to edit the setup string for your own high-speed modem to disable error-checking at low speeds, to add a dialing prefix to get an outside line on your company PBX, to access a long-distance carrier, or to add a dialing code that disables the call-waiting feature.

To submit the order, select the Send button. If you selected Modem, the program will use its built-in communications software to start and complete the transmission automatically.

If you selected Diskette, you will be prompted to insert a blank, formatted diskette in the drive. Type the device letter and path in the Output Directory box, then select OK. The data file and order instructions will be written to disk, which you must then ship to a service center. (No transmittal is required, since the order instructions are embedded in the disk file.)

*N*OTE *The disk preparation procedure described here is similar to that required to create a disk for processing by other types of film recording software. For example, Lasergraphics film recorders require installation of a Windows printer driver that creates files in Binary Lasergraphics Language (.BLL extension). The device name is BLL Generator For WinRascol and the Windows printer driver file name is BLLONLY.DRV. Agfa Matrix film recorders use the SCODL driver, which creates .SCD and .BIN files. (The .BIN format is used for files that contain 24-bit color bitmaps.) The device name is Stingray SCODL and the driver file is SR_SCODL.DRV. The film recorder file created by the driver must then be input to a separate RIP program provided by the recorder manufacturer to generate the signals that drive the CRT in the recorder.*

Do You Want to Squeeze Your Files?

Both modem transmissions and disk files can be compressed automatically by the utility PKZIP.EXE, which is included with ToAGX. The command File ➤ Compression permits you to turn off this feature or to enter a specific path on your hard disk for use as a temporary work area for the compression program. (You would not normally turn compression off unless you suspected that it were causing problems with RIP processing.)

Slides that contain large bitmaps, backgrounds built from bitmaps (such as gradient fills), or both can result in very large film-recorder files. For example, a complex slide that also contains a large bitmap easily could exceed 1 MB as a .CPS file. The PKZIP compression utility will shrink such a file to about 200 KB, which will still require approximately 15 minutes to transmit at 2400 bits per second (bps). Higher transmission speeds, such as 9600, 14.4 K, or 19.2 K bps, might be used as they become available at processing centers. However, at higher speeds the transmission time might not be any less if the telephone connection is noisy. For a large number of slides, it might be more practical to send a disk by an express shipping service and then use the modem to transmit any last-minute revisions.

Problems of Font Compatibility

You might notice that the fonts on your screen don't match the slide output. Remember that most film recorders use hardware fonts. If a font you have specified does not reside in the recorder, one of two things will happen:

- The Windows font will be translated to a bitmap font embedded in the print file. The print file will be downloaded to the film recorder.

- The closest-match hardware font will be used, based on a *font substitution table* in the driver software.

A mismatch between fonts might be particularly noticeable with True-Type fonts. To determine the source of an error, you can inspect the options for the way the Autographix PostScript driver handles these fonts. In the Windows Control Panel, do Printers ➤ Autographix ➤ Setup ➤ Options ➤ Advanced. The Advanced Options dialog box will appear, as shown in Figure 10.10.

Notice in Table 10.1 that Autographix requires you to set the True-Type Fonts option to Send To Printer As Adobe Type 1. (The other selection is Bitmap (Type 3).) You are also required to mark the option Use Substitution Table. As a result, for a TrueType font the driver will look up the corresponding PostScript Type 1 font in its substitution table. If the name of the TrueType font is not in the table, the driver will embed the font in the print file as a bitmap (PostScript Type 3) font.

FIGURE 10.10

Options for handling
TrueType fonts in
printing PostScript
files to disk are
among the settings
here.

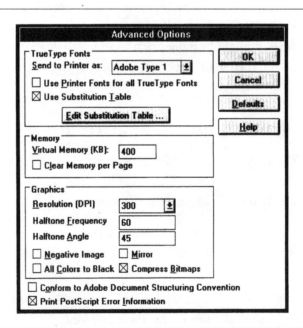

Autographix recommends using only the default settings in the substitution table. However, it is possible to make changes to the substitution table by selecting the Edit Substitution Table button. These changes affect the behavior of the driver in your computer system, not the RIP processing at the service center. The Substitution dialog box is shown in Figure 10.11.

For any TrueType font in the list on the left, you can reassign its PostScript Type 1 equivalent on the right. When you select the name of a TrueType font, the name of a Type 1 font will be highlighted if there is a default assignment in the substitution table. If there is no entry in the table and if there is no close match for a TrueType font, the correct choice is Download As Soft Font, which has the same effect as specifying Bitmap (Type 3) as the conversion option, but for that font only.

Remember that by changing the substitution options you are changing the table inside the PostScript driver of your own computer system. The font substitution will be made *after* you have created the graphic in the application but *before* your graphics file has been printed to disk. The WYSI-WYG display in the application may not be reliable, and there is no guarantee that a Type 1 font you select will actually match the TrueType font. You must therefore be careful to select a font for which the letterspacing is the same.

FIGURE 10.11

TrueType fonts installed in your system are shown in the list on the left, PostScript Type 1 fonts on the right.

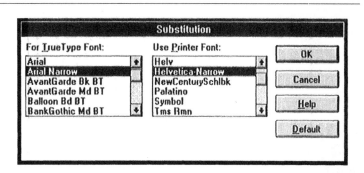

In general, processing will be more efficient if you specify a closely matched Type 1 font than if you pick Download As Soft Font. Using bitmap fonts can greatly increase the size of the print file and will increase transmission and processing times. You might use bitmap fonts sparingly, for the display type in logos, for example. (To reset the conversion options according to the predefined lookup table in the driver, select the Defaults button.)

CHAPTER 11

Dressing Up Fonts

or

Font Party Tricks

HE DISCUSSIONS and examples in previous chapters have managed to avoid many of the technical details of font construction. (I don't know about you, but I find it much more pleasant to drive a car if I'm not worrying about what's going on under the hood.) In this chapter, I'll bravely plunge into the internals of font files—not because it's interesting in itself, but because in special circumstances, that's the best way to get things done. You might confront this stuff if you ever

❡ Find that a much-needed character, such as a fraction, is missing from a particular font.

❡ Want to create logos, symbols, or special characters that can be contained within a font and available at a keystroke.

❡ Want to enhance the letterspacing of a font so that it is kerned automatically.

❡ Try to use a commercial or shareware font file that causes errors, perhaps even causing your system to crash.

I did the examples in this chapter with Fontographer 3.5 for Windows, an application that its manufacturer describes as a "professional font editor." It is available in both Windows and Macintosh versions, and it can handle both PostScript Type 1 and TrueType font files, as well as its own proprietary format for creating custom fonts.

Font File Types: Only What You Need to Know

Each font that is installed in your system exists as at least two files—a file containing character outlines and a file containing information that applications need to interpret the outlines as images in a particular size.

TrueType Font Files

TrueType fonts can be installed through the Control Panel and usually reside in the subdirectory WINDOWS\SYSTEM. If you look at a file listing of this subdirectory, you will see .FON, .FOT, and .TTF extensions. The .FON files are bitmapped screen fonts that are used by Windows for display and usually not for printing. The .TTF are outline font files. For each .TTF there must be a corresponding third type of file, a *font resource file* (.FOT extension). The font installation software uses the .FOT file to interpret the .TTF outlines. From the .TTF file, both screen and printer fonts can be generated as they are needed by Windows.

PostScript Type 1 Font Files

Adobe PostScript Type 1 fonts (such as those supplied with Adobe Type Manager, or ATM) are also of two varieties: an outline file—.PFB

(PostScript font Bézier) and a metrics file— .PFM (printer font metrics) or .AFM (Adobe font metrics). The .PFM contains bitmapped characters, as well as other information needed to scale and letterspace the font correctly.

PostScript Type 1 fonts are supplied in both file formats. ATM usually installs the .PFB files to the directory PSFONTS, the .PFM files to the subdirectory PSFONTS\PFM. Fontographer reads the .PFB files but can also open the .PFM files to get the kerning information.

TrueType, Type 1, and Your Type

Fontographer can open three types of files: the .TTF of TrueType, the .PFB of PostScript Type 1, and its own internal format .FOG. The .FOG files are used for fonts that you create from scratch with Fontographer, as well as for internal working versions of TrueType or PostScript Type 1 fonts that you have modified with the program.

B-Spline, Bézier—What's the Difference?

For the technically inclined, characters in .TTF files are described as mathematical curves called *quadratic B-splines*. A B-spline is defined by two points on a curve and a third point off the curve that controls the curvature through the two other points. (See Figure 11.1.)

By contrast, for each Bézier curve used in a Type 1 font, there must be one point, or vertex, on the curve and two *control points* off the curve. The control bar, a line segment drawn between the two points, is tangent to the point on the curve. The curvature at that point is determined by the length of the control bar and its angle with respect to the point on the curve. In Fontographer, the endpoints of the control bar are called Bézier control points, or BCPs.

From a practical standpoint, all of this means that TrueType and Type 1 font characters differ fundamentally in their construction and aren't directly compatible with one another. However, since both kinds of outlines are described mathematically, one type of font can be converted to the other with a little calculating, as long as the processor of your computer has nothing else to do for the few minutes it might take.

Fontographer interprets and can manipulate fonts as the same Bézier curves used in PostScript Type 1. Therefore, when you open a TrueType font, the program first must convert the character outlines from B-splines to Bézier curves. Since B-splines can be more complex, the conversion process can remove some of the subtleties of the TrueType letterforms. Because the conversion must be done in reverse to create a new .TTF file, other slight variations in the letterforms can appear.

Some font utilities can convert a font from one format into the other. However, for the reasons just stated, the translation isn't always perfect. You can convert a font using Fontographer by loading it (which converts it to .FOG format), then generating a new font file in either .TTF or .PFB format. Some other font utilities for Windows that can convert among multiple formats are listed in Table 11.1.

FIGURE 11.1

Two ways of defining the outlines of letterforms: Quadratic B-spline (TrueType) and Bézier curve (PostScript Type 1)

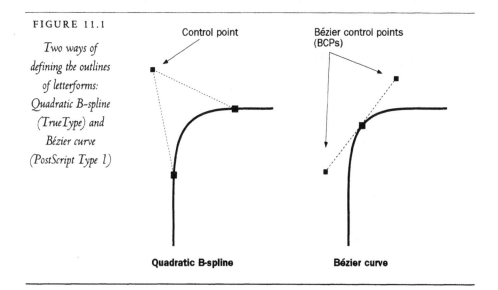

Control point

Bézier control points (BCPs)

Quadratic B-spline　　　　**Bézier curve**

PRODUCT NAME	VENDOR NAME	VENDOR PHONE
AllType	Atech Software	800 786-3668
FontMonger	Ares Software Corporation	415 578-9090
Metamorphosis Professional	Altsys Corporation	214 680-2060

TABLE 11.1: *Some Font Conversion Utilities for Windows*

Font Metrics

The .FOT and .PFM files of TrueType and PostScript Type 1 fonts contain font *metrics*, or parameters for rendering the accompanying outline .TTF or .PFB file. Aspects of font metrics are kerning, tables, and *hints*. Hints are algorithms (mathematical formulas) for improving the appearance of characters that will be printed at resolutions lower than 1,000 dpi (less than publication quality). Like kerning, hinting is an enhancement that is not implemented in all font designs.

Using Fontographer to Inspect Font Files

Start Fontographer in Windows by double-clicking its icon (which is usually installed in its own program group):

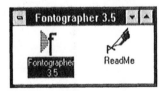

The program menu bar will appear:

You needn't be concerned about accidentally corrupting a font file if you load it into Fontographer. The program interprets and manipulates TrueType and PostScript Type 1 fonts in its own internal font format (.FOG). You must then go through a separate font-generation procedure on a previously saved .FOG file to create an installable .TTF or .PFB file. You can give this file a new, unique name, so even after you've modified a font, it would normally reside on your system in both the old and new versions. You would then be able to select either the unchanged font or your modified font from the Font options in any Windows application.

To load a font file, do File ➤ Open Font. The Open dialog box will appear. Here you can navigate the file system to log onto the directory that contains the font files you want:

DIRECTORY	FONT FILE FORMAT (EXTENSION)
FONTOG35	Fontographer (.FOG)
PSFONTS	PostScript Type 1 (.PFB)
WINDOWS\SYSTEM	TrueType (.TTF)

Some other sample font files supplied with the program can be found in FONTOG35\SAMPLES.

Looking at the file listings in the Open dialog box, you'll notice right away that the file names aren't always very descriptive. Some aren't difficult to decipher:

- ARIALNI.TTF is Arial Narrow Italic.

- All TrueType fonts from Bitstream have the form TT0498M_.TTF (Americana BT), where the four digits are the Bitstream catalog number.

- Fonts supplied by Swfte International, Ltd. have names like BOBSWFTE.TTF (Bongo).

- PostScript Type 1 fonts from Adobe have even more inscrutable names: CA_____.PFB (Caslon Open Face). The underscore extends the file name to a full eight characters.

Fontographer 3.5 does not permit you to inspect the full name of the font until its file has been loaded into the program and fully interpreted, which can take a minute or so, depending on the speed of your processor and the amount of free memory. If you don't want to guess which file goes with what font name, you might use a font management utility like Swfte Typecase, in which the command Fonts ➤ Properties displays information for a selected font, including its file name and style. (Typecase works only with TrueType fonts, however.)

In the Open dialog box of Fontographer, select a font name, then select OK. If you select anything but an .FOG file, it will take some time to load. The outline information must be interpreted, then a bitmap must be generated for each character in the font. The result is a character map of the font, as shown in Figure 11.2.

FIGURE 11.2

On loading and interpreting a font file, Fontographer generates a character map.

Settings control display of code above character slot

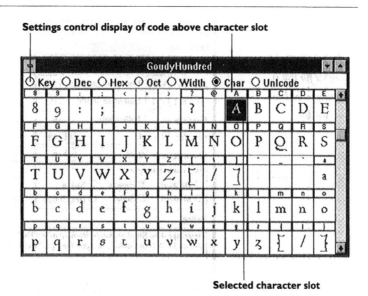

Selected character slot

When the Font window (character map) is open, the command Edit ➤ Font Attributes will display information about the font, as shown in Figure 11.3.

The numeric measurements in the Font Attributes dialog box are in *em-units.* An em-unit is dimensionless: The actual distance is calculated when you select a point size for the font in an application. The point size fixes the dimensions of the *em-square,* the square area occupied by a capital M, including some white space (called the shoulder) above the letter. This distance equals the height of the ascent added to the height of the descent of lowercase letters (Figure 11.4). So, the em-units contained in the font file are scaled, or given absolution dimensions, by the point size you select. (Fontographer reports all font measurements in em-units.)

331

FIGURE 11.3

Fontographer reports this information about the file that is currently in the Font window.

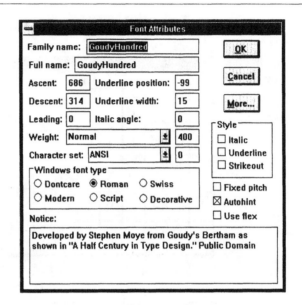

FIGURE 11.4

Em-units are dimensionless distances in relation to the em-square measurement, which is scaled when you select a point size for displaying or printing the font.

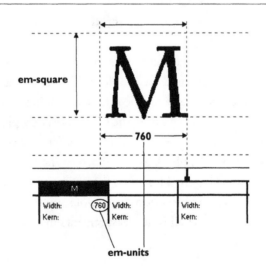

Among the check boxes here is the Autohint option. Normally, you would leave this option on, activating any hints that might be designed into the font. (If you turn this option off, you have to specify hinting yourself by the command Special ➤ Expert ➤ Hinting Setup.)

Selecting the More button will open the More Font Attributes dialog box, which shows information about hinting and all of the various names by which the font is referred to in different applications. These Name Table listings include Font Manufacturer Name (assigned by Microsoft), PostScript Font Name, Font Style Name (such as Normal, Bold, Italic, or Condensed), TrueType Unique Name, TrueType Release Name (a date and time stamp), File Name Prefix (the name you selected when you opened the file), Windows Font Menu Name (in Control Panel ➤ Fonts), Ventura Publisher Name, and PostScript Weight Name.

When the character map window is open, the command Edit ➤ Character Information will display the Character Width in em-units, the Unicode Number, and the Character Name for the currently selected character. The Unicode number is a unique character identifier in an international standard system, corresponding to one slot in the Font window. You can change the name or number of the character, but if you do, the font will not follow standard keyboard coding and will be treated as a set of symbols (like Wingdings). To restore standard keyboard coding for the font, reselect ANSI for the Character Set option in the Font Attributes dialog box.

Modifying Characters

To modify a character displayed in the Font window, double-click the character or do File ➤ Open Outline Character. The Character Edit window will open, as shown in Figure 11.5. This outline view of the character shows the points, or vertices, that lie on its Bézier curves.

FIGURE 11.5

The Character Edit window shows the Bézier curves of the character outline.

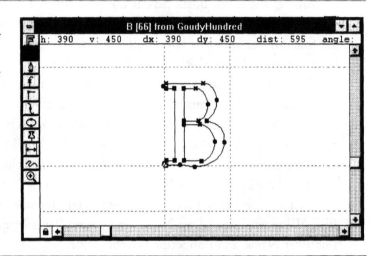

Here are some of the ways you can change the shape of a character:

Move a point By dragging it to a new location. Or, select Point ➤ Location and enter the distance in em-units. Here's the result:

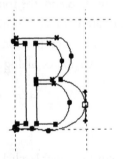

Change the vertex type By the commands Point ➤ Tangent Point, Point ➤ Corner Point, or Point ➤ Curve Point. Different types of connecting lines, curves, and intersections are permitted for each type of vertex.

Remove a point By clicking on it and doing Point ➤ Merge Point.

Change the curvature Of a point on a curve. When you click on a point, its two nodes (BCPs) and control bar will appear. Drag either of the BCPs to change the curvature. (Pressing the Shift key as you drag will constrain the control bar to right angles.) Here's the result:

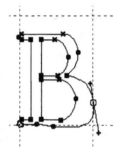

Add a cusp By bending the Bézier control bar at an angle. (A *cusp* is a sharp bend in a curve.) If the point is not at a corner, click on the point and do Point ➤ Corner Point. Then drag one of the BCPs to bend the control bar. Here's the result:

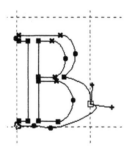

Transform the character By any of the commands from the Special pull-down menu: Special ➤ Set Width (character width in em-units), Special ➤ Scale (increase or decrease character proportionally in size), Special ➤ Rotate, Special ➤ Skew (adding a slant, as in an Italic style), Special ➤ Move (all or selected points by em-units, an alternative to dragging), or Special ➤ Flip (mirror-image).

Change character weight Can be done for selected parts of a character by the command Special ➤ Expand Stroke or overall by the command Special ➤ Change Weight.

Creating Custom Characters: Fractions

For an example of a custom character, I created a fraction. These useful characters are often missing from font character sets. You can use much the same procedure in Fontographer to create other kinds of custom characters that are combinations or modifications of existing characters in the set.

 *FontMonger (Ares Software Corporation) will create fractions automatically. On your command, the program will select numerals from the font, scale them, add the divisor line, and assign the new character to the key code you specify.*

Loading the Font

To create a custom character, begin by starting Fontographer and doing File ➤ Open Font. The Open dialog box will appear. For this example,

---

Oops! What an Ugly Character!

When you're playing around with these characters, they can turn ugly on you. Don't fret—do Edit ➤ Undo to reverse the effect of the last command or operation you did. Or, to be really conservative, do File ➤ Revert (Yes), and Fontographer will restore the last version of the file that was saved to disk. (Whew!)

I used one of the sample fonts supplied with the program. Go to the FONTOG35\SAMPLES subdirectory and choose GOUDYHUN.FOG. The Font window for the selected font, GoudyHundred, opens. (Refer back to Figure 11.2.)

Copying a Character as a Template

Adjust the scroll bar in the Font window until the en-dash character appears. (It's located between the plus sign and the em-dash.)

Double-click the en-dash character slot:

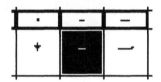

The Character Edit window will open, showing the outlines of the en-dash character.

Now, the technique I recommend, which is by no means the only way to work, involves copying an existing character as a template for the new one. This way, you are working with known character attributes, including character width. In this example, the en-dash is particularly handy because it can also be used as the divisor bar in the fraction. (Depending on the style of the font, a forward slash might be a better choice.)

To copy the character outline to the Clipboard, with the Character Edit window open, do Edit ➤ Select All, then do Edit ➤ Copy. You can now close this window by double-clicking in its control box (top left corner).

Pasting the Template into the Empty Fraction Slot

The Font window containing the character map for GoudyHundred reappears. Adjust its scroll bar until you see a row of empty character slots for the fractions $\frac{1}{4}$, $\frac{1}{2}$, and $\frac{3}{4}$:

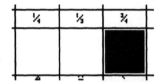

Double-click on the $\frac{3}{4}$ character slot and its Character Edit window will open. Do Edit ➤ Paste and the en-dash outline will be pasted into the Threequarters window, changing the character width in the process, as shown in Figure 11.6.

FIGURE 11.6

Paste the en-dash outline into the $\frac{3}{4}$ *Character Edit window.*

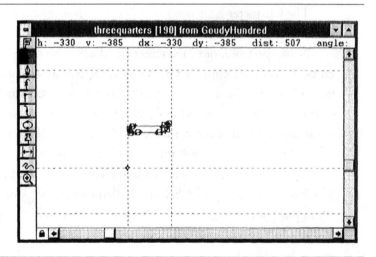

Copying and Pasting the Numerals of the Fraction

Switch back to the Font window and adjust the scroll bar until you see the numeric digits of the font, which precede the capital letters. Click the 3 character slot:

Then, do Edit ➤ Get Part. (You don't want a full copy in this case, which would include the character width. This command copies only the outline of the numeral.) Click in the Threequarters window to activate it. Then do Edit ➤ Paste. The 3 appears, superimposed on the en-dash:

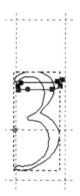

Reduce the size of this character by doing Special ▶ Scale, typing in 50 for Uniform Scaling, and selecting OK. The 3 reappears, reduced in size by 50 percent:

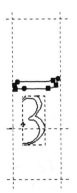

The dotted box surrounding the 3 indicates that the character is selected for manipulation. To change its position, drag it to the top of the character space:

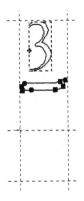

Now, move the en-dash (which will be the fraction divisor bar) up to almost touch the bottom of the 3. Drag a dotted box around the en-dash, selecting all its points, which will change to small, hollow squares:

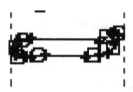

Drag any one of the hollow squares upward to move all of the selected points together:

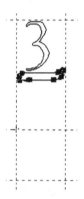

Go get the 4 the same way you got the 3, by clicking its character slot in the Font window:

Do Edit ➤ Get Part. Switch to the Threequarters Character Edit window, and do Edit ➤ Paste. The full-sized 4 appears in the character space. Reduce it in size by doing Special ➤ Scale with Uniform Scaling set to 50 percent. (You can just click OK in the Scale dialog box, since the program has already entered 50 percent for you as a result of the previous scaling operation.)

A dotted box surrounds the 4, indicating that it is selected for manipulation. Drag it upward and slightly to the left so the top of the numeral just touches the en-dash and aligns vertically with the 3:

This step completes the creation of this custom fraction. To preview it, do File ➤ Open Metrics.

When you close the other open windows, the new character appears in its slot in the character map of the Font window:

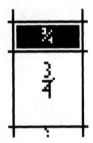

Saving and Generating Font Files

To save your new version of GoudyHundred, do File ➤ Save As. When you are modifying any font, you should rename it so that the old version remains unchanged. Then, if you experience problems with the new font, you can always revert to the distribution version. In this case, you might use a file name like GOUDYHU1.FOG, since all eight characters of the file name prefix were already used up.

Again, Fontographer saves your working copies of fonts as .FOG files. You must go through a separate procedure to generate an installable font file.

Generating an Installable Font File

To convert an open .FOG font to TrueType or Type 1, with the Font window open, do File ➤ Generate Fonts. The Generate Fonts dialog box will open, as shown in Figure 11.7.

FIGURE 11.7

Options you set here determine the file format that will be created by converting the currently open .FOG font.

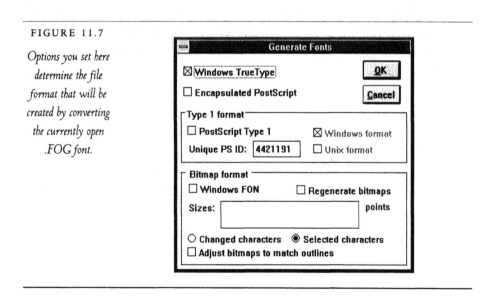

By marking the check boxes in the Generate Fonts dialog box, you can generate the font as any one of the following:

❡ TrueType (.TTF)

❡ Encapsulated PostScript (.EPS), a collection of graphics

❡ PostScript Type 1 (.PFB for Windows or in UNIX format)

❡ Bitmap (Windows .FON screen font; specify the point size)

The program will not prompt you for a file name. Rather, it will use the file name prefix of the .FOG file and append the correct new file extension.

The new file will be saved in the same directory as the source .FOG file. You must then use a font installer, such as Control Panel or ATM, to install and activate the font for use in Windows applications.

Need to Get Serious about Kerning?

Steps for kerning type manually in CorelDRAW are covered in Chapter 2. You should consider kerning type manually if it is larger than 18 points. In particular, you will want to kern display type used for headlines and logos. Some enhanced fonts, particularly those used for publication text, contain kerning tables by which proportional letterspacing can be adjusted automatically to compensate for unsightly gaps between letters.

Kerning tables usually give custom spacing in em-units for each problem pair of characters, or *kerning pair*. Each pair has a positive spacing value if the spacing is greater than the default, or a negative value if the spacing is less than the default. Most kerning values are negative, since the purpose is usually to close a gap that would be made by default spacing.

Some publication-quality text fonts contain as many as 1,000 kerning pairs, but the more sophisticated fonts for Windows have only about 250. Most fonts have none. The kerning values are usually different for each font because of variations in the letterform designs.

 *Among Windows applications, WordPerfect and QuarkXPress recognize and implement the kerning pairs contained in a font. QuarkXPress also permits you to edit the kerning table in a font. A shareware program for editing the kerning tables of PostScript Type 1 fonts is PFMEdit from Dennis Harrington, the developer of FontManager and other font utilities. (FontManager is the earlier shareware version of the application that is now available commercially as Fontographer.)*

Inspecting and Adjusting Kerning in Fontographer

With Fontographer, you can inspect the kerning pairs in a font, if any exist. After loading the font, with the Font window open, do File ➤ Open Metrics. The Metrics window will open for the selected character in the map. (To access kerning pairs quickly, start by selecting the first letter in the pair.) When the Metrics window is open for any character, you can do View ➤ Next Kern Pair and View ➤ Prev Kern Pair to open metric views of the kerning pairs in the font. If the font contains no kerning information, these commands will be dimmed. However, these commands are always dimmed if the metrics window is not open. For example, there is no kerning information in the TrueType font Courier New, since it is a monospace font.

When the metric view of a kerning pair is open, as shown in Figure 11.8, you can adjust the letterspacing, thereby changing the values in the kerning table. To adjust the kerning by em-units, do View ➤ Set Width. To adjust it interactively by eye, drag the *T-bars* that control letterspacing, which are located just below the metric characters in the window.

345

FIGURE 11.8

For each kerning pair, Fontographer presents this metrics view in which letter-spacing can be adjusted.

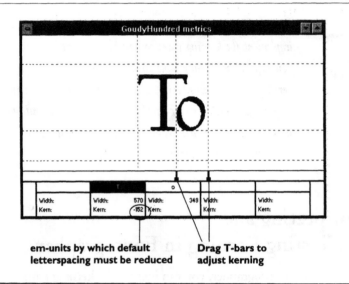

**em-units by which default
letterspacing must be reduced**

**Drag T-bars to
adjust kerning**

Fontographer provides an alternative for deeply serious editing of kerning tables. You might do this if you are dissatisfied with the kerning overall (or if the font has none). To clear any existing kerning table from the currently open font, do Edit ➤ Clear Kerning Pairs. You can then do File ➤ Import ➤ Import Kerning to import the kerning table of any other Post-Script Type 1 font from its .PFM or .AFM file. Since kerning requirements vary among font designs, if you import the kerning table from another font, you will have to "fine tune" the letterspacing by doing File ➤ Open Metrics and then View ➤ Next Kern Pair, as just described.

Fontographer can give you a printout of the current font's kerning table, if there is one. Do File ➤ Print and set the Sample Type option to Kerning Pairs. Make sure your printer is on-line, then select OK.

Do You Care for Homemade Fonts?

A custom fraction is just a tasty sample of the font treats you can cook up with Fontographer. You can also create your own fonts, logos, and graphics with this program. The advantage of creating logos and graphics in Fontographer instead of in an application such as CorelDRAW is that you can assign a new logo, for example, to a key code in an installable font file. The logo can then be retrieved by keystroke and scaled by point size to be inserted in any Windows application.

There isn't space in this modest book to cover font creation from scratch, but Figure 11.9 shows a letter *A* that I drew (okay, maybe it's not wonderful) in Fontographer.

FIGURE 11.9

You can use the drawing tools on the left to get creative with new letterforms.

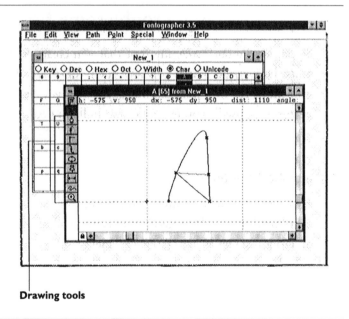

Drawing tools

Start by doing File ➤ New Font and double-clicking the slot in the character map of the letter you want to draw. The Character Edit window will open, and you can use the drawing tools at the left of the window to create the Bézier outline. Then, do File ➤ Open Metrics to see the fully rendered character. Here's how mine looks:

Tips on Tracking Troublesome Fonts

Be cautious about using any font that you create or that you obtain from other homemade sources. Many such fonts are available as shareware (download for free, mail in your payment if you use it) or as freeware (no strings, supposedly) on networks and bulletin boards.

What's the Problem?

Here's the problem: Many of these fonts—as well as some commercially distributed ones—don't necessarily contain all of the information required by a font installer such as Control Panel or ATM. Installing and using such a "bad font" in a Windows application can cause your system to crash. (The display will freeze, the keys will lock up, and your mouse will play dead. You may or may not get a terse and technical error message that will be decipherable only by a Windows programmer.)

*Even if a font file you get from a bulletin board isn't defective, there remains the possibility that it is carrying a computer virus. Download new files to a clean, formatted diskette, then immediately use an antivirus utility to check the diskette before copying any of the files to your hard drive.*

As a preventive measure, after you install *but before you actually use* a possibly suspicious font (including one you've proudly crafted yourself), you can check it out with a freeware font utility called OKFonts. Its developer George Campbell claims that it is the only Windows program that will do this type of verification.

The program reads selected font files (which must be an installed font) or all your installed fonts and prints each character, one at a time, to the screen and to the printer. That is, it interprets, renders, and scales each character just as an application would do. (This process will take some time, particularly if you've selected more than one font.) If there is an error in a character, the program will usually crash, just as a print job might if you used that font. You can then reset the system and delete the offending font from your disk and from your life.

The program provides no tips on font repair, and neither can I. If the file is going to do such nasty things to your system, just get rid of it!

OKFonts and other utilities (not necessarily free) are available from the following address:

OsoSoft
1472 Sixth Street
Los Osos, CA 93402
BBS: 805 528-3753
CompuServe ID: 71571,222

Here's Another Diagnostic Tool

A useful shareware font utility for Windows is Printer's Apprentice, with which you can inspect installed TrueType and ATM font files. Among its features, the program permits you to view characters, character maps, typeface styles and sizes, keyboard assignments, and kerning pairs, as well as print font inventories. Its developer is Brian Kinkel. You can reach Brian at the following address:

> Brian Kinkel
> Lose Your Mind Development
> 506 Wilder Square
> Norristown, PA 19401-2643
> 215 275-7034
> CompuServe ID: 70564,2372

CHAPTER 12

Love Notes
for the
Technically-Inclined

How to Cope with
Some Ugly Characters

 CAN'T RESIST adding some technical notes in this concluding chapter. These are topics that I scrupulously avoided in previous chapters because a detailed knowledge of how Windows gets things done isn't essential to using its applications productively. My purpose here is to give you enough background to at least *feel* better prepared to make a call to the vendor's technical support hotline, should it ever become necessary.

However simple fonts might be to use, when problems arise, the complexities can be annoying. And the cause isn't always obvious: I know some programmers who describe such problems as "POM-dependent." POM stands for "phase of the moon," a cute phrase for admitting that the expert is stumped because the cause doesn't follow any known pattern.

The most important clue to diagnosing what seems to be a technical problem is *repeatability:* If you know exactly what procedure you used when the problem appeared, you stand a better chance of being able to re-create it. If you can get the problem to appear consistently, you have removed it from the gray mists of POM-dependent phenomena and are well on your way to solving it, or at least to describing its symptoms accurately to someone who can help.

PostScript Type 1 and TrueType: Together Again

In theory, PostScript Type 1 under Adobe Type Manager (ATM) and TrueType fonts can coexist happily on the same system. You can even intermix them in the same document. However, the marriage of these two competing formats in Windows was something of a shotgun wedding: Neither family is entirely thrilled that the other was invited.

One set of rules by which the two sides cooperate is found in the WIN.INI file, which resides in the WINDOWS directory.

 *In the religion of computer software, the .INI files of your Windows system are sacred places; violate them at your peril. Always make a backup copy of any such file before you open it. As a general rule, change only one line (statement) in a file at a time. You can then restart Windows and verify the effect of your change. If you make too many changes at once, you might never find the source of an error. The only reliable solution in that case would be to reinstall Windows and start afresh. Whenever you make a change to an .INI file, you must restart the corresponding program for the changes to take effect.*

[FontSubstitutes] in WIN.INI

If you open the WIN.INI file in a text editor such as Notepad, you will see the following section:

```
[FontSubstitutes]
Helvetica=Arial
Times=Times New Roman
Tms Rmn=MS Serif
Helv=MS Sans Serif
```

This font substitution table is necessitated by differences in screen fonts between Windows 3.0 and Windows 3.1. Version 3.0 used the Adobe

353

PostScript names for its screen fonts. In the table in the graphic above, these are found on the left side of the equal sign. With version 3.1, Microsoft implemented TrueType. The names of the screen fonts changed to those on the right.

If the font named on the left is not installed, Windows will substitute the TrueType font on the right. If the font on the left *is* installed, as may be the case if you have ATM, the substitution will not be made. (To complicate matters, ATM may make its own substitutions, as described below.) This is how ATM can improve the appearance of Windows 3.0 screen displays: You see the scalable PostScript Type 1 font instead of a cruder bitmap font. You can't see much difference in version 3.1 because the TrueType fonts are also scalable.

The four substitutions listed above were required by the change from Windows version 3.0 to 3.1. If you find any others in your WIN.INI file, some programmer or some application program put them there, and these substitutions might be the cause of "nonWYSIWYGability," or a mismatch between what you see on the screen and what you get on paper.

To disable a statement in the FontSubstitutes section, or in any section of any .INI file, don't delete it. Rather, change it to an inoperable comment by inserting a semicolon (;) at the beginning of the line. Then, save the file as WIN.INI (remembering to keep an unchanged backup copy) and restart Windows. Repeat the procedure that caused the problem. If the screen display or the printout is different in any way, you may have found the cause.

[TrueType] Options in WIN.INI

While you have the WIN.INI file open, take a look at the statements under the heading [TrueType]. This section can contain the following statements:

OutlineThreshold=<Number> Defines the Number of pixels per em-unit, or the minimum size at which Windows will render

TrueType fonts as outline fonts instead of as bitmaps. Bitmaps give faster performance but require more memory. The default value for Number is 256. The maximum is 300. Don't change this setting unless your system is low on memory. The only way to make the change is to edit the statement in the WIN.INI file.

TTEnable=<0 or 1> Is set by a check box in Control Panel ➤ Fonts ➤ TrueType: Enable TrueType Fonts. A value of 0 means No (TrueType off) and 1 means Yes (TrueType on). Don't edit the statement. Turn off TrueType through the Control Panel if you want to see the effect of using ATM fonts only.

TTIfCollisions=<0 or 1> Is missing from your file if you installed Windows with default settings, but inserting this statement can be a solution to some problems. It tells Windows how to handle conflicts between TrueType and any other kind of font that has the *same font name.* Precisely to avoid such collisions, font manufacturers have tried to give their products standardized, unique names. (You can inspect a font's various names in Fontographer by the command Edit ➤ Font Attributes, as covered in the previous chapter.) However, some duplications can arise. For example, there are at least two fonts named Symbol: One is the Windows bitmap version and the other is a TrueType font. If the setting is 0 (the default), the TrueType version will be used exclusively. Edit the statement to change the setting to 1 if you believe a font has a name duplication with a TrueType font and you want to enable that font.

TTOnly=<0 or 1> Is set by a check box in Control Panel ➤ Fonts ➤ TrueType: Show Only TrueType Fonts In Applications. A value of 0 means No (permitting TrueType and ATM to coexist) and 1 means Yes (TrueType on exclusively). Don't edit the statement. Make the change through the Control Panel. If you enable this option (setting the statement to 1), you should also turn off ATM through the ATM Control Panel. You will have to restart Windows for these changes to take effect.

The [Fonts] Table of WIN.INI

This section tells Windows which *screen fonts* to load at startup. If you see a long list here, it's no wonder Windows seems to be taking so long to load. The font names are on the left and the font resource (bitmap and metrics) file names are on the right. The font names appear as the Installed Fonts list in Control Panel ➤ Fonts.

To increase system performance and to conserve memory, only the fonts you use frequently should be in this list. Although removing (or commenting out) a statement will disable a font, *adding* a statement will not result in a correctly installed font. Whether you are deleting or adding fonts, you should not attempt to edit the list in WIN.INI. Rather, use the Remove or Add buttons in Control Panel ➤ Fonts to delete or add fonts.

What's the Maximum?

According to Microsoft, no more than 1,170 TrueType fonts should be installed in Windows 3.1. The maximum number of Type 1 fonts under ATM is 400. You should consider uninstalling some fonts to improve system performance if you have 200 or more.

Font Substitution by the Printer Driver

Another means of exchanging one font for another is through the font substitution table for a particular printer driver. The details of this are covered in Chapter 10 in connection with modifying TrueType-to-PostScript substitution to be compatible with the hardware fonts in color film recorders.

As I mention in Chapter 10, one way to edit the font substitution table for PostScript printers is through Control Panel ➤ Printers ➤ <Printer Name> ➤ Setup ➤ Options. Select the Advanced button in the Options dialog box, then mark the Use Substitution Table check box and select the

Edit Substitution Table button in the Advanced Options dialog box. The Substitution dialog box appears, as shown in Figure 12.1. There you can specify a Printer Font substitute (list on the right) for each TrueType font name (list on the left).

FIGURE 12.1

Access this dialog box through Control Panel ➤ *Printers to change font substitution by the printer driver.*

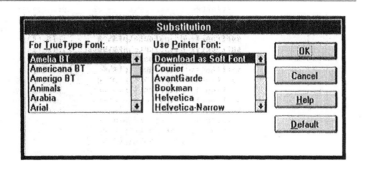

If you have downloaded soft fonts for a printer, the assignments will appear under the device name section in WIN.INI, as shown in Figure 12.2. These specific entries were added during ATM installation by the option Install As Autodownload Fonts For The PostScript Driver. Downloading these soft fonts can increase performance if the PostScript printer does not contain Base35 fonts, which are standard on later models:

AvantGarde	Palatino
Bookman	Symbol
Courier	Times
Helvetica	ZapfChancery
Helvetica Narrow	ZapfDingbats
NewCenturySchoolbook	

FIGURE 12.2

*Downloadable font
substitution in
WIN.INI for the
PostScript printer
driver*

```
[PostScript,FILE]
ATM=placeholder
softfonts=21
softfont1=c:\psfonts\pfm\gnbc____.pfm,c:\psfonts\gnbc____.pfb
softfont2=c:\psfonts\pfm\gnc_____.pfm,c:\psfonts\gnc_____.pfb
softfont3=c:\psfonts\pfm\gneb____.pfm,c:\psfonts\gneb____.pfb
softfont4=c:\psfonts\pfm\gnub____.pfm,c:\psfonts\gnub____.pfb
softfont5=c:\psfonts\pfm\gnubc___.pfm,c:\psfonts\gnubc___.pfb
softfont6=c:\psfonts\pfm\mtbc____.pfm,c:\psfonts\mtbc____.pfb
softfont7=c:\psfonts\pfm\mtc_____.pfm,c:\psfonts\mtc_____.pfb
softfont8=c:\psfonts\pfm\mtci____.pfm,c:\psfonts\mtci____.pfb
softfont9=c:\psfonts\pfm\ox_____.pfm,c:\psfonts\ox_____.pfb
softfont10=c:\psfonts\pfm\tbscr___.pfm,c:\psfonts\tbscr___.pfb
softfont11=c:\psfonts\pfm\_a_____.pfm,c:\psfonts\_a_____.pfb
softfont12=c:\psfonts\pfm\bdbc____.pfm,c:\psfonts\bdbc____.pfb
softfont13=c:\psfonts\pfm\bs_____.pfm,c:\psfonts\bs_____.pfb
softfont14=c:\psfonts\pfm\dc_____.pfm,c:\psfonts\dc_____.pfb
softfont15=c:\psfonts\pfm\lg_____.pfm,c:\psfonts\lg_____.pfb
softfont16=c:\psfonts\pfm\mtb_____.pfm,c:\psfonts\mtb_____.pfb
softfont17=c:\psfonts\pfm\mtbi____.pfm,c:\psfonts\mtbi____.pfb
softfont18=c:\psfonts\pfm\mti_____.pfm,c:\psfonts\mti_____.pfb
softfont19=c:\psfonts\pfm\mtr_____.pfm,c:\psfonts\mtr_____.pfb
softfont20=c:\psfonts\pfm\ng_____.pfm,c:\psfonts\ng_____.pfb
softfont21=c:\psfonts\pfm\ptrg____.pfm,c:\psfonts\ptrg____.pfb
```

Metric file   **Outline file**

The items to the left of the equal sign are the names by which the driver refers to soft fonts, SOFTFONT1–SOFTFONT21, in this case. For each soft font name, the corresponding file names are given on the right—here the ATM metric file (.PFM), followed by the outline file (.PFB).

For ATM to download and use the fonts in the printer, the following statement must appear in the ATM.INI file:

```
[Settings]
DownloadFonts=On
```

You will see a similar substitution table under the HP driver section in WIN.INI if you have installed Hewlett-Packard PCL downloadable fonts for the LaserJet II series. Unless you have a special reason (see the Tip below), you shouldn't be using these fonts anyway. Instead, print ATM and TrueType as graphics and give yourself a break. In fact, some PCL clone printers, which generally do LaserJet II emulation, do not support downloaded fonts and will substitute an internal font, further obstructing the road to WYSIWYG.

To experiment with disabling PCL soft fonts, you can precede each SOFTFONT statement in the substitution table with a semicolon. However, it will usually be more reliable to use the HP Font Installer in the Control Panel to add or delete downloadable fonts.

 *You will get the most reliable WYSIWYG performance if you tell Windows to handle all fonts as graphics. (There's more about this in Chapter 1.) For Type 1, mark the Print ATM Fonts As Graphics check box in the ATM Control Panel. For TrueType, mark the Print TrueType As Graphics check box in Control Panel ➤ Printers for each printer driver. The main reason to use printer-resident (hardware) fonts is to increase system performance (speed), especially if the computer or the printer or both are low on memory. However, beware that most font gremlins are born in font substitution tables!*

Font Substitution Tables in ATM.INI

If you have installed ATM, you have some other places to look for screwy font substitution. The file ATM.INI, which is also located in the WINDOWS directory, contains startup information for Adobe Type Manager. ATM.INI has two font tables that control substitution. The first is headed [Aliases] and the second is [Synonyms], as shown in Figure 12.3.

FIGURE 12.3

Font substitution

tables in ATM.INI

```
[Aliases]
Helv=Arial MT
Tms Rmn=TimesNewRomanPS
Courier=Courier
Times Roman=Times
Helvetica=Arial MT
Times=TimesNewRomanPS

[Synonyms]
Helv=Arial MT
Tms Rmn=TimesNewRomanPS
Courier=Courier
Times Roman=Times
Helvetica=Arial MT
Times=TimesNewRomanPS
```

[Aliases]

The aliases work somewhat differently from the FontSubstitutes table in WIN.INI: Whether or not the font name on the left is installed, the font name on the right is *always* substituted. The substitution usually serves one of two purposes:

- ❡ If a Windows bitmap font such as Helv is requested for display, ATM can substitute Helvetica and generate sharper characters.

- ❡ If an application requests a font name that is not installed, such as Helvetica, ATM can substitute its supplied font Arial MT.

If the Use Pre-Built Or Resident Fonts check box is marked in ATM Control Panel, ATM uses the bitmap version if one exists for the point size requested by the application. If the option is unmarked, ATM generates all sizes of the font from its outline file. (The recommended setting is Off when using ATM fonts as graphics.)

[Synonyms]

The use of synonyms works this way: The names on either side of the equal sign are interchangeable. These substitutions apply mainly to Windows 3.0 bitmap fonts. In a default installation, the Aliases and Synonym sections contain the same lists. (Refer back to Figure 12.3.)

If you have all of the required Type 1 fonts installed (Helvetica, Times, Arial MT, and TimesNewRomanPS), the substitutions for these fonts should be as follows in *both* Aliases and Synonyms sections:

```
Helv=Helvetica
Tms Rmn=Times
```

One possible source of error is that the substitutions in WIN.INI and ATM.INI don't match. The result can be a font name collision, which might cause you to see a different font displayed or printed from the one you selected in the application.

[Fonts]

As in WIN.INI, the [Fonts] section defines the font files that are loaded on startup. The font names on the left are those listed in the selection window of the ATM Control Panel.

The fonts in this list are available to all non-PostScript devices for display and printing. However, the fonts that will be used for PostScript printers are determined, not by the table in ATM.INI, but by the SOFTFONT statements in the printer driver section of the WIN.INI file. If you are using a true PostScript printer, ATM is not involved in printing. The Windows PostScript driver uses the table in WIN.INI, and ATM need not even be running.

As a result, you might not see bold or italic attributes on a PostScript printer unless separate outline fonts for those weights or styles are resident.

However, on non-PostScript printers, ATM comes into the picture and modifies the normal font to simulate the bold and italic styles.

Don't edit the Fonts list in the ATM.INI file. Add or delete fonts through the ATM Control Panel.

The font utilities FontMinder and AllType also can update the ATM.INI file, so you might want to recheck the settings in it after you have installed either of these programs. As with ATM, you must restart Windows for any changes to take effect.

Adobe Systems advises that some memory-resident virus protection programs will not permit modification of the ATM .EXE and .INI files during installation of a newer version. (Any unauthorized modification of an .EXE file can be an early warning sign of viral activity.) You may have to temporarily disable the virus protection software to complete the installation. Adobe recommends immediately re-enabling the virus program and re-scanning your hard disk before using any applications. (In such cases, you can expect that the virus protection program will warn you that the .EXE file has been modified, presumably by an unknown virus.)

For other suggestions on the fine-tuning of ATM, including adjusting the size of the font cache, see Preventing Those Pesky Printer Problems *in Chapter 1.*

Hiring a Good Font Manager

Some font utilities can place fonts in subgroups that you can install or un-install depending on the requirements of the application you are using. For example, if you always use the same six fonts in a newsletter, you might create a subgroup named NEWS, and install it through the font-management utility just before starting a desktop publishing application. Some font utilities that can create and install font groups are given in Table 12.1.

The FontMinder utility (yet another font program developed by Dennis Harrington) extends the font grouping capability to printers, as shown in Figure 12.4. When you select the name of an installed printer from the Install Fonts For drop-down box in the top right corner, its list of installed fonts appears in the Installed PostScript Fonts box. Notice in the figure that the PostScript printer driver has been selected. The font list contains the font names that correspond to the 21 SOFTFONT entries in WIN.INI— the same list shown in Figure 12.2.

A real virtue of FontMinder is the ability to inspect the font lists that are installed for each of several printers. You can then reconcile those lists to avoid the unpleasant results of requesting a font that is not available on the selected printer. This feature is particularly handy when you are dealing with outside service bureaus, some of which offer only PostScript hardware fonts over which you have no direct control.

PRODUCT NAME	VENDOR NAME	VENDOR PHONE
Facelift	Bitstream Inc.	800 522-3668
FontMinder	Ares Software Corporation	415 578-9090
Typecase	Swfte International Ltd.	302 234-1740

TABLE 12.1: *Some Font Managers for Font Groups*

Disabling ATM for Troubleshooting

If you think ATM is getting in the way, you might want to disable it while you run tests with only TrueType fonts. However, turning off the ATM

FIGURE 12.4

The FontMinder utility permits you to install fonts selectively in groups, by application (font pack) and by printer.

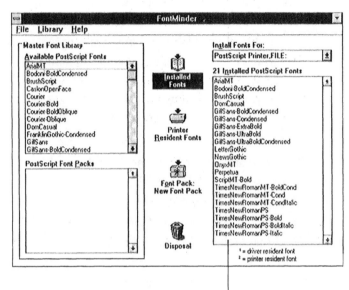

Same list as Figure 12.2

Control Panel and restarting Windows doesn't reset the system completely. To be sure that ATM's changes are not affecting Windows system files, do the following:

1. Open SYSTEM.INI with a text editor such as Notepad. (Be sure to keep a copy of the unchanged file.)

2. Change the entries in the [boot] section by commenting out two existing lines (preceding them with a semicolon) and adding a third:

```
;SYSTEM.DRV=ATMSYS.DRV
;ATMSYS.DRV=SYSTEM.DRV
SYSTEM.DRV=SYSTEM.DRV
```

3. Make sure that the file SYSTEM.DRV resides in the WIN-DOWS\SYSTEM subdirectory. If not, reinstall it from the distribution diskette.

4. Save the edited file as SYSTEM.INI.

5. Open WIN.INI with the text editor. (Again, keep a backup copy.)

6. Insert a semicolon (;) as the first character in any printer driver statements that begin with SOFTFONT.

7. Save the edited file as WIN.INI.

8. Restart Windows.

To restore ATM, reinstall the backup copies of SYSTEM.INI and WIN.INI, turn the ATM Control Panel back on, and restart Windows.

TrueType Troubleshooting

Here are a few tips on tracking down the source of trouble if a TrueType font does not display or print correctly:

§ Upgrade your computer's memory to more than 2 MB. True-Type fonts are unstable if memory is low.

§ Avoid using TrueType fonts that have been converted from other formats, such as PostScript Type 1. (You need not convert Post-Script Type 1 fonts if you are using ATM.) Use a font utility such as OKFonts to check for a defective font, or follow these steps:

1. Create a full page of MS Sans Serif text in Windows Write.

2. Save the file.

3. Select all the text in the document.

4. Do Character ➤ Font.

5. Select one of the converted fonts.

6. Print the document.

7. If the font is bad, printing may cause a General Protection Fault (program crash).

8. Repeat the above steps 3–7 for each converted font.

9. Uninstall any bad fonts.

❡ If the problem is in the display, check the source and version of your video driver software. Some third-party drivers that have not been updated for Windows 3.1 cannot handle TrueType fonts correctly. If the driver is current, reinstall Windows to be sure you have an uncorrupted file.

Working in Other Languages

As complicated as this subject of fonts might seem at times, things can really get out of hand if you have to use different languages on the same computer system.

Using the DOS KEYB Command to Change Code Pages

Today's keyboards are soft, or programmable by the system. On a PC, the language your keyboard speaks—meaning the interpretation that is given to each key on the keyboard—is determined by the IBM Code Page, a table that translates numeric key codes into characters. The default in DOS for U.S. English is Code Page 437. If you work in several languages, you might find it more convenient to set up your system to use Code Page 850, Multilingual.

What about Windows? Well, Windows takes its cue from DOS, so first things first.

For systems in the United States, Code Page 437 is the default when you install DOS. However, the code page assignment can be changed in DOS by inserting a KEYB command (with parameters) in the AUTO-EXEC.BAT file. You must also then put the command INSTALL KEYB.COM (with parameters) in the CONFIG.SYS file. (See the *MS-DOS User's Guide* for parameters and options.)

Switching Languages

The main reason to use the KEYB command is to convert the entire computer system for primary use in another language. To reset Windows temporarily for working in another language, make your changes through the Control Panel instead to *temporarily override the DOS setting*—as long as Windows is running and until you reset the option.

You don't have to sweat the details of changing code pages for international keyboards. Key Tronic Corporation provides setup disks for all foreign-language keyboards it manufactures. The setup disk has .BAT installation files that insert the correct KEYB syntax for each code page. For more information, contact Key Tronic at the following address:

Key Tronic Corporation
Accessories Department
P.O. Box 14687
Spokane, WA 99214-0687
800 262-6006
509 927-5395 (within Washington state)

If you reprogram your English-language keyboard by the KEYB command, its keys will assume the character definitions of the code page, but remember that the labels on the keys won't match. However, this needn't stop you from typing in Greek, if you so desire. Just refer to the keyboard diagrams in the Appendix "Keyboard Layouts and Character Sets" in the *MS-DOS User's Guide* for information about what each foreign character key stands for.

Having reassigned the keys with KEYB, you can switch back to the default code page any time in DOS by pressing Ctrl-Alt-F1. To resume typing in the foreign language, press Ctrl-Alt-F2.

Windows Setup for Language

As I said before, the Windows Setup program takes its cue from DOS. Technically, if the DOS Code Page setting is anything other than 437 (U.S.), Setup looks in the SETUP.INF file under the heading [codepages]. By the statements in this section, Setup installs the correct translation table and system fonts. (Settings can also affect the DEFXLAT= statement in the [data] section, which determines how external text files are to be translated on import.)

However, as with so many other things, Windows can simplify this. You can override the DOS KEYB setting by the command Control Panel ➤ International. The International dialog box will appear, as shown in Figure 12.5.

The options in this dialog box include the following:

Country Also resets the Measurement option and the default Page Size used with printers.

Language Affects operations such as sorting and conversion between capital and lowercase letters.

Keyboard Layout Changes the Code Page.

FIGURE 12.5

Settings here override the DOS Code Page setting as long as Windows is running.

IBM Code Page

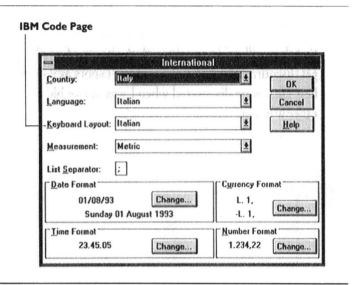

Other Options Affect country-specific conventions for units of measure, as well as the formats of list separators, currency amounts, numbers, dates, and times.

Believe me, it will be less confusing if the DOS KEYB setting and the International settings in Windows match.

Don't assume that, having transformed your keyboard layout, you will be able to type merrily along in your chosen language. The fonts you use must contain the characters for the codes you type. Inspect the character set in a selected font by displaying its character map, as described in Chapter 1.

If you routinely work in different languages, consider changing the Code Page (Keyboard Layout) setting to 850, Multilingual, which covers English and other European languages. Increasingly, font sets implement the characters in the multilingual table so as to be useful in as many languages as possible.

369

In conclusion, I want you to know that most of the pointers in this book were discovered by trial and error. I offer them to you in the sincere hope that they will guide you through the basics of working with fonts. But don't get discouraged if you run into rough spots as you experiment. A lot of my best ideas were discovered when I was in trouble and there seemed to be no other way out!

Index

Note: Page numbers in **bold** refer to primary discussions or definitions of a topic. Page numbers in *italics* refer to figures.

A

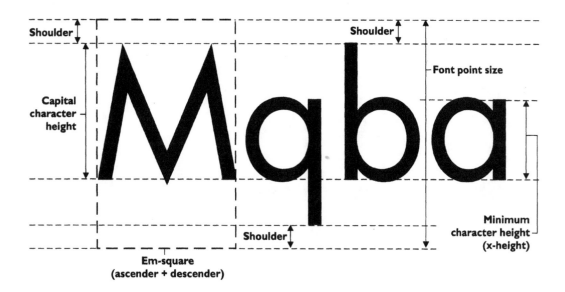

Shoulder

Capital
character
height

Shoulder

Font point size

Shoulder

Minimum
character height
(x-height)

Em-square
(ascender + descender)

ligature In a font, a design that links two characters to form a single, special character, such as *æ*.

link The portion of a letterform that joins one closed curve to another.

metrics Auxiliary information for an outline font that tells computer software how the font will be rendered, including hinting and kerning information, if any.

minimum character height The height of the smallest letterform in a font; usually, the x-height.

monospace A font in which each letter occupies the same amount of horizontal space.

nudging In Windows graphics applications, moving a text or graphic object by small increments using the arrow keys.

outline A representation of letterforms in a font as vectors, or points and closed curves.

pica A unit of measure that equals $\frac{1}{6}$ inch.

point The smallest typographical unit of measurement: 12 points = 1 pica; in Windows, 1 point = $\frac{1}{72}$".

point size For typeset text in a specific size, the distance from the tip of the ascender to the tip of the descender, in units of $\frac{1}{72}$ inch; for a font in a specific size, the height of its em-square, including the shoulder.

proof A hard copy of typeset text used for error-checking before printing.

proportional spacing The variation of the width of characters to achieve more pleasing letterspacing of words.

river Problem text composition resulting from too much space between words or sentences so that the gaps throughout a paragraph appear vertically through text columns.

www.ingramcontent.com/pod-product-compliance
Lightning Source LLC
Chambersburg PA
CBHW081505050326
40690CB00015B/2926